D1458146

DOMESTIC VIOLENCE AND PSYCHOLOGY

This book rethinks the way psychological knowledge of domestic violence has typically been constructed. It puts forward a psychological perspective which is both critical of the traditional 'woman blaming' stance, as well as being at odds with the feminist position that men are wholly to blame for domestic abuse and that violence in intimate relationships is caused by gender-power relations. It is rather argued that to neglect the emotions, experiences and psychological explanations for domestic violence is to fail those who suffer and thwarts attempts to prevent future abuse.

Nicolson suggests that domestic violence needs to be discussed and understood on several levels: *material* contexts, including resources such as support networks as well as the physical impact of violence, the *discursive*, as a social problem or gendered analysis, and the *emotional* level which can be both conscious and unconscious.

Drawing on the work of scholars including Giddens, Foucault, Klein and Winnicott, and using interview and survey data to illustrate its arguments, *Domestic Violence and Psychology* develops a theoretical framework for examining the context, intentions and experiences in the lives of women in abusive relationships, the men who abuse and the children who suffer in the abusive family. As such this book will be of great interest to those studying social and clinical psychology, social work, cultural studies, sociology and women's studies.

Paula Nicolson is Professor of Critical Social Health Psychology at Royal Holloway, University of London and is also a trainee at the Tavistock in psychodynamic organisational consultancy.

DOMESTIC VIOLENCE AND PSYCHOLOGY

A Critical Perspective

Paula Nicolson

Routledge
Taylor & Francis Group

LONDON AND NEW YORK

Published in 2010
by Routledge
27 Church Road, Hove, East Sussex BN3 2FA

Simultaneously published in the USA and Canada
by Routledge
270 Madison Avenue, New York, NY 10016

Routledge is an imprint of the Taylor & Francis Group, an Informa business

Copyright © 2010 Psychology Press

Typeset in Times by Garfield Morgan, Swansea, West Glamorgan
Printed and bound in Great Britain by TJ International Ltd, Padstow, Cornwall
Cover design by Anú Design

British Library Cataloguing in Publication Data
A catalogue record for this book is available from the British Library

Library of Congress Cataloging in Publication Data
Nicolson, Paula.
Domestic violence and psychology : a critical perspective / Paula Nicolson. – 1st ed.
p. cm.
Includes bibliographical references and index.
ISBN 978-0-415-38371-4 (hardcover) – ISBN 978-0-415-38372-1 (pbk.) 1. Family violence–
Psychological aspects. I. Title.
HV6626.N567 2010
616.85'822–dc22
2009048239

ISBN: 978-0-415-38371-4 (hbk)
ISBN: 978-0-415-38372-1 (pbk)

CONTENTS

ACKNOWLEDGEMENTS

This book is the result of a long-standing interest in the application of feminist ideas to the psychology of abusive heterosexual relationships. It has been particularly helpful to draw upon data from the DASH study (*D*omestic *A*buse: Women *S*eeking *H*elp) funded by the National Lotteries Charities Board Health and Social Research Programme while I was working at the University of Sheffield. So first I would like to acknowledge my colleagues there, particularly Louise Brenard, Kathy Doherty, Caroline Dryden, Caroline O'Keefe, Jenny Powell, Graham Smith (now at RHUL), Sue Ward and Richard Wilson, all of whom, in their different ways, supported the conduct of the DASH project.

I would also like to acknowledge people who have worked with me on the study of domestic violence and abuse since then, especially Anna Gupta, Liz Hudson and Alix Walton from Royal Holloway, University of London and Kristin Heffernan (now at SUNY, Brockport). Liz in particular organised a highly successful conference for social workers, lawyers, doctors, police and health care professionals in central London during the summer of 2006 to showcase the DASH and other relevant work. Tracey Newby's and Betsy Stanko's contributions ensured the success of that day.

Many others have supported me in writing this book. Colleagues at the University of Malta (Jacqueline Azzopardi, Maureen Cole, Marceline Naudi and Sandra Scicluna) have discussed ideas over coffee and lunches and provided original material on domestic violence in their country. My colleagues in the Department of Health and Social Care at Royal Holloway, University of London have supported the sabbatical leave which enabled me (at last) to finish this work. Particular thanks there go to Toni Bifulco and Anna Gupta. Colleagues and staff at the Tavistock Portman Foundation Trust in north London have been inspirational and evidence of thinking in this regard is clearly visible in what follows. Of others who have supported me in writing this book I would particularly like to acknowledge Erin Pizzey. It goes without saying that those women who told their stories of living with abuse deserve gratitude.

ACKNOWLEDGEMENTS

Jane Ussher, series editor, and the Taylor & Francis team have shown amazing patience, so thank you!

Finally, as ever, friends and family, particularly Derry, Kate, Malachi and Azriel, have been there to keep me amused and sane. Love to you all.

Paula Nicolson
August 2009

INTRODUCTION

This has been the most difficult book I have ever written. Thinking and talking about psychology and domestic violence and abuse is harrowing. The experiences women describe are brutal, malicious and unforgiveable. Even as I am writing this, more stories of domestic violence flash up on the home page of my computer screen. Twenty-five minutes ago for example the trial of a man in Bedfordshire (England) for killing his ex-girlfriend by stabbing her more than forty times was reported as postponed until November 2009. His counsel have pleaded diminished responsibility and the court has requested psychological reports. What could possibly cause a man to inflict such a vicious and frenzied attack on someone he was once so close to? Just a few days ago in the English Midlands a 9-year-old girl was found strangled in a lorry and the driver (her mother's boyfriend) was found hanged in a field nearby having presumably taken his own life after killing the young girl. A couple of days later:[1]

> Detective Chief Inspector Tricia Kirk, of Northamptonshire Police, said today that police could not rule out that there was some sexual touching involved in the incident that led to her death. Ms Kirk also revealed Walker, 40, the boyfriend of Stacey's mother Roxanne, had a history of a domestic incident involving his wife of three years who he was currently in the process of divorcing. She said: 'He was cautioned for that offence and we have no other criminal records for him.' She said the incident involved an assault on his wife in 2006.

It is sickening to hear of such things and domestic abuse and violence seem to be all around us. But writing about domestic violence and abuse has been made much harder because of the politics surrounding it and how I have understood my own position within them. In the past I have found it (relatively) easy to take a clear stand across the complex matters which have involved women's psychological and physical oppression by individual men, patriarchal institutions and professions (such as universities, psychiatry or obstetrics and gynaecology). I have been in the role of a pro-feminist psychologist taking account of (what I have understood to be) women's voices in the context of gender-power relations across the transition to motherhood and as professional women climbing the career ladder.

It took relatively little time though before I recognised that for some activists and campaigners in the area of domestic violence and abuse *I* was positioned as the enemy – as a psychologist and an academic who was not at the 'front-line'. It seemed that it was unnecessary to know anything else about me. What on earth could (yet) another academic (and psychologist to boot) do to *help women*? Ironically I began my studies of domestic violence and abuse from the perspective of a relatively strong pro-feminist, influenced over thirty years ago by Erin Pizzey's first film of the Chiswick refuge for battered women. I can still recall the images and some of the stories. The extent to which other women had experienced extreme violence at the hands of their male partners was almost incomprehensible. A further 'political' surprise came when I was firmly advised that (twenty-five years later) Erin Pizzey's work was a 'taboo' subject among those currently in the foreground of domestic violence activism.

There had been many questions I wanted to ask as a researcher when I decided to work in this area and after working on this book I know these may have been (politically) a little naive. What causes domestic violence? How can we make it stop? Are women equally as violent as men? Are children brought up with violence more at risk of becoming perpetrators or victims/survivors of domestic abuse and violence? What are the emotional and psychological effects of violence upon those involved? Are women's lives better for public awareness of domestic violence than they were when it happened quietly 'behind closed doors'? And the most common question – *why does she stay?*

Starting to address them from the position of psychology, it is clear now, was highly controversial. Many pro-feminist academics continue to argue that any attempt to *explain* domestic violence potentially condones men's violent and abusive behaviours (Kelly and Radford 1990; Kirkwood 1993; Humphreys and Thiara 2003; R.E. Dobash, Dobash, Cavanagh and Lewis 2004). Any connection drawn between 'domestic violence' and 'psychology' is anathema because a focus on psychology or individual differences moves attention and blame away from men, the agents of patriarchy. There is no middle ground. Men are violent and instil fear in order to control women. Violence must stop. Men must take responsibility for their behaviours and women (and children) must be heard, believed and made safe (Hague and Malos 2005; Hague and Mullender 2006). Who, feminist or not, could disagree with the latter sentiment? Women and children need to be made safe from male violence. We need to hear and understand what they want. While it is demonstrably not so easy for women to leave their home to seek safety for themselves and their children, we also need to look beyond the limited resources, cynicism and poor practice of health, social care and law enforcement professionals as being the only causes of women remaining with a violent and abusive man (Erez 2002; J.R. Gillis *et al.* 2006). We need to explore the emotional side of the coin.

There are many reasons that make women stay with violent men, which include shame, fear and the social pressure not to declare the abuse (Buchbinder and Eisikovits 2003). The reasons also include attachment to the abuser, which has its origins in low self-esteem (both from the time of their childhood and from years of being abused in adulthood by that man), and love (Ferraro and Johnson 1983; Henderson, Bartholomew and Dutton 1997; Allison, Bartholomew, Mayseless and Dutton 2007).

But here contention lies. Is there a need to explore the context and content of individual relationships? Is it relevant to consider whether 'types' of domestic violence might be categorised as different from each other? And should any explanation and analysis take account of anything beyond men's control of women under patriarchy?

As I shall both argue and demonstrate in this book, intimate heterosexual relationships are complicated. They are in themselves, of course, a product of patriarchy, and women's lives and the choices women make are constrained and regulated within patriarchal power relations. But we cannot leave the analysis at that. Neither can we deny the agency of those who seek a reparative relationship with an abuser. The debate between psychologists and feminists has become rancorous, with the protagonists in many cases being side-tracked into mutual hostilities rather than focusing upon understanding the different layers of the complex problem (Dekeseredy and Dragiewicz 2007).

What are these complexities that might be offered in mitigation for male violence? There is evidence that male violence might be mediated and exacerbated through his being out of work, under the influence of drugs or alcohol, stress or coming from an abusive background (Bhatt 1998; Quigley and Leonard 2000; White and Chen 2002). These factors cannot be disregarded, and considered as *absolutely irrelevant* to making sense of aspects of male violence in the context of a relationship *that a woman wishes to sustain*. None of this excuses men's responsibility for the violence and abuse.

Even so it is also important to acknowledge that mutual violence in a heterosexual relationship (D.G. Dutton and Nicholls 2005) or female heterosexual or lesbian violence *does take place* (Renzetti 1998; Kimmel 2002; Johnson 2006) and further that different types of violence within relationships may be 'classified' (Johnson and Ferraro 2000).

If we *do* listen to women's voices it is likely that we will hear many different things. This is not to be glib. Suzanne Martin's (2009) account of her experiences as both an activist against domestic abuse and a psychologist working therapeutically with couples where the woman has suffered abuse characterises the emotional split for many of us. As an activist the natural reaction is to abhor men who have been violent. As a psychoanalytic therapist one can see the complexities within relationships and support the desire of both partners for reconciliation and reparation.

Domestic violence is not only a psychological, health and social problem. It is indisputably a crime (Morley and Mullender 1992) and perpetrators should be punished. But domestic violence takes place, by definition, in a relationship, and as such there are complicated emotions, meanings and behaviours that underpin those relationships and support or prevent women leaving to achieve safety or prosecuting the man involved.

Violence is a tragedy for everyone involved whether perpetrators, victims or witnesses (Garcia-Moreno, Heise, Jansen, Ellsberg and Watts 2005; Chrisler and Ferguson 2006; Ellsberg 2006b). Violence is also endemic across cultures and history and within different kinds of relationships, from war (Caprioli and Boyer 2001) through to political conflict, bullying (Baldry 2003) and moral violence in organisations (Diamond and Allcorn 2004), as well as between intimate partners (Yllö 1998; Bullock and Cubert 2002; Bostock, Plumpton and Pratt 2009).

This book specifically focuses upon *women's* experiences of living with violence, although it is mostly women in heterosexual relationships. Violent and abusive behaviours in relationships are rarely isolated events. The patterns of violence both perpetrated and experienced, just like any other feature of a relationship, *evolve*. Even in short-term relationships the dynamics have to change fundamentally in order for the relationship to end. As affections change, other people enter and influence the experience of the relationship partners; as the material context changes over the course of a relationship, so do experiences of abuse and violence. A relationship may involve physical violence, as many do, when the woman becomes pregnant or when children are young (Peckover 2003), but as time passes physical violence and aggression may change into verbal abuse, or conversely the physical violence might escalate as women get older (Straka and Montminy 2006). The very first experience of violence in a relationship changes the quality of that relationship for ever and what happens next will be as a consequence of the couple (and others involved) negotiating around that violence and the meaning they give it. By this I mean the woman may resolve to leave, or find a way of being with that man that somehow might mitigate the event for her at that time. The man, of course, is also involved in the negotiation of the violence dynamic.

Violent relationships, like any other, have phases. This alone makes the study of domestic violence and abuse a complex process which needs to take account of history and culture, gender-power relations, and the material context, as well as the changing dynamics of emotion and psychology.

It is the aim of what follows in this book to address these complexities with the overall intention of shifting thinking that informs contemporary research and practice towards a more pragmatic, effective and multifactorial understanding of how to prevent and support those who live, or who have lived, with domestic violence and abuse.

Contemporary reporting of domestic violence and abuse shows it has reached epidemic proportions. The facts and figures remain startling (Saltzman, Green, Marks and Thacker 2000; Walby 2004; Skinner, Hesler and Malos 2005). For instance as many as one woman in every three across the world is estimated to experience *violence* from a male partner at some time in her adult life (see Chapter 1). This by itself speaks clearly as to why academics, practitioners and the lay public have to continue to pay attention to this 'hidden' crime in order to identify a knowledge-base to stop domestic abuse.

Within the facts and figures, though, lie the human stories and *psychological* questions that need to be addressed. In particular the stories of the children living with their mother's abusive and violent partner who are likely to see and hear the attacks and possibly experience violence and abuse themselves (Martin 2002). Even if they are not subject to direct violence, the anxiety and emotional pain of their mother's suffering will have a complex and long-term emotional impact on them which may not be anticipated in its incidence, nor be predictable in its expression (Dryden, Doherty and Nicolson 2010). The stories of women who have left abusers only to be forced to return through lack of material resources and social support, because they are forced back by the man, or their own wider families experience levels of distress that destroy their lives, need to be heard. Women who do succeed in leaving the abuser but who have lost trust in themselves and others and fear entering new relationships are also in need of long-term psychological support.

What are the specific reasons given for ambivalence towards psychological and emotional explanations? One reason given is the distaste among feminist commentators for individualistic explanations. Mullender and Morley (2001), commenting on the lack of links between child care specialists and those concerned with preventing domestic violence, note that

> the only specialist book available has been the Canadian one, *Children of Battered Women* by Peter Jaffe *et al.* (1990). Its clinically oriented, individualistic model has never fitted well with typical British approaches – especially in refuges where the major work with children escaping violence here has taken place.
>
> (2001: 3)

But this typical British approach does not have all the answers and lets many women down.

Mullender and Morley also cite another book (Peled and Edleson 1994) which they consider combines useful North American material, although

'It is unfortunate that, judging from its title: *Ending the Cycle of Violence*, it appears to accept this "cycle" as its *raison d'être*' (2001: 4).

So why do British researchers in the field of domestic violence eschew the individualistic approach? It isn't as if the British academic or clinical/ practice work to prevent domestic abuse or heal the scars is beyond criticism. And why should there be such an aversion to the idea of a 'cycle of violence'? Why is it dismissed as 'simplistic' (Kelly 2001)?[2]

In what follows I focus upon the psychology of women's experience of heterosexual violence and abuse by intimate partners and ex-partners. I explore why this violence and abuse might happen, how women get involved with such men and how they (may) free themselves from these relationships. I also examine the psychological and emotional causes and consequences of both leaving such a man and staying with him, for the woman herself primarily, but also for her children. To do this I use real-life case studies – some well publicised cases from the media but mostly anonymised[3] cases from the DASH study.[4]

The DASH study

The DASH study was in several parts across three years. The first year involved two surveys both of which are discussed in Chapter 4 below. The first was an e-mail survey to elicit responses to a vignette, and the second a postal survey of a representative community sample (Nicolson and Wilson 2004). The second-year in-depth interviews were conducted with twenty-six women survivors who had left their abusive partners (see Chapters 6 to 8 in particular). We also independently interviewed eight children of those survivors (Dryden *et al.* 2010). Finally in the third year of the study in two separate postal surveys we collected data from health and social care organisations about their policies and practices and from front-line workers about their views, training and experiences related to domestic violence and abuse. From this latter survey we identified health and social care professionals prepared to be interviewed in more detail about the same topics.

A critical psychology of domestic violence and abuse

There are three elements to this book that distinguish it from previous psychological approaches to domestic abuse and violence. They are, first, the consideration of domestic abuse on three inter-related levels (the material, discursive and intra-psychic). The *material* context(s) (e.g. resources of the family and community, quality of the relationships and support networks), including the physical impact of violence such as burns and broken bones, is typically the focus of much contemporary knowledge. The level of the *discursive* context (e.g. rhetorical, ideological, attributional and gendered analysis) examines the social construction of domestic abuse, the meanings attributed to it by those who experience, witness or think about what it means, as well as the discursive regulation of gender-power relations. The *intra-psychic* context examines both conscious and unconscious ways (e.g. feelings, guilt, shame, self-esteem and emotional ways) in which we experience abuse and violence, with a particular emphasis here on the psychodynamic aspects of intergenerational transmission of violence, and its relevance for women living with and leaving abusive partners.

The second element is the development of a psychological perspective which takes account of the complexities *within* gender relations and the various ways in which patriarchy has impacted upon the psychology of being a woman.

Substantively, several facets of women's experience pass through different states of explanation. Violence is a feature of every society. It is present in social institutions from the family through to the workplace as well as deeply embedded in the human psyche. Women leave, enter and remain in abusive relationships not only because of *material* resources to support their leaving but also because of *discourses* such as 'shame' and the moral imperatives of 'marriage', as well as the primitive intra-psychic mechanisms such as early attachment experiences.

Third, the book is informed by empirical evidence from surveys and in-depth interviews with women which throw the traditional sociological feminist position into sharp relief.

In what follows I explore the diversity of contemporary knowledge-claims and beliefs. I unpack existing 'mythologies' about psychological approaches to understanding domestic violence and abuse and reconsider the complexity of heterosexual relationships. Psychology frequently stands accused of focusing on the *experiences* of domestic abuse from a position of curious or forensic neutrality/objectivity while turning a blind eye to evidence that it is a gender issue and a crime by men towards women based on misogyny. As Loseke (2001) posits, however: 'The wife abuse formula story that has flourished in recent decades is told in terms of clearly immoral behaviour, with pure victims and evil villains' (2001: 107). This is not the case with this book.

In Chapter 1 I outline the material context of domestic abuse with evidence and detail of attacks on women by their male partners around the world and accounts of how governments and non-governmental agencies have tried to combat violence to women.

Chapter 2 examines the definitions and meaning of domestic violence and abuse and discusses how different research questions and methods underlie diverse theoretical positions.

In the third chapter I look critically at the ways in which ideological differences have constrained the research and practice agenda in the area of domestic abuse, particularly across the feminism versus psychology debate, and then the debates within psychology itself.

In order to bring domestic abuse and violence into the public domain and achieve support for abused women, myths and formula stories of domestic violence have been made explicit. In Chapter 4 the politics of these mythologies are examined, arguing that while the purpose of highlighting domestic violence has been served, paradoxically the most vulnerable women are more than ever at risk.

Chapter 5 looks at public awareness, perceptions and everyday explanations from research in North America, Europe and the UK in particular. It draws attention to the different 'moralities' implicit in how we perceive the perpetrators and survivors, and this lends clues to the experiences of women living with domestic abuse who share the culture.

The lived experience of domestic abuse and violence, the focus of Chapter 6, begins to draw together the theoretical perspectives, particularly examining the role of unconscious processes, memory and narrative of the self.

Chapter 7 takes up this theme, looking specifically at the impact and legacies of intergenerational experiences of living with abuse and neglect, focusing upon the work of the psychoanalysts Erik Erikson, John Bowlby, Donald Winnicott and Melanie Klein in particular.

Finally in Chapter 8 the dilemmas of care and questions of blame are explored, with a focus on the dilemmas facing women living with violence in the couple relationship and the role of the health and social care professionals in this context.

Part 1

THE CONTEXT

1

DOMESTIC VIOLENCE: THE MATERIAL CONTEXT

Introduction

To begin with, a work of fiction from a best-selling and troubling novel about women's experience of marriage under the rule of the Taliban in Afghanistan. It tells the story of Rasheed's two wives – Mariam, who had been his wife for many years, and Laila his new wife. Laila had come from a kind, educated family in which her father valued women and girls. She married Rasheed only after a series of related tragedies. This cruel and selfish man knew he could do whatever he chose to his wives because women counted for nothing under traditional culture which had been made worse under the Taliban. Laila had never experienced personal violence before. She was not prepared for what happened.

> Laila didn't see the punch coming. One moment she was talking and the next she was on all fours, wide-eyed and red-faced, trying to draw a breath. It was as if a car had hit her at full speed. . . . She tried to breathe again and could only make a husky, choking sound. Dribble hung from her mouth. Then she was being dragged by the hair.
>
> (Hossein 2007: 239–240)

Mariam on the other hand had led a tragic life of loneliness and poverty. Her mother had been the mistress of a rich man who for a while had visited Mariam but ultimately, for his own ends, had handed her to Rasheed in marriage. Mariam had experienced many years of being beaten and abused, and she had also experienced Rasheed's marriage to Laila as an additional humiliation. The events described here, though, took place because Laila had tried to protect her, which had never happened to her before. Even Mariam's mother and father had ultimately let her down.

> He let go of Laila and turned on her. . . . At first, he looked at her without seeing her, then his eyes narrowed, appraised Mariam with interest. . . . Mariam saw now in those same eyes what a fool she

had been. Had she been a deceitful wife? she asked herself. A complacent wife? A dishonourable woman? Discreditable? Vulgar? What harmful thing had she wilfully done to this man to warrant his malice, his continual assaults, the relish with which he tormented her? Had she not looked after him when he was ill? Fed him, and his friends? Had she not given this man her youth?

(Hossein 2007: 309)

These two women's experiences of their shared husband's violence, juxtaposed in time, had different meanings. Laila was stunned, not only physically but because she had never been attacked before. Mariam, a veteran of living with violence, questioned herself about why she had deserved the years of abuse and violence. Unlike Laila, Mariam's reaction exposed her view that some wive's/women's behaviours might indeed justify this treatment. For Mariam violence was a fact of Afghan women's lives. If someone had not been a good wife maybe a man had a right to beat and abuse her? However, following Laila's lead, she admonishes herself for being Rasheed's victim for so long. Rasheed himself it seems was shocked that Mariam had begun to fight back as he too had the expectation that women were property and available for him to take out his frustrations through violent rage.

Women's experiences of living with violence vary, as with Mariam and Laila. Removing themselves and their children from a violent partner also demands different strategies in different cases. Some women can leave the man immediately. Most women do not and take varying amounts of time and endure different experiences before they either leave (NiCarthy 1987) for a place of safety, develop effective coping strategies or work with their partner (and often a psychological therapist) to change the quality of the relationship and stop the violence (Vetere and Cooper 2003). Erin Pizzey (1974/1977; Pizzey and Shapiro 1982) has argued that in certain cases a woman will opt to remain in and engage in a violent relationship. Pizzey also believes from her observations at the Chiswick refuge that some women are themselves 'naturally' violent and almost thrive on violence in their lives and need specialised support.

Women from different backgrounds also experience and make sense of their partner's behaviour in different ways, as with Laila and Mariam – the former neither expected nor was prepared to put up with violence; the latter did put up with it for years and it took that time and an event of significance to make her question why she should have to continue to do so (see Chapter 7).

What is the material context?

The material context of domestic violence and abuse comprises a complex interconnected set of factors which include the physical world and the social, health and economic resources available to women who live with or leave abusers (Larsen, Broderson, Larsen and Bendtsen 1985; Kirkwood 1993). For example, many women are not financially independent of their partner; refuges for abused women are scarce and not always pleasant to live in, and the likelihood of being re-housed is low. All of these things impact upon a woman's decision to leave (and frequently return to) the abuser. The material context also includes personal experience and biographical factors throughout a woman's life history. This context has brought the woman to the situation and influences how she sees and deals with it. The material context involves corporality through which physical injury and pain are experienced as a result of an attack.

Violence(s) against women around the world

Violence is endemic and violence against women is widespread whether or not it be against an intimate partner (WHO 2006). Violence against women is the primary means of controlling women's behaviour (and minds) in abusive misogynist cultures (Palmer 1998). Examples are legion.

One recent example was widely reported in August 2009. Lubna Hussein, a Sudanese woman who had worked for the United Nations, went on trial[1] for being unsuitably dressed because she and other women had been wearing trousers in a café. As a result of this she was in danger of being flogged as have been many others before her. Police in Sudan make random sweeps of popular leisure locations regularly looking for women who transgress their views of suitable female behaviour under Islam. The thirteen women arrested with Lubna Hussein had already received ten lashes and a large fine but Hussein has been one of the few prepared to challenge the authorities and go to trial. Hussein believed that the western democracies would take notice of what was happening to women if she took the action she did. She said she was not afraid of physical pain and no longer wanted to live under the conditions women in Sudan were forced to endure.

Although the last thirty or so years have seen legislative and behavioural changes around the world which have sought to eradicate such violences against women, including domestic violence, 'Still there is no shortage of causes for concern [as]. . . . Many of these achievements are proving to be fragile or contradictory' (Romito 2008: 1). In the (so-called) post-feminist era of the early twenty-first century a survey conducted by the British Home Office (2009) revealed that one in five adults thought it acceptable for a man to strike his partner if she wore 'revealing clothes' in public. Further, ironically, despite the removal of the Taliban regime from Afghanistan with their severe constraints upon women's lives and abuses of their human rights, the Afghan government is trying to reinstate a new law to regulate the personal status of Afghanistan's minority Shi'a community members, including relations between women and men, divorce and property rights.

> The new law denies Afghan Shi'a women the right to leave their homes except for 'legitimate' purposes; forbids women from working or receiving education without their husbands' express permission; explicitly permits marital rape; diminishes the right of mothers to be their children's guardians in the event of a divorce; and makes it impossible for wives to inherit houses and land from their husbands – even though husbands may inherit immoveable property from their wives.[2]

Women's bodies, women's appearance, women's rights and women's property are abused by misogynist regimes and misogynist individuals who constrain women's lives. Under such political and personal regimes women are diminished and rendered powerless. They are also *psychologically* mute despite those like Lubna Hussein whose acts of bravery remain few and far between. It took Mariam in the novel nearly twenty years and the experience of living with another wife who had had a different kind of background from her own that imbued greater self-esteem, before she challenged her husband's right to beat and abuse her. Even so the questions she asked were about herself and her possible failings, not about his right to be an abusive and violent man.

Much has been written about why men batter. Much has been written about why women don't leave but far less has been written about the *psychological* implications of living with abuse and what it means in the medium and long term.

Material constraints

Most feminist academic and campaigning literatures on domestic violence and abuse focus firmly on the material context at the (deliberate) expense of the psychological. That is the material *constraints* within which people live, including the physical context, such as housing, food, hygiene and safety and economic resources, as well as the physical body or 'corporality'. The material context both enables and limits capacity for development and change. Being physically fit, strong and affluent makes it easier for a woman to choose her future than does being unwell, pregnant or caring for young children. Examination of the material context of women's lives exposes the gendered power relations involved in the perpetration of physical violence and abuse upon women, in families, communities, law enforcement, education, health and social care organisations. Women rather than men are judged. As with Mariam above, the law enforcers and social care agencies will implicitly ask questions about what *she* has done to deserve the abuse. The material context therefore not only includes the abusive behaviours *per se*, but intersects with how and why those behaviours occur and how they are judged.

Over the past twenty years information about prevalence, type and (to an extent) impact of abuse towards women has been highlighted, and support for women's emancipation from abuse is now firmly on the human rights agenda (Andrews and Brown 1988; Perilla 1999; Dasgupta 2000; Danielsson, Olafsson and Gådin 2005; Chrisler and Ferguson 2006; Schuler, Bates and Islam 2008; Bostock *et al.* 2009).

> Statistics on the prevalence of the problem indicate that domestic violence is a worldwide epidemic. Studies show that between one quarter and one half of all women in the world have been abused by intimate partners. Worldwide, 40–70 per cent of all female murder victims are killed by an intimate partner.[3]

Violence and abuse towards women is well recognised to be a world-wide problem (Walker 1979) 'that persists in all countries of the world, and the perpetrators of that violence are often well known to their victims. Domestic violence, in particular, continues to be frighteningly common and to be accepted as "normal" within too many societies' (WHO 2006: vii). Recently 'published' websites provide contemporary snapshots of culture, attitudes and resistance to violence towards women from a number of political, social and religious perspectives. A typical feminist position (immediately below) is now very close in kind to official international standpoints on women's rights:

> Around the world, across geography, language, race, religion and culture, domestic violence is all too often defended in the name of law, culture, tradition, or just life. The numbers are staggering. In the United States, a woman is battered every 15 seconds. In India, 40 percent of adult women reported physical assaults by a male partner. In Sweden, one of every six murders is committed by a man murdering his partner. In Nicaragua, nearly thirty percent of women reported partner abuse. In South Africa, one women is killed approximately every six days by her male partner. 38 percent of Korean women reported battering by their spouse in the past year.[4]

Domestic violence, then, is truly a global problem of epidemic proportions. Even so, statistics on domestic violence, while consistently shocking, are typically understated because victims do not report all incidents, as for example in the United Kingdom (Home Office 2003). Public health studies globally also reinforce the message that domestic violence is under-reported and/or not recognised. A study published by Johns Hopkins School of Public Health undertook the task of documenting the international prevalence of domestic violence. In roughly fifty population-based surveys from around the world, the Centre for Health and Gender Equity found:

- 1 in every 3 women worldwide has been beaten, raped, or otherwise physically abused.
- Between 10 per cent and 50 per cent of women report having been physically assaulted by an intimate male partner at some point in their lives.
- These are not isolated events, however; 60 per cent of the women sampled had been repeatedly abused.
- Physical violence was often combined with psychological and sexual abuse in one-third to over one-half of the cases.

(Heise, Ellsberg and Gottemoeller 1999)

This confirms similar studies which show that nearly one in three adult women experience at least one physical assault by an intimate partner during adulthood (American Psychological Association 1996); between one in eight and one in ten women will have experienced domestic violence over the previous year in England and Wales (Criminal Statistics 1997); and between one and four million women experience a violent assault by an intimate partner each year in the USA (Bureau of Justice 1995; American Psychological Association 1996); of 224 female homicide victims 47 per cent are killed by their partner (Criminal Statistics 1997);[5] 43 per cent of all violent crime experienced by British women is domestic (British Crime Survey 1996); women were twice as likely as men to have been injured by a partner; and the estimate for the total number of incidents (male and female victims) in 1995 was 6.6 million (Mirrlees-Black and Byron 1999).

A survey in the USA (Coker, Smith, McKeown and King 2000) indicated that of 1,401 eligible women surveyed, 772 (55.1 per cent) had experienced some type of intimate partner violence in a current, most recent, or past intimate relationship with a male partner; 20.2 per cent were currently experiencing intimate partner violence. Among those who had experienced partner violence in any relationship, 77.3 per cent experienced physical or sexual violence, and 22.7 per cent experienced non-physical abuse. Alcohol and/or drug abuse by the male partner was the strongest correlate of violence.

The WHO (2006) population-based household surveys[6] also indicated that violence by a male intimate partner was widespread. The proportion of women who had ever suffered domestic violence varied from 13 per cent in Japan to 61 per cent in a Peruvian provincial area, with most sites falling between 23 per cent and 49 per cent. The prevalence of severe physical violence (being hit with a fist, kicked, dragged, choked, burnt on purpose, threatened with a weapon or having a weapon used against her) ranged from 4 per cent in a Japanese city to 49 per cent in provincial Peru (WHO 2006: xiii). The violence used against women by their intimate male partners is very much the same across the world.

16

Cultures of violence and social exclusion

Nowhere is the self-defeating factor in the victory of violence over power more evident than in the use of terror to maintain domination.

(Arendt 2008: 242)

Violence, as Arendt asserts, is the extension of attempts to gain and maintain power over others, although, as she argues, violence ultimately destroys power because power and violence are opposites and where the one rules absolutely the other is absent (2008: 242). A man who can only keep his position as 'head of the family' through violence is not exercising or gaining power. He is demonstrating his failure (Russell, Van de Ven and Gena 1988; Walker 1989; Worden and Carlson 2005). But what of situations and cultures where violence is legitimated by those who have political power?

During the middle ages, it was both legal and 'normal' for women to be burned alive for threatening their husbands, talking back, adultery, having children outside marriage, masturbating, lesbianism, or miscarrying, even if this was the result of a kick or blow from their husband (Dodge, Bates and Pettit 1990; Erez 2002).

In the following centuries there were only relatively minor changes in how women were treated, and in most contemporary societies, although cruelty of all sorts to women is illegal, there are still 'traditional' enclaves where, for example, women are burnt alive on widowhood – the Indian rite of 'suttee' – or girls have their genitals mutilated (see Daly 1984).

Other contemporary illegal violence(s) include trafficking in women from Eastern Europe and the former Soviet Union to work as slave prostitutes in the west (Raymond 2002), so-called 'honour' killings and kidnappings, particularly among the Muslim community (Nasrullah, Haqqi and Cummings 2009), and rapes and torture of women in conflict and war zones (Brownmiller 1975/1993; Niarchos 1995; Caprioli and Boyer 2001; Douki, Nacef, Belhadj, Bouasker and Ghachem 2003). There are also numerous cases of rape of women in apparently stable, peaceful conditions, named by Betsy Stanko (1985) as the 'ever present terror' (Pearshouse 2008).

However, in the twenty-first century in western democracies and beyond there should be no excuse for ignorance of what constitutes a breach of the law in relation to violence between partners. If one partner intimidates, humiliates, or gratuitously torments the other mentally or physically in any way then it is defined ethically, legally and emotionally as domestic violence and abuse.

Cultural contexts, then, clearly constrain the way women are valued and treated, and the extent to which this is 'acceptable' depends upon the politics, religion and culture (Sokoloff and Dupont 2005; Sullivan, Senturia,

Negash, Shiu-Thornton and Giday 2005; Yoshihama 2005; Weidel, Provencio-Vasquez, Watson and Gonzalez-Guarda 2008).

In Cambodia, for example, the brutality of the Khmer Rouge regime continues to reverberate. According to one website[7] the *nature* of domestic violence can be assessed from personal stories. For example it reported the story of one woman[8] in 2008 who was hit by her husband for the first time when she was just 23 and he returned home drunk. It was reported that this young woman had been angry with him for spending the little money they had on alcohol, when the couple's son was, in her words 'weak with hunger'. When her husband slapped her in the face, the woman was afraid but not surprised, and she stated that, 'Men think that a woman is their property once they are married.' 'They think they have the right to hurt us.'

The website continued to propose that this was not unique and claimed that reports suggest one in four Cambodian women have experienced abuse at the hands of their partner. But, despite these appalling statistics, the Cambodian government has done little to stop the violence. A law on the prevention of domestic violence, passed in 2005, has:

> barely scratched the surface of such an endemic, and complex, violation of human rights. Female inferiority is instilled at all levels of society in Cambodia – women receive a second-class education, marry early, and are expected to serve and respect their husbands.
>
> Add to this the culture of violence – perpetuated by the brutal Khmer Rouge regime – which continues to reverberate in Cambodia. Often the shame of exposing marital problems is enough to keep women quiet.

This one example alone emphasises some of the complexities associated with living with domestic abuse exacerbated by the material conditions of developing post-conflict societies. These are shown here as endemic violence, poverty, hunger, worries about children, alcohol abuse, and few educational opportunities, on top of the straightforward neglect and denigration of women's lives and women's rights even as rhetoric and legislation appear to espouse emancipation and change. On top of it all is the shame women would have in exposing the fact that they are being abused by their husbands. The same website[9] provides a comparable account of domestic abuse in Kenya:[10]

> Traditional and cultural attitudes to women in Kenya can be summed up in a quote from an elder of a nomadic community; 'Women belong wholly to men except their teeth. If you break a woman's arm you don't pay for it, if you break her teeth, you do.' Against this backdrop of violence, Eva Darare, a dynamic and

committed woman, supports both men and women through gender development initiatives. The Rendille are a marginalised group within the community and women are second class citizens, they often suffer domestic violence and are discriminated against in so many ways. 'For example, they don't own anything, they don't inherit anything. There is a lot of wife beating – all those injustices which women go through in the name of culture.'

This example shows that although domestic violence occurs across the spectrum in Kenya there are some groups, such as the nomadic ethnic Rendille, where women's value is even less than in others, and that domestic violence is one more inequality and discrimination for women to live with.

Another website about Korean women's experiences[11] indicated a differentiation between sub-cultural groups, with a growing awareness and resistance to being abused by urban women while rural life still meant that women were not in a position to ask for divorce and thus gain a degree of safety. Statistically in rural Korea:

1   Forty to sixty per cent of married women have been physically abused by their spouse.
2   Nine per cent have been beaten badly enough to need medical treatment.
3   One out of six married people has suffered from domestic violence.
4   The Korean Women's Hot Line revealed that 42 per cent of those interviewed had been assaulted more than once a week.

Russell *et al.* (1988) documented crimes against women from around the world re-emphasising the double oppression of 'Third World' women and the silences of governments in Australia, South Africa, Egypt, Saudi Arabia and the USA about the violence towards minority ethnic groups such as Aboriginal, Black, Arab and Native American women. This study covers rape and sexual abuse as well as domestic violence and abuse but clearly indicates the different layers of disadvantage to women that privilege men and patriarchy, reinforcing men's domination over women.

A collection of essays and research reports on family violence (Klein 1998) illustrated the variation in the ways and extent to which different cultural groups and researchers in different communities identify and report family violence, although it is still clear that mostly men are violent towards their intimate female partners. Official statistics in Poland from the early 1990s identified male to female violence occurring in about 30 per cent of heterosexual relationships in urban areas and around 40 per cent in rural areas. Forty-one per cent of divorced women had experienced regular physical attacks by their husbands, although this was not the main reason given for the divorce (Kwiatkowska 1998). Statistics from Greenland were less robust although it is clear from both statistical and anecdotal evidence that the phenomenon of men beating their wives is commonplace there (Sorensen 1998). Evidence from Greece, France and Germany in the same anthology reinforces these points.

Awareness of the prevalence of domestic violence was not matched by high-profile initiatives to combat it even in western industrial democracies until the mid- to late 1990s despite at least twenty years of academic discourse (e.g. R.E. Dobash and Dobash 1984). Equally, domestic violence and abuse are still taken for granted as part of married life in some non-democratic and developing societies, although one outcome of globalisation is for international initiatives to increase awareness among victims and government and non-governmental agencies. A north Indian study (S.L. Martin *et al.* 2002) of married men demonstrated intergenerational trans-mission of wife abuse. In South Africa one woman in every six is assaulted regularly by her partner (Russell 1991). In Bangladesh 50 per cent of married women who are murdered are killed by their husband (Neft and Levine 1997). The World Bank survey of 1993 showed that violence was a contributing factor to maternal mortality. Furthermore abused women were less likely to seek antenatal care and more likely to give birth to low birth-weight babies (Heise, Pitanguy and Germain 1994).

Challenging domestic violence

The *rhetorical* emphasis on women's rights in relation to domestic violence has changed dramatically over the past forty years. In 1971 Erin Pizzey established the first refuge for 'battered women' in the UK which famously became Chiswick Women's Aid. At that time the subject of domestic violence was both novel and controversial in that it was widely believed to be rare and directed to poor women living in inadequate housing. This meant it was of little interest across the general population.

In her first book on the subject Pizzey graphically describes not only the beginnings of her own awareness of the endemic nature of domestic violence but also the scandalous lack of resources to provide refuge and support for women and their children. She evoked the serendipitous example of an older woman who lived down the road from the refuge, who suffered from agoraphobia and was walked round by a neighbour for a cup of coffee every so often. This woman, who had brought up nine children, told Pizzey almost as an afterthought:

'My husband's beaten me all our married life'.
   It had started nineteen years before, when she was pregnant with the first child and he took up with another woman. When he came

home from the pub or from his job in a bad mood he just laid in to her.
 . . . 'Why didn't you leave him?' I asked not thinking.
 'Where do I go with my children?'

(Pizzey 1974/1977: 19)

This extract resonates with the stories from Cambodia described above – a drunken assault by an uncaring husband, worry about the children and serious material constraints. Later, in another example, Pizzey describes a middle-class mother who arrived at the refuge with four children. This woman's husband had been violent for quite a while but she had put up with it until he tried to throttle the eldest child. Pizzey then realised that 'a lot of women will put up with unimaginable cruelty to themselves but once the man attacks the children they leave for good' (1974/1977: 20). The simple need for a refuge from violence and abuse became abundantly clear.

As soon as the word got round that there was somewhere that women who suffer violence could take refuge, women were coming and they have never stopped coming. By May 1973, we were taking nearly 100 telephone calls a day. The little house was getting so full that we had to put mattresses down in the hall for people to sleep on. The usual number of residents was about thirty women and children.

(Pizzey 1974/1977: 43)

Lay, professional and academic interest in domestic violence, abuse and cruelty reflects the zeitgeist. Activism and support for women who are abused in a relationship has been strongly associated with the UK particularly because of Pizzey's pioneering work. However, therapeutic work, social action and research in the USA have developed and flourished since the 1970s (Walker 1979, 2000; Fincham and Beach 1999).

Now in the twenty-first century any internet search reveals literally thousands of websites across the world defining, challenging and providing information about how to combat domestic violence and abuse through reaching a place of safety and drawing on law enforcement and social care agencies. For instance the content of the *Women's Aid*[12] website (http://www.womensaid.org.uk/) is typical and provides details of the twenty-four-hour hotline, definitions, information about the frequency of violence, the fact that it is illegal and what a victim needs to do, as well as giving further information on the impact on survivors (including children).

All the websites make it clear that domestic violence should not be tolerated. Some refer to specific campaigns and partnerships against domestic violence and abuse.[13] For example in 2007 the police in Surrey (UK) undertook a 'day of action' to arrest those believed to be involved in serious domestic violence cases. They arrested six people during that day although the arrests did not result in prosecutions for domestic violence. In 2008 a partnership was formed between the Metropolitan Police (in London) and a National Centre for Domestic Violence with the aim that reported cases would result in an injunction within twenty-four hours, something which would not have happened otherwise. Normally a woman would have had to seek an emergency injunction through a solicitor and (probably) have to pay the fees.

In Australia the Partnerships Against Domestic Violence Taskforce is based on research evidence on what actually constitutes domestic violence and who perpetrates it and in what ways (Bagshaw and Chung 2000). The Council of Europe has established a Task Force to Combat Violence against Women, including Domestic Violence, and in November 2007 it launched a European-wide campaign at a conference in Madrid. The campaign is intended to ensure all European member states have effective legislation and action plans to combat domestic violence. Hagerman-White (2006) on their behalf had established that between 12 per cent and 15 per cent of European women over the age of 16 suffer domestic abuse in a relationship and many continue to suffer physical and sexual violence from former partners even after the break-up, and too many have died.

Rhetoric of punishment, protection and prevention also prevails (see Chapter 4) and is well expressed in the consultation paper on ending violence to women and girls issued by the British Government in 2009 (Home Office 2009). The aim of the consultation had been to:

> take more action to prevent violence against women and girls, help them feel safer when they are out, especially at night, further improve the help women and girls get when it is needed and act to catch and convict perpetrators.
>
> (Home Office 2009)

Jacqui Smith, the Home Secretary at the time, claimed that the British Labour Government over its three terms of office had worked with voluntary organisations to deliver a 'packet of measures' which had halved the number of domestic violence incidents and increased convictions, and that in 2007/8 the number of women killed by their partners and ex-partners was the 'lowest recorded figure for more than a decade'.

The achievements claimed were expressed in the language of *criminalisation* of domestic abuse (and other violences to women), emphasising the number of convictions and support for women to prosecute the perpetrators. The emphasis on prevention is about women/girls as 'victims'. But the ability and willingness to *understand* the abusive *relationship* is missing from all contemporary political and activist discourses. As argued in Chapter 2 below, while the phrase 'domestic abuse' has ensured that violence and other controlling and abusive behaviours are identified as reprehensible, there are *differences* in the experiences of women in different types of abusive relationships. Attending to these differences is more likely to result in effective use of resources, which may not necessarily be 'material' ones in the sense of refuges or the training of those concerned with the criminal justice system, but conjoint therapeutic services that work to change and support some relationships (Almeida and Durkin 1999; Rivett 2001; Stith, Rosen and McCollum 2003).

The relationships between recognition, understanding and beliefs about domestic violence then derive from the variation in socio-legal and historical endorsements of the conduct of intimate relationships which engage with a range of ideological positions, such as feminist and religious standpoints.

Domestic violence observed

Naming the problem reflects the socio-political context. This has been influenced by the growing amount of data collected from around the world demonstrating the extent of domestic abuse and its similarities and differences from other violence(s) against women. It has now been widely accepted by activists and policy makers that domestic abuse and violence comprise a (reasonably) unitary 'category' and are generally understood to be part of women's oppression under patriarchy and a legacy of women as men's 'chattels'. This was vividly expressed in some of the women's stories described above.

Domestic Violence Forums[14] in the UK have been renamed Domestic *Abuse* Forums to reflect an acknowledgement that violence in heterosexual relationships is part of a wider pattern of male behaviour. The front page of the Dundee Domestic Abuse Forum (http://www.ddaf.co.uk/) for example introduces the problem to its stakeholders thus:

Domestic Abuse Is:
Physical, emotional or sexual abuse of one person by another. It can happen with a partner or ex. partner.
Remember:
You are not alone and it is not your fault. Domestic Abuse is an Abuse of Power.

Contemporary and well-publicised definitions of domestic violence and abuse are now unequivocal. Thus the following description on the *Shelter* website:

Domestic abuse is when someone close to you (usually your spouse, partner, ex-spouse, or ex-partner) behaves towards you in a way that causes physical, mental, or emotional damage. It need not necessarily be physical violence.[15]

Hitting, punching, name calling, forcing sex, enforcing pregnancy or abortion, isolation, financial control, using contact with children to abuse you or them, blatant infidelity, humiliating, controlling and more: the gender politics of the naming of all these behaviours as domestic abuse represents a triumph for feminist activists. It adds more weight to their assault on patriarchy. There is some evidence of a continuum of cruelty from name calling to violence and aggression (see Chapter 2). However there is also an important difference between financial control and name calling (which are none the less unacceptable in a relationship) and a series of violent assaults and possibly murder. Women living with the possibility that their partner will beat them up if they say the wrong thing or the man has had a bad day at work will probably be traumatised and suffer mental health consequences (Herman 2004). A woman who is constantly undermined and humiliated by her partner may also suffer mental health consequences, but are these similar events and experiences?

The case of Leslie illustrates this. Now in her late fifties she married Christopher when they left college thirty-five years ago. He used to describe her as the 'prettiest woman on campus' and was proud to be seen with her and made this clear at their wedding. After their two children were born his career in publishing flourished and Leslie stayed at home until the girls started school. She was reasonably happy but put on weight and was less conscious of her appearance generally, not worrying too much about whether her clothes were fashionable. Her and Christopher's interests grew apart, although for a few years when she returned to teaching they lived peacefully, both taking a pride in their children and their own careers. When he was in his mid-forties Christopher's job was threatened. He moved to another newspaper (less prestigious but still interesting) but the print media was in decline and by the time he was 55 he had taken an early retirement package. He was financially secure but saw himself as a failure and instead of trying to find a role for himself he verbally attacked Leslie as often as he could. He would make rude comments about her appearance and was careless about how he treated her in public, often humiliating her in front of friends. He told his friends that she was a burden to him and he wished he could leave her. He became a nuisance to his old colleagues and gradually became more isolated and more unpleasant. They continue to live together although with largely separate lives and her friends don't understand why she doesn't leave.

Not every abusive marriage involves undermining and humiliation. Andy hit Briony on the jawbone, knocking out two teeth and leaving her with a bitten tongue and bruises. This happened within a year of their marriage when she came home late one night, slightly drunk and very happy, after being out with friends. She had no idea what had happened and why. He himself only knew that he had felt a sudden fury and jealousy that he had been deliberately left out of something good. He also felt she had been laughing at him and talking about him to her friends. Andy had lost control of his anger but expressed remorse. They both decided this should never happen again and have sought psychological therapy. The prognosis is unclear.

These cases are not the same and despite the potential for a generally abusive man to escalate his behaviour from name calling to slapping and for a man who has once hit a woman to become more frequently violent and out of control there is no evidence to indicate that any of this will lead to violent assault with a weapon or murder (D.G. Dutton and Kropp 2000; Kropp and Hart 2000; Kropp 2004).

It is therefore important to consider how far the more inclusive category of 'domestic abuse' is actually helpful to women. On the one hand it highlights that women should be treated equally and with respect by their partners. It also demonstrates that control and humiliation are not acceptable and women do not have to put up with such behaviour as an inevitable consequence of a heterosexual relationship. It provides a name for this behaviour, enabling women to lay blame where deserved. However such a catch-all category also has negative consequences. The public in the main and the mass media frequently fail to name couple violence(s) as domestic abuse. It does not always happen in 'predictable' contexts and the profiles of perpetrators are not necessarily immediately obvious. Old, young, educated, rich, poor, middle- and working-class men and (less often) women from a range of religious backgrounds and political affiliations can perpetrate or become victims/survivors of domestic violence and abuse. Individual examples seem to be treated as single, albeit shocking, events and constructed as special 'newsworthy' cases of violence, cruelty or criminality, as of course they are. The following was reported in the *Yorkshire Post* in 2003 for example:

A highly-educated professional man in Leeds had beaten his wife for years when she had a stroke which left her struggling to walk.

She needed a Zimmer frame, but he disliked her using it. Health visitors were horrified to witness the old man pull her frame away, shouting 'you don't need that, you must walk properly'.

He then kicked her as she lay on the floor.

Health visitors also suspected he was refusing to get her drinks or take her to the toilet in the night, as they frequently found her in the mornings lying in a soiled bed. Ms Ingram said: 'She didn't have the mental ability to make her own decisions because she had had a stroke but she was plainly very scared. She would clutch at the hands of the home care workers because she didn't want them to leave her.' The woman was ultimately taken away to a residential care home.[16]

This case, as characterised here, is a series of 'surprising' contradictions that reinforce the prevalence and pervasiveness of domestic violence. Older people are not expected to abuse their partners, or to be abused, particularly if the perpetrator is 'highly educated' and the survivor disabled. The health care workers were 'horrified' although it appears from this extract that it took quite some time before anyone of them took action to have the woman 'taken away' from the abusive context. This is a puzzling case. From reading this report it would appear that the man's behaviour had been known for some time (since his partner's stroke at least). Her weakened body prevented her from defending herself – all she could do was to clutch at the hands of possible rescuers, but they did not seem to act. This happened in an affluent British city with two universities, modern hospitals, contemporary shopping arcades, theatres, cinemas – not at all similar to a developing country.

This case may stand out because the couple were older, but it is not without precedent for older people to experience violence at the hands of their partners or other relatives (Pillemer 2005; Steinmetz 2005). It was perhaps the blatant violence that the man demonstrated that brought the details into the public domain.

However, more recently another incident where a 69-year-old man tried to poison his estranged wife on more than one occasion was described as an 'ill-thought-out act of love', for which he received a suspended sentence.

The case of William and Maureen Dowling was reported on a website (by Steve Addison and edited by Tim Castle)[17] headed: 'Pensioner who tried to poison his estranged wife so he could win back her love by nursing her to health escaped jail on Friday'.

This was an account of the trial of 69-year-old William Dowling, held recently in Preston Crown Court in the north of England. Dowling had slipped mercury into his wife Maureen's tea on at least five occasions. Maureen had suffered symptoms including forgetfulness, indigestion and headaches but the mercury had apparently had no serious adverse effect on her health. Dowling was given a 350-day prison sentence, suspended for two years, according to the Press Association. Judge Robert Brown also imposed an eighteen-month supervision order.

Dowling had admitted administering a poison or noxious substance with intent to injure, aggrieve or annoy. Prosecutor Mark Lamberty stated in court that Maureen Dowling, aged 64, would regularly visit her old home and had gone to see her estranged husband in February 2008. The judge in the trial is reported to have said:

> The defendant made her a cup of tea and, as was customary, poured that into a white china beaker with a yellow floral motif. While she was drinking it, she noticed what appeared to her to be ball bearings at the

bottom of the cup. She showed it to her daughter Julie and commented she had noticed that in her cup before, and it always appeared to be the situation that the defendant made the tea.

It seemed that there had been four or five previous occasions when Maureen had noticed the same thing. She allegedly commented about this to her estranged husband who replied that, 'they must be coming off the kettle', or on another occasion, 'they must be coming off the teabags'.

Lamberty is reported to have said that when Julie, the couple's daughter, examined the contents of the cup, which appeared to be liquid metal, 'the defendant seized the cup from her, threw the contents into the bin and appeared agitated'. When Mrs Dowling noticed the silvery substance in her tea cup the following week, the defendant told her he really must clean the kettle, Lamberty said. He also reported that the effects of this on Mrs Dowling had been 'devastating' and had caused her to lose her self-confidence and created a family rift.

Paul Lewis, for the defence, said in mitigation: 'the actions he undertook were only intended to annoy his wife so she would feel the need for him to care for her and so resurrect their relationship. He had no intention to cause her any significant harm. His actions were ill-thought-out.'

Judge Brown is reported to have told Dowling that his wife of twenty-eight years had left him because 'she had become fed-up of what she regarded as your controlling attitude towards her'. He continued:

> In judging the seriousness of the crime you committed, your . . . wanting her to return to your care is irrelevant. What is relevant is that you are not a medical expert and it follows from that that it was more by good luck than anything else that your wife did not suffer serious harm.

From the judge's comments we know the man was 'controlling' and his wife of many years had left him. His actions (ill-thought-out perhaps) were designed to cause her serious harm and were repeated several times. The woman suffered physically and doubtless emotionally as well and yet the perpetrator's excuse was taken at face value (or so it appears from the outcome of the trial). The words domestic violence/abuse were not mentioned.

When domestic violence becomes murder

Murder of women by their partners and ex-partners also gets a great deal of publicity, but although sensational, such murders are not on the whole isolated or discrete crimes of passion (R.E. Dobash et al. 2004). Evidence

27

suggests that it often takes much time and suffering before suspicions about the circumstances are raised and taken seriously by law enforcers (as well as friends and neighbours). Homicide is rarely named as 'domestic violence' even when a man murders his intimate partner. Murders of women by their partners exemplify this, as with the following examples, one in the UK and the other in the USA.

First is the case of Hayley Richards[18] from Wiltshire who, aged 23 and pregnant, reported an attack by her boyfriend to the police in 2005. This was six days before he murdered her. The day before the murder happened, the police had questioned Hugo Quintas, Hayley's boyfriend and murderer, but then released him, although he was subsequently charged and convicted. The 24-year-old man had denied murder during the trial, but pleaded guilty to manslaughter, claiming that his victim Hayley had provoked him to such an extent that he eventually killed her. However, five of the seven members of a Bristol Crown Court jury believed the prosecution had proven their case that Hugo Quintas had indeed murdered Hayley by slitting her throat in a premeditated fashion. After murdering his pregnant girlfriend, Quintas fled to Spain via Portugal. He was arrested in Madrid after an international manhunt was launched by Europol.

The second case is that of 27-year-old, pregnant Lori Hacking whose husband was arrested in August 2004 in Utah, on suspicion of her aggravated murder. Lori's relatives had been aware of his violent behaviour towards her but didn't know what to do about it or who to tell. It was some time before her body was found (dumped in a rubbish container) and before she could be given a formal burial. She had been shot in the head while she was sleeping. Her husband received a six-year prison sentence.

These examples (one woman with her throat slit and the other with a gunshot wound to the head) demonstrate some of the contradictions in public attitudes and discourse about domestic violence and abuse. In the case of Lori Hacking no one knew what do about her husband Mark Hacking's violence towards his pregnant wife. Hayley Richards had actually reported an earlier attack by her boyfriend Quintas to the police, but nothing was done to help her find safety.

The abusers in both cases believed they could get away with the murders. Quintas argued that he had been provoked and believed that was adequate mitigation. Mark Hacking's case was more complicated in that Lori had found him out in a lie. She had been told by Hacking, and believed him, that he had been accepted as a medical student. When she discovered that this was not, and could not be, the case it seems he murdered her to save his own face. He also claimed insanity at one point. He still only received a six-year jail term.

In both cases, once they had come to trial, the jurors took a hard line on their descriptions of the men's behaviour. But why did these innocent women have to die?

Another recent British case[19] where a woman was violently abused indicated that a similarly hard line was taken by the judge even though the woman was reconciled with the abuser and a lesser charge was eventually negotiated:

> Boyfriend is jailed over 'torture' (from the archive, first published Tuesday 18th Sep 2007).
>
> A boyfriend who scalded his girlfriend with boiling water has been jailed for 20 months.

Katie Cussans, who was pregnant by the time of the trial, went into the witness box at Bradford Crown Court to tell Judge Roger Scott that she was now reconciled with James Walsh, aged 45. Walsh, who had worked with vulnerable adults, however was given a custodial sentence, and Judge Scott declared that his behaviour towards his partner had been akin to torture. Prosecutor Jayne Beckett had apparently told the court that the couple had been arguing because Walsh wrongly believed his girlfriend was having an affair. At one stage he threatened to pour boiling water on himself, but then shook the kettle over his girlfriend as she crouched on the floor.

Judge Scott said: 'You accept she was screaming. It is a horrible, horrible picture and that was torture. There is no other word for it and torture should be dealt with by a custodial sentence.' Miss Beckett said the complainant had suffered burn marks to her back, arms and leg. Barrister Michelle Colborne, for Walsh, had urged Judge Scott to consider an intensive supervision programme.

Miss Colborne said: 'He's concerned that whatever incorrect and warped thinking was there on this occasion does not repeat itself.' Walsh had originally faced a charge of wounding with intent to cause grievous bodily harm, but at trial his plea to the lesser charge of causing grievous bodily harm was accepted by the prosecution after consultation with the victim. Judge Scott is reported to have said that he took account of Miss Cussans's forgiveness and the fact that the couple were reconciled, but said he had a duty to the public.[20]

High-profile cases that come to court are positioned as exceptional behaviours or 'real' crimes as distinct from 'commonplace' domestic violence. Bullock and Cubert (2002) emphasise that newspaper coverage of domestic violence fatalities tends to take each of them as separate incidents rather than show the pattern of (mostly) male violence to women. Such cases therefore are probably understood as the exceptions.

It is also important to note that in the two murder cases described the women were pregnant (Renker and Tonkin 2006; Cook and Bewley 2008). There is evidence to show that in many relationships domestic violence begins or is exacerbated when the woman becomes pregnant (Peckover 2003; Cook and Bewley 2008). In the case of Katie Cussans she became pregnant soon after the reconciliation, showing that many women in abusive relationships are sexually active and many claim to love the abusive partner.

'Victim' or 'survivor'?

The term 'victim' is an emotive one in the context of domestic abuse and violence (Kirkwood 1993; Ferraro 1996). It broadly means someone who has suffered an injury or injustice from some act, condition, or circumstance. Was the older woman who was taken into residential care a victim? Was Katie Cussans a survivor? Both of these women lived after their abuse and in the latter case Cussans continued to live with and have a sexual relationship with her abuser. However the first woman was frail and had had to be rescued. Cussans returned to her abuser even though she had been seriously harmed.

Feminist-inspired discourses around domestic abuse focus on the word 'survivor' in preference to 'victim'. The Women's Aid website makes the following point in explanation:

> The terms 'victim' and 'survivor' are both used, depending on the context. 'Survivor' is, however, preferred as it emphasises an active, resourceful and creative response to the abuse, in contrast to 'victim', which implies passive acceptance. If you are reading this, then you are – at least to some extent – a survivor.[21]

Ferraro (1996) reiterates that victimisation carries notions of 'deservedness', with a public and legal image of a victim influenced by class and race. This rhetoric also resonates with Walker's (1979) model which proposes that abused women are subject to a pattern of 'learned helplessness'. As Kirkwood (1993) posits, however, although this perspective moved psychological analyses of battered women forward from female masochism theories, it introduced the idea of women as helpless victims which did not resonate with the vision of the woman surviving against the odds.

Critics in the past have identified feminism itself as working from a standpoint in which all women are victims of male violence inspired through the operation of patriarchy, and this indeed raises questions about the ways in which some feminist discourses position themselves. For the purposes of this book I have chosen to use the terms 'victim' and 'survivor' dependent upon the material circumstances of the matter under discussion. For example a woman in a violent relationship suffering abuse and violence, at the time is a victim and so I use that word in that context.

A woman who has left a violent relationship and emotionally and physically lived to tell the tale is clearly a survivor.

Conclusions

Why is there such an interest in domestic violence? And why now? Men have always battered the women they live with in all societies across the ages. The 'cartoon' image of the cave-man with his club dragging an unconscious woman along behind him by her hair is a familiar archetypal 'humorous' image which is also a representation of 'love' and marriage. This has not evaporated with the knowledge of brutality to women across the world. For some, 'wife beating' remains a joke. But the evidence is increasingly clear that domestic abuse and violence if not prevented end in murder. The material constraints under which the majority of women live in affluent and developing countries have ensured their oppression and place them at risk of abuse and violence.

2

WHAT IS DOMESTIC ABUSE?

Introduction

> Thirty years ago 'wife abuse' didn't exist; there were no 'battered women' or 'abusive men'. Of course that doesn't mean that men were not being violent toward women. Rather it means that the social problem . . . was not yet in the public consciousness.
>
> (Loseke 2001: 107)

Histories of family life and gender-power relations have revealed that physical and mental cruelty to women and children are typically taken for granted as part of 'normal' family relations (Gordon 1988). Domestic violence and abuse, by definition, take place away from the public gaze and so are easy to ignore, diminish and/or deny (Jecker 1993; Heise *et al.* 1994; Zink, Jacobson, Regan and Pabst 2004). Therefore, even in sophisticated democratic societies, recognition that violent behaviour in the private sphere 'counts' along with publicly committed violence is a relatively new concept.

However, the last part of the twentieth and into the twenty-first century saw changes so that now, in law and in general, violence, abuse and cruelty in the home are without doubt understood to be as 'bad' as they are in the community, and the perpetrator seen as equally as culpable as when similar acts occur in a public place (Romkens 2006; Pearshouse 2008). It is only during the past twenty-five to thirty years though that domestic violence and abuse have reached the top of the public health, legal, social care and academic agendas, with research evidence now providing the core of practitioner training and guidelines for good practice (Coker *et al.* 2000; Ellsberg, Heise, Pena, Agurto and Winkvist 2001; Peckover 2003; Humphreys 2007).

A burgeoning combination of campaigning (Heyzer 1998; Murray and Powell 2009), advocacy (Gilson 1998; Hague and Mullender 2006) and research on domestic violence and abuse across the world (J.C. Campbell 1990; Walker 1999; Carrillo 2002; Bostock *et al.* 2009) has been successful in placing concern over domestic abuse and violence high on the political and public agendas. This work has had a direct and irrevocable influence on health and social care practice (Heise *et al.* 1994; Peckover 2003; Jenkin and

32

Millward 2006; Humphreys 2007), justice (Frattaroli and Teret 2006; van Wormer 2009), resource allocation and policy (Pahl 1985; Breckenridge and Mulroney 2007). It has also made an impact on attitudes (Worden and Carlson 2005; Muhlbauer 2006). Thus it is true to say that:

> advocates for battered women some thirty years ago took a strong and uncompromising stance that all violence against women is best dealt with as a crime, that it reflects the patriarchal nature of society, and that any attempt to examine couple dynamics in domestic violence adds to battered women's victimisation. At the same time, some aspects of domestic violence were, of necessity, left out of the advocacy movement's analysis. In order to advance an important social change agenda, advocates downplayed . . . the wish many victims have to stay with their abusive partners, albeit without continued violence.
>
> (Stith *et al.* 2003: 423)

The conundrum of matching the pro-feminist ideologies with those of other groups who take a less uncompromising stand on how to manage the variety of needs of those involved in domestic violence and abuse is the challenge I try to meet in this book: how to walk a line through the dilemma of being pro-feminist while seeing that what women frequently say they want collides with the underlying tenet of feminist ideology – that is that many women wish to remain with their partners and be assisted to cope in doing so.

Methodological and ideological disagreements which have emerged between groups of academics and also between some academics and women's advocates (see for example Kirkwood 1993; Mullender and Morley 2001; Felson 2002; Loseke, Gelles and Cavanaugh 2005; D. Dutton and Corvo 2006; Gondolf 2007) have reached an impasse. Questions about the nature and extent of women's violence to men (Gelles 1980; Straus 2005), whether growing up with domestic violence influences the future behaviour of men and/or women (Markovitz 2001) and the impact of patriarchy on gender-power relations in the analysis of intimate relationships (R.E. Dobash and Dobash 1984; Yllö 2005) have not been resolved and do not look as if they will be in the near future.

Navigating this complex area, which in part is about psychology versus sociology, feminism versus traditional psychology, and qualitative versus quantitative research, and making a contribution to knowledge and to women's lives, poses a major challenge to any discipline. However, psychology in particular has been positioned as unhelpful and vilified as 'anti-feminist' (Kirkwood 1993; Mullender and Morley 2001; see Chapter 3).

In this book I reconsider the role psychology has played in making sense of domestic abuse in order to prevent it and support survivors, but also the role that the stand-off between psychology and pro-feminists has played in

33

making a critical applied psychology problematic (see for example Bostock *et al.* 2009).

In this chapter I examine some of the social, cultural and historical connections between all the key players as they impact upon naming, defining, identifying and understanding the scope and impact of what is most commonly referred to as *domestic violence* and/or *domestic abuse*. I then outline the possibilities provided by a material-discursive-intrapsychic theoretical approach which will be the framework for what then follows.

Describing domestic violence

Despite the detailed descriptions outlined in Chapter 1, it remains hard to explain exactly what constitutes domestic violence, why it happens and what it feels like to live with it. Women's experiences of life prior to an abusive relationship vary to such an extent that there is no *global* 'template' or clearly defined line that is crossed between violence and non-violence (Bifulco, Bernazzani, Moran and Ball 2000; Ehrensaft, Brown, Smailes, Chen and Johnson 2003; Fernandez 2006; Bayer, Hiscock, Ukoumunne, Price and Wake 2008). This is partly because of social norms which vary between countries, communities and social groups (Perilla 1999; S.H. Martin *et al.* 2002). It has already been suggested in Chapter 1 that in post-conflict and developing societies, violence itself has different levels of meaning (McFarlane, Groff, O'Brien and Watson 2005; Craig, Robyak, Torosian and Hummer 2006). This is true for relationships as well so that giving an experience *meaning* in any relationship requires pre-existing repertoires of meaning for individuals to enable them to name their experience. Linda Green (2008), talking about the experience of living with violent civil conflicts across the world, makes the point:

> How does one become socialised to terror? Does it imply con-formity or acquiescence . . .? While it is true that with repetitiveness and familiarity people learn to accommodate themselves to terror and fear, low intensity panic remains in the shadow of waking consciousness. One cannot live in a constant state of alertness, and so the chaos one feels becomes diffused throughout the body.
>
> (Green 2008: 186)

This paragraph could well be describing domestic violence and abuse. This 'socialisation' and 'familiarity' sometimes makes it difficult for women to see themselves as experiencing it until some time after it has happened, and often they don't recognise the full extent of the abuse until they are free from the perpetrator (Muehlenhard and Kimes 1999). They may at the time experience the upsetting events simply as individual incidents which don't necessarily paint the picture of themselves living in a violent relationship.

Also it is possible to get used to someone's bad and abusive behaviour so you see it as just 'the way they are'. Connie[1] was typical in that:

> at the time I didn't really know, I didn't recognise it for what it was because I mean it was things like not speaking to you, like nudging you and bumping into you and at one point he pulled my hair and pushed me over, things like that. I just thought that was sort of like a bit over zealous but I didn't really recognise it for the start off.

Most women, across many studies, report that it was difficult to name what was happening to them as abuse or domestic violence (Ferraro and Johnson 1983; Frost 1999; Zink *et al.* 2004; Hague and Mullender 2006). As Lara reported:

> In my case where there weren't a lot, well it sounds a bit contradictory cause when I listen to what I am saying it sounds like there were a lot of physical abuse, but I didn't think at the time there were a lot of physical abuse. And I didn't sort of class myself as a person suffering domestic violence, just that I had got a really abusive husband, that's all. . . . Because most of his abuse were verbal. . . . And I didn't sort of when I first started going to the domestic violence project I used to feel a bit like sort of guilty, that I shouldn't be there you know because I had not been getting beaten up everyday I thought it didn't count . . . when you leave you actually realise how bad things were.

In fact Lara had been beaten up and thrown against a wall on the several occasions that her ex-husband had been out drinking. Somehow though it took a 'shift' in her sense of herself to understand that she was experiencing domestic violence. The psychological aspects of victimhood in this (horrendous) context make it hard for someone to be objective and reflect upon their own situation. The awareness that you are living with an abuser (rather than someone who behaves in certain ways) often comes slowly into consciousness, by which time it is too late to simply leave. And then there is a sense of shame that this happened.

Marilyn had had two abusive partners. Recognition of what was happening (particularly with the second man) left her with 'Shame. I think that's the big one.' But for her there was also the 'wake up call' and then the 'Fear – the fact that if you do tell somebody then you have got to do something about it really. You're . . . there's no back up . . . you and your children living in the dark.' Marilyn's previous experience of a violent man had made recognition that she was living with the experience again even more frightening in that she knew she had to name the experience but that would also compel her to act (particularly on behalf of her children) and then somehow, it seemed from her narrative, flood gates would open and take away control (see also Chapter 8).

Experiencing violence

Descriptions of incidents that women in the DASH study introduced into the interviews show the *variety* of abuse and violence that the men perpetrated and differences in how they dealt with it (Ferraro and Johnson 1983). Some women had always known their partners could act in violent ways while others had never expected to witness or experience abuse. Two women participants exemplify this.

Sandra, who was 22 when she was interviewed, described seeing her ex-partner of five years, before they began living together, 'try and poke people's eyes out and bite people's noses off in fights', so she was convinced his threats were authentic when 'daily he used to tell me that if I leave him he knows where my nan lives, he'll set their house on fire, he'll kill my sister and he'll cut my face wide open'. She did manage to leave him after he was imprisoned for assaulting someone else but was persuaded to go back to him after his release. Following their reconciliation they went to another city to visit his mother but as they were driving back home (they were both drunk) he stopped the car and:

> I was really drunk out of my head like concussed and he like pinned me down, do you know and ripped my tights and everything. . . . And I don't know why I stayed with him after that because after he'd started, but didn't do it properly, he started to have sex with me. I started crying and everything so he got off, so there's me thinking 'oh it's right good that he stopped' . . . and there's me thinking 'he must care 'cos he stopped'. But after we got home he lost something in the flat and couldn't find it so he started throwing the plates down stairs, at my head. You know the dinner plates and I was jumping like that and I was crying and he still had sex with me even though I didn't want to and I was crying all the way through.

Sandra's description and reflection on how she coped demonstrate violent and abusive behaviour on the part of her partner but also hint at how she was looking for some evidence, however small, that he cared for her. She thought he had stopped his sexual advance at first, which was the evidence she sought, but that he later continued while she cried and resisted remained crucial to her narrative and possibly how she identified what he did as abuse and violence, and also brings to the fore what some commentators position as the 'relational' side of abusive couple relationships (Kearney 2001; Wood 2001; Allison *et al.* 2008).

Mary, a woman in her late fifties from a middle-class professional background, had a different but equally harrowing story to tell. Geoff, her husband of nearly thirty years by the time of the incident, frequently yelled and swore at her. On one occasion they were shopping and she dropped a bottle of wine as she was putting it in the supermarket trolley and it broke. 'He just stood there and yelled "you silly fucking bitch". You name it and it came out in this torrent.' She was used to his abusive language. However, later they were on holiday with their three teenage children:

> and this particular evening we'd had dinner and I was really feeling hot and bothered with the atmosphere and the kids and so on but there was nothing particularly wrong. I went up and had a shower and I was sitting on the bed with a towel around me and he came in and he never said anything and he just picked up the pillow from the bed and brought it down on my head and I was so surprised. I must have had my mouth open to say something because when he hit me with the pillow my jaw clamped together and I cracked this tooth and I was in enormous pain for three days . . . and then he stamped on my foot and threw a book at me and I can see myself now. . . . I started to scream because I was quite frightened and we were in one room and the children were next door so I shot out of our room . . . he'd sort of made three attacks and I didn't really know what he was going to do next so I shot into the other room screaming and I can't really remember what I said but as a result of what had happened the boys were aware of what had been going on.

Neither Sandra nor Mary talked specifically about domestic violence or abuse, but there is no doubt their experiences qualify. The *context* of their experiences and the particular incidents described above have much in common and demonstrate that men and women from all backgrounds are able to both be perpetrators and be victim/survivors. However there are also differences in their relationships and expectations about relationships that might shed light on matters such as risk factors, emotional dependence and other vulnerabilities that are absent from much contemporary literature (Ferraro and Johnson 1983; Goldner, Penn, Sheinberg and Walter 1990).

Meanings

The words used by academics and practitioners to describe the phenomenon once known generally as 'wife battering' serve as metaphors representing the potentially diverse ideologies among those who work in the areas of abuse and violence between intimate partners (Margolin, Burman and John 1993). Embedded within the words which name the problem are powerful gender and socio-historical politics. Are all men 'naturally' predisposed to violence? Are men and women equally capable of violence? Does verbal aggression or controlling another person represent an inevitable first step towards physical violence? Is patriarchy to blame for inevitable violence against women? Do women collude in their own abuse? The questions and their answers are all highly emotive and uncompromisingly contested among practitioner agencies and academics.

Some words position men as maliciously culpable, allocating most of the blame to them, as in 'wife abuse/battering' (Walker 1979; R.P. Dobash, Dobash, Wilson and Daly 1992). This label appears to position the 'wives' as (relatively) blameless, defenceless or passive in the face of the abuse. Other descriptions, for instance 'family violence', *spread* blame, although this label also potentially obscures the evidence that men, on the whole, are the perpetrators and women the victims of violence in the home between intimate partners. More recently, the terms 'domestic violence' and 'domestic abuse' have replaced 'wife battering' or similar phrases. Although 'domestic abuse' has strong connotations and is a term that does not 'tolerate' any form of coercion by the perpetrator, paradoxically it is also euphemistic, particularly with regard to lay perceptions, whereas 'battering' provokes a more chilling evocation. 'Domestic violence' has the clear connotation that, 'In everyday speech and even in most social science discourse, "domestic violence" is about men beating women' (Johnson and Ferraro 2000: 948). Ferraro also indicates that, 'In the United States, at the end of the millennium, "domestic violence" is a code for physical and emotional brutality within intimate relationships, usually heterosexual' (1996: 77). 'Domestic abuse' appears to extend the potential types of act that might make one person a 'perpetrator' and the other a 'victim' or 'survivor'. Most recently however the phrase 'domestic violence against women' has been used (Bostock *et al.* 2009), suggesting that perhaps the expressions 'domestic violence' or 'abuse' have now extended their meaning beyond man to woman violence, requiring more precise terminology.

'Violence' itself though is a multi-faceted term with little consensus about its meaning. Barnett and colleagues cite research in the USA (Adams 1986) which indicates clearly that:

> the battering of women is not just perpetration of a list of physically abusive behaviours. Instead true battering includes the instilment of fear, oppression, control of the victim and assault.
>
> (Barnett, Miller-Perrin and Perrin 2005: 252)

The phrases 'domestic violence', 'domestic abuse' (R.E. Dobash and Dobash 1984) and 'woman abuse' (Mullender and Morley 2001) are used more frequently in the UK and Europe (Borg 2003), while 'family violence' and, more recently, 'intimate partner violence' (IPV) are used more in the USA (e.g. R.C. Klein 1998; Barnett *et al.* 2005; Loseke *et al.* 2005).

The transition on both sides of the Atlantic from the common term 'battered' wives, or women, is indicative of changes in the ideological, legal and political climates across the last (approximately) thirty years. That the talk of 'wives' is now excluded demonstrates changes in domestic arrangements (or at least the formal recognition of them), so that unmarried heterosexual and gay relationships are now included (Letellier 1994; Ristock 2003).

Although IPV is now the preferred North American term, there is no consensus on what this actually means (Barnett *et al.* 2005). Generally in the USA IPV refers to a range of actions from 'mild verbal abuse to severe physical violence and even death' (Barnett *et al.* 2005: 251), and therefore includes acts of emotional or psychological abuse, stalking, physical assaults, sexual assaults (i.e. marital rape), injuries and homicides, and includes victims and perpetrators from both heterosexual and homosexual relationships (R.P. Dobash *et al.* 1992; Abrams and Robinson 1998; Nasrullah *et al.* 2009).

Domestic abuse (DA) (rather than violence), the term most commonly and currently used in the UK and Europe (Mullender 1996), has equivalent sub-categories to those set out in definitions of IPV. DA involves the emotional, physical, sexual and/or economic abuse of one or more members of a family by another within the domestic sphere (R.P. Dobash *et al.* 1992; Grace 1995; Richardson and Feder 1996; Bates and Brown 1998; Hearn 1998; Department of Health 2001) and involves a number of forms of violence including physical assault, sexual abuse and rape, threats and intimidation. Furthermore:

> Physical violence may be accompanied by other forms of intimidation such as degradation, mental and verbal abuse, humiliation and deprivation (which can involve keeping women without money and in isolation), and may also include systematic criticism and belittling.
>
> (Home Office 2003: 3)

It is thus likely that physical, psychological and sexual abuse is experienced in more than one way in most cases (Eriksen and Henderson 1992).

Categories of domestic violence?

Are there different types of domestic violence? Certainly personal narratives of living with violent men indicate that patterns of abuse vary with the relationships. A review of the psychological research on domestic violence during the 1990s (Johnson and Ferraro 2000) indicated two broad themes. The first included the importance of distinctions between types and contexts of violence. The second was about the interplay between violence, power and control in relationships and included the 'gendered' context of abusive relationships (Bettman 2009) including the psychological and social consequences of domestic violence (Coker *et al.* 2000; Humphreys and Joseph 2004; Kasturirangan, Krishnan and Riger 2004). These themes have remained a feature of subsequent studies.

Johnson and Ferraro concluded in their review that:

> in spite of increasing evidence of the importance of distinctions, almost all of our general theoretical and empirical work is severely handicapped by the failure to attend to these distinctions. . . . Everything from lists of risk factors, to inferences about causal processes from multivariate analyses, to statements about differences in incidence across groups or across time – all of it – is called into question.
>
> (Johnson and Ferraro 2000: 959)

While Johnson and Ferraro argue that it is important to distinguish different *types* of violence against partners if our knowledge and potential to predict and successfully intervene are to progress (Murray and Powell 2009), other writers see no distinctions to be made (Skinner *et al.* 2005; Sokoloff and Dupont 2005). Johnson and Ferraro (2000) confirmed Johnson's earlier work identifying four types of partner violence: '*common couple violence*' (CCV), '*intimate terrorism*' (IT), '*violent resistance*' (VR) and '*mutual violent control*' (MVC). Particularly important also was that such distinctions are not based on a single incident but on more general patterns of control across the 'many encounters that comprise a relationship, patterns that are rooted in the motivations of the perpetrator and his or her partner' (Johnson and Ferraro 2000: 949).

In summary the distinctions they make are as follows:

CCV (common couple violence): This arises out of the context of a specific argument in which one or both of the partners lash out physically at the other. It is not likely to escalate over time, nor to be severe and is more likely to be mutual.

IT (intimate terrorism): Here violence is but one tactic in a general pattern of control. It is likely to escalate over time, less likely to be mutual and more likely to result in serious injury. However it is not just severe violence. It might result in murder or it might be low-level violence but it does come from a motive to control.

VR (violent resistance): This is perpetrated almost solely by women. There is relatively little research done on this.

MVC (mutual violent control): Johnson describes this as a couple who 'could be viewed as two intimate terrorists battling for control'. Once again relatively little research has been done on this type of couple violence.

How useful is it to make these distinctions? Do we learn about the complexities of relationships from these typologies? How far does the classification of abusive relationships lead to further understanding of why
violence occurs and how to prevent it? Is there a 'sliding scale' between
lashing out in an argument as in CCV and intimate terrorism? The stand-
off between pro-feminist authors and the psychologists conducting large-
scale studies has not assisted an advance in knowledge or practice.

The majority of research on domestic violence, most of which does not
make such classifications, focuses on the causes and consequences of what
Johnson and Ferraro have labelled CCV and IT (Johnson 2006). Both types
are more likely to be perpetrated by men towards women, although where
there are cases of women who are abusive to their male partners the
physical violence on the whole is likely to be far less damaging (Hamberger
1997; R.E. Dobash *et al.* 2004; Swan and Snow 2006).

Common couple violence or intimate terrorism?

In the DASH study there were examples of both of these kinds of abuse
although it was unclear how far CCV might have become IT if there had
not been an end put to the violent relationship. Surely it is also a moot
point? Once the line has been crossed and a blow has been struck the fear of
subsequent violence will persist (Goldner *et al.* 1990; Walker 2000).

One case illustrates the *distinction* between types of violence that women
make for themselves however. Sasha talked about her first husband of
thirteen years who had died. She said that when they argued he would hit
her 'and then it were all over and done with. But he weren't like that all the
time and I would never have left him.' She said that she had loved him and
as he became weaker because of his illness his capacity for violence was
much diminished. However the relationship she began with another abusive
man was different. Shortly after they married, he

> began knocking me about . . . he never marked my face, usually my
> neck but he had a fad about strangling me you know. He used to like
> strangle me so I used to have a lot of marks on my neck. So I would
> just wear a scarf or polo neck. Once though he belted me with his
> belt, but he were blind drunk and he'd cut all my back with his belt and
> my legs and that's really when it came to a halt cause I kept saying to
> him it didn't hurt so he'd do it all more.

Sasha continued on to say that that particular incident made her contact
the women's refuge and eventually she left that man. What was not clear
was the connection between her telling him it didn't hurt, which clearly
increased his efforts to hurt her, and why that in particular was the last

41

straw for Sasha. This lends some support to the notion that there is an implicit hierarchy of violence in women's stories and also for almost all a 'tipping point'.

Other women in the DASH study reported a sense of the man's motive to terrorise and control them. Tricia for instance had remained married for thirteen years and during most of that time she lived in fear. She didn't report the violence, because of 'fear more than anything. Knowing that if I did speak to anybody I would get another crack or . . . I did leave him three years ago but. . . .' She returned to him because there seemed nothing else for her to do, nowhere to go with her young family. On one occasion:

> He threatened me with a knife, cut through the phone wire then threw me in another room and then threw the knife at the boys. He had the knife and was waving it everywhere. I just did whatever he said.

Another explicit example comes from Erin Pizzey's first book, which is equally evocative of terrorism:

> Years and years of cruelty and vicious persecution can knock the determination out of anybody. One woman who wrote to us had endured a nightmare marriage for thirty years. Time and again she'd tried to break out. She often went to her mother's but her husband had broken in there and taken her back. The police never did anything because it was a marital quarrel. Nobody else wanted to be involved. After all she did have a roof over her head didn't she? He always kept her short of money.
>
> (Pizzey 1974/1977: 43)

This is a particularly evocative example: thirty years of suffering and effective imprisonment with no one prepared to support the woman to leave. This situation may be dismissed by some as a story from the 1970s, with the advent of women's refuges and the increased profile of domestic violence in the community as the definitive moment when women's lives changed. But as shown so far from the literature and the stories above, this was the beginning – the tip of the iceberg – and as shown in Chapter 1, not all societies have reacted to support women's rights to a life untrammelled by such abuse (Palmer 1998; Krantz and Garcia-Moreno 2005; Ezer 2008; Suffla, Van Niekerk and Arendse 2008; Nasrullah *et al.* 2009).

Violent resistance

Women do resist violence sometimes in violent ways. In Hossein's novel (2007) about Laila and Mariam's marriage to Rasheed they eventually killed him, although Mariam had to pay the ultimate price. Many women don't get the chance to retaliate in kind. One DASH respondent, Mary, outlined her fantasy of violent resistance (VR), also known as the 'slow burn' because the resistance usually occurs after a long period of enduring violence and abuse. She had tried to serve her husband with divorce papers but he had ignored them. He swore and shouted obscenities in public which made her feel totally humiliated. He had a terrible temper that he would take out on her physically as well as through insults. She described her feelings after watching a fictional television programme in which an elderly woman stabbed her husband to death after many years of suffering his physical and psychological abuse.

> I just felt that one day that's what I would do [stab him] and he would push me to a point where I would just go for him and I wasn't prepared for that. I was never prepared to leave because as far as I was concerned I'd put an awful lot into that marriage and I'd created two really lovely homes and I wasn't going to walk away from that so what I had to do was to get him out and when I served the third lot of papers on him he didn't do anything about it, he just ignored it and I tried to talk to him about it and he used to say things like 'I don't understand what the problem is' and I'd tell him and then he'd say 'that's rubbish' and I'd say 'you cannot say that, it may sound like rubbish to you but that's how I feel'.

Mary fantasised about murdering her way out of the frustration caused by his controlling and abusive behaviour. But she never did it. However, women do take their revenge in relatively rare but dramatic cases, though frequently they suffer legal penalties for doing so because their methods are often more draconian than those of men.

Southall Black Sisters have been involved with supporting and arranging legal defences for several women who have killed or attacked a violent husband over recent years. The first highly publicised and successful case they took up was that of Kiranjit Ahluwalia, an Asian woman, who set fire to her husband Deepak in May 1989 after suffering his brutality for ten years. The story is now being made into a film, described in the extract below:

> Back in September, 1992, Regina vs Kiranjit Ahluwalia made English legal history when Kiranjit was released after serving three-and-a-half years of a mandatory life sentence for murdering her husband, Deepak, whom she had drenched in petrol while he was asleep and set alight. Her retaliation followed 10 years of systematic abuse but what caused her to flip on that fateful evening was that he had pressed a hot iron against her – she still bears the scars.

Kiranjit was released by Appeal Court judges on grounds of 'diminished responsibility' but her case, taken together with those of other women, all white, who had also killed their partners, has helped bring about a change in the law.

Today, if a battered woman strikes back and kills her husband or partner, the 'slow burn', the time period between the acts of abuse and retaliation, is taken into account. Unlike a man, who is physically stronger and can instantly lash out in a moment of anger, a woman smoulders inside but often waits before she seizes her opportunity. The law previously construed this to be pre-meditation and found women guilty of murder but after Kiranjit's case, the charge can be the lesser one of manslaughter which does not automatically carry the mandatory life sentence. It is a sobering thought that once upon a time, before the death penalty was abolished, Kiranjit would probably have gone to the gallows.

However, thanks to the campaign conducted on her behalf by the Southall Black Sisters, a women's rights group in west London, and a dynamic young Indian lawyer called Rohit Sanghvi, English law, while not giving battered women a licence to kill their men, is a lot more understanding about their plight.[2]

Mutual violent control and gender symmetry

Much political capital continues to be made about how far domestic violence includes mutual heterosexual couple violence as well as the related matter of whether the woman can be the main protagonist in a violent relationship (Gelles 1997; D.G. Dutton and Nicholls 2005; Motz 2008; Straus 2008) and whether gay and lesbian relationships provide additional data on heterosexuality and patriarchy (Hammond 1989; Letellier 1994; Ristock 2003). The violence(s) that Johnson and Ferraro classified as mutual violent control (MVC) represent the highly contentious view that women could engage in ongoing, seriously violent behaviour towards their partners rather than violent resistance as described above (Hamberger 1997; Dasgupta 2002; Gondolf 2007; Swan and Sullivan 2009). And there remains the question of 'who started it?'

A major point of contention is whether there is symmetrical or asymmetrical violence and whether frequency of violence and relative damage in violent encounters needs to be unpacked (R.E. Dobash *et al.* 2004; Johnson 2006).

There is little doubt that *some* women can be extremely and gratuitously violent, but far less evidence that the frequency of such behaviour in any way equals that of the violences of men (Motz 2008). Mostly such events

44

make news headlines. For example in a recent case reported in the media in which a woman was jailed for three years, Tracy Davies bit off her boyfriend's tongue. Both journalists and Mr Coghill, the boyfriend, described the event graphically:[3]

> A recovering alcoholic, Davies had become upset because she wanted a baby and wasn't pregnant. When Mr Coghill comforted her, she told him she loved him and asked him to kiss her.
>
> But she soon turned into a 'massive monster', Mr Coghill told the court, biting down hard on his tongue after she lured him into putting it in her mouth. He screamed in pain and tapped her on the head in a bid to make her release him. Instead she chewed through his tongue, and spat it out on the floor.

Apparently they had consumed at least two bottles of vodka between them that night, and the incident, as with the murders and serious assaults to women described in Chapter 1, was seen as a novel crime rather than domestic abuse and violence. The older (now almost apocryphal) story of John Wayne Bobbit[4] was a case where domestic violence and abuse was claimed by both partners:

> Who can forget John Wayne Bobbit, male victim of one of the most infamous domestic violence incidents of the last twenty years. In case you have, here's a quick recap:
>
> On the night of June 23, 1993, John Wayne Bobbit was fast asleep after allegedly engaging in non consensual intercourse with his wife. (He says it was consensual, she disagrees, however he was charged and subsequently acquitted.) Whilst he slept, Lorena Bobbit took a knife to his manhood, severed it from his body and took it for a drive, eventually tossing it into a field.
>
> After coming to her senses, Lorena realized what she had done, called 911 and aided the police in recovering John's member. It was reattached after a six hour operation, Lorena was taken into custody, charged and subsequently found to be mentally incompetent to the point where she was unable to take responsibility for her actions. According to her, she had been subjected to mental, emotional and physical abuse for the duration of her marriage to John Wayne, abuse which went so far as to include a forced abortion. At the end of the trial she was ordered into 45 day observation and then released.

In both examples (Bobbit and Davies/Coghill) the women were portrayed as somehow 'wronged' (by nature in that Davies could not get pregnant and by being a victim of Bobbit's abuse in the Bobbit case). They were also

45

positioned as out of their own control (under the influence of alcohol and through victimhood) at the time of the incident. Despite this apparently sympathetic portrayal the subtext of the stories placed the women somehow as aberrant harridans who abused men.

There were reports of mutual violence in the DASH study although few and far between. In one case Charlotte talked about her family of origin:

> My childhood background was that my dad was an alcoholic and he was extremely abusive toward my mum. Never to us as children. I never felt at risk from him at all and to some extent it was fifty of one and half a dozen of the other. I saw just as much abuse from my mum as what I saw from my dad and I did see some! I actually saw my mum stick a poker out of the fire and into my dad's side and another time I saw her throw a knife across the room and into his neck. On the other hand I saw my dad be extremely abusive to my mum. When he drank he would just flip. She would go at him, fling his dinner at him or whatever.

Johnson and Ferraro (2000) make the plea for distinguishing between types of domestic violence as an essential prerequisite for future research and clinical/legal practice (Flitcraft 1995; Babcock, Jacobson, Gottman and Yerington 2000). How far though is it valuable to have predefined categories, in contrast to the approach that there are different qualities within different abusive relationships that need to be understood (Ferraro and Johnson 1983; Wood 2001; Bacchus, Mezey and Bewley 2006; Swan and Snow 2006)?

Ideologies and classification

There is some evidence that classifying types of behaviour and relationships that sustain them does provide greater opportunities to explore the impact of different types of lived experiences and what leads to staying with or leaving abusive partners. This helps in the development of supportive services (Vetere and Cooper 2003), but categorising in itself can produce dilemmas for those engaged in supporting women (and men) who have lived with violence (Sonkin 1986; Goldner *et al.* 1990).

Throughout what might seem to be questions of 'semantics' or 'linguistic fashion' in naming and classifying, there are ideological and epistemological struggles, avowals of meaning and 'operational' definitions applied by social scientists, lawyers and those involved in preventing violence and abuse between intimate partners (Gelles 1980; Brush 1990; Muehlenhard and Kimes 1999; Peled, Eisikovits, Enosh and Winstok 2000; Fennema-Notestine, Stein, Kennedy, Archibald and Jernigan 2002; McCosker, Barnard and Gerber 2004).

The links between 'naming', explaining and challenging domestic violence however are crucial to understanding why domestic violence continues to happen across the world (Schuler, Hashemi, Riley and Akhter 1996; Walker 1999; Gelles 2000; Bettman 2009). Gender-power relations play a major part in its persistence and social attitudes and beliefs about women are the main influence on how seriously any society or social group challenges domestic violence (see Chapter 1). However there is also no doubt that interpersonal dynamics also play their part in the trajectory of any relationship regardless of gender-power politics (Henderson *et al.* 1997; Hare 2006; Malik, Silverman, Wang and Janczewski 2008).

Research and theories

The complexity of family violence and the many questions it raises also have drawn the attention of people who approach their work from different perspectives and with different goals.

(Loseke *et al.* 2005: xv)

My aim in this book is to re-situate psychology's contribution to understanding, predicting, preventing and healing across the spectrum of domestic violence and abuse from one which attempts 'objectivity' to one that is pro-feminist while at the same time accounting for the relationship struggles and nuances of power shifts for women before, during and after leaving abusive men. The focus on women's experiences cannot be understood outside gender-power relations. However these relations are complex and there are different perspectives across the academic debates drawing from different epistemological and ideological traditions (Bentzel and York 1988; R.P. Dobash *et al.* 1992; Mullender and Hague 2005; Moe 2007).

Governments and charities across the world, until recently as a consequence of the global recession, had gradually made funds available for research projects, particularly those that focus upon criminality (Morley and Mullender 1992; Liebling and Stanko 2001; Stanko 2007).

There are two closely related components underpinning the controversies surrounding domestic violence and abuse. The first relates to the quality and type of data that define and describe domestic violence. The second (and not necessarily mutually exclusive issue) concerns the epistemological underpinnings of the thinking about domestic abuse and the methodologies that produce those data.

Researching violence of any kind raises conceptual, ethical and practical difficulties, but the past decade or so has given rise to helpful texts and papers across the field, particularly related to gender-based or sexual violence(s) (Schwartz 1997; Lee and Stanko 2003; Skinner *et al.* 2005). Writers in these areas focus on a number of broad issues, one of which being the politics of funding. This had been less of a problem since the mid-

1990s than previously although the recent 'credit crunch' has put a new squeeze on money for research.

In 1997–2002 in the UK, for example, the ESRC (Economic and Social Research Council) funded the *Violence Research Programme* with twenty linked projects, and much of the current consideration of researching violence has resulted from that initiative. Part of the concluding remarks from that programme were:

> Violence means different things to different people, and the impact of inequalities on people's lives gives us clues as to how violence makes difficult lives even more difficult. Violence has a differential impact on groups of people, especially the most vulnerable. Violence falls heavily on the shoulders of the young, and young adults in particular. It is often compounded by the interactive effects – living in violence, living with violence, adapting to abuse, being abusive. While these patterns are not predictive, they are clearly known as part of the provision of services for those committing or experiencing violence. Violence is often targeted at vulnerability. Women – young or old – are still most at risk from known men. The youngest target of homicide – babies under one year old – are most at risk from their carers. It is therefore important when dealing with the impact of violence to understand as best possible the context within which it takes place. It is this context riddled with information of how the structures and spaces of inequalities sustain violence and abuse that enables us to devise protective factors to minimise the harm – and the sustenance – acts of violence take from the situation/environment within which they take place. For example, racist violence may be exacerbated by housing policies, school policies or prison policies. We must continue to ask why the contexts of violence are invisible to social service and other statutory agencies and demand that the context of violence is known as much as is possible. Recognising inequality can assist in exploring long term solutions rather than short term responses which neglect structural or policy change.[5]

The message, in some ways a general one, does identify the inequalities and structural/political contexts in which violence flourishes. However there seems to be a subtext to this suggesting that human lives 'interact' with social structures to produce a vulnerability to violence(s) – both as victims and perpetrators. Has that message been followed up in subsequent research on domestic violence? It is difficult to unpack the (very) different messages that are coming from the academic studies.

Debates about researching violence have explored the traditional qualitative versus quantitative considerations and positivism versus standpoint (particularly feminist standpoint) issues including whether feminism (and women) can be served through collecting statistical data or whether all research on gender-based violence should be overtly 'political' and qualitative enterprises (Renzetti 1997; Griffiths and Halna 2003).

Practical matters include ethical ones about confidentiality and anonymity and the potential backlash for participants which might cause unexpected stress, including flashbacks (e.g. Kirkwood 1993; McCarry 2005); access to 'hard to reach' participants; or achieving a good enough response rate from a population survey to make it viable (Nicolson and Wilson 2004; O'Brien, Black, Carley–Baxter and Simon 2006). Inevitably when researching violence there are also questions of safety – not only for the researcher but also for the respondent who might be subjected to increased abuse if it were discovered by her partner/ex-partner that she had revealed information about the abuse (Fontes 2004). The benefits to research participants are that they could become emotionally strengthened with greater access to information and resources and increased self-knowledge (Renzetti 1997).

Quantitative research

Research questions and/or hypotheses, epistemologies and methodologies are intrinsically linked so it is inevitable that the findings from different research approaches should have emerged from and bring in different considerations to the topic. The large-scale projects based on quantitative survey methods (Steinmetz and Tabenkin 2008), some using the Conflict Tactics Scale (CTS) (Straus 1979; Kilpatrick and Williams 1998; D.G. Dutton and Nicholls 2005), have been seen by pro-feminist researchers in particular to depoliticise domestic violence (Loseke and Cahill 1984). The work of North American researchers (known as the Family Violence Research Group), including the work of Gelles and Straus (1988), developed and then employed the Conflict Tactics Scale which was used to gather data to *measure* violent behaviours in a number of surveys across the United States including the National Family Violence Survey (1985) and the 1990 National Survey of Families and Households (Brush 1990). Straus, Gelles and Steinmetz's (1981) *Behind Closed Doors* used the CTS which revealed widespread violence towards women by men, towards children by their parents and towards men by women – the latter being an ongoing controversial finding (for reasons discussed below in Chapter 3) but one which Straus defends for a great part via his use of a scientifically validated scale.

Qualitative research

Qualitative data, collected mostly via in-depth interviews and focus groups (Moran and Skeggs 2003), is frequently the 'preferred' feminist approach (e.g. Mullender and Hague 2005; Bostock *et al.* 2009). The idea of 'listening to voices' is appealing and potentially emancipatory. All data though (qualitative and quantitative) are subject to interpretation or 'bias' by even the best-intended researcher, and Kirkwood (1993) for instance, following Kelly (1988), identified the need to address the responses of the researcher to the research process, which she terms 'reflexive experiential analysis' (Kirkwood 1993: 38). This process enables the researcher to be sensitive to what the psychoanalyst Melanie Klein, in another context, would have called 'counter-transference' (Heimann 2003; Spillius 2007). That is the possibility for the researcher themselves to 'experience' the participant's pain and feeling of helplessness during the telling of the story (see Chapters 6 to 8). This is a powerful experience and one that more recently has come to be taken seriously in psychological research (see Hollway and Jefferson 2000/2001).

Finding what you know and supporting what you find

Researchers *do* know what they want and need to find. Even so, it is possible that the data may not provide the researcher (or their intended audience) with what they wish to hear, creating ethical and ideological dilemmas, particularly about what issues should be made public and the impact of revelations. Buchbinder and Eisikovits (2003) for example have explored the ethical responsibilities of researchers whose results might place abused women's parenting practices in a negative light.

I myself have been vilified by a few pro-feminists for asserting the importance of a psychological understanding of domestic abuse and violence: first by an activist who challenged me for continuing to acknowledge the importance of Pizzey's pioneering work (because Pizzey had been positioned by some activists in the UK as a traitor to the cause[6]); and second by Sandra Horley (of *Refuge*) for presenting findings indicating that some women were more likely to experience victimisation and re-victimisation than others. I have also been 'accused' by pro-feminists of 'psychologising' (proposed as a negative activity) as a consequence of presenting evidence from the DASH study.

The DASH study had had at its core twenty-six in-depth interviews with women who had left abusive men. The aim of these interviews had been to explore their routes to safety and the human and material resources they had accessed to achieve their goals. What happened though was that over a third of the women interviewed told the interviewer (unasked) that they had had between two and six abusive partners, and almost all the twenty-six women had had violent, abusive or in some way negligent and dysfunctional backgrounds, as had many of their abusive partners. Furthermore some of the women were convinced that this pattern was 'typical' of others in their situation.

My argument, that some women are more vulnerable to living with abusive partners (sometimes more than once) than others and as such need to be given extra support to help them leave and remain safe, has been (wrongly in my view) positioned as one that flies in the face of the idea that anyone can become a victim of domestic violence and abuse (see Chapter 4). Being told that 'I must be mistaken' (during a live BBC Broadcast on *Woman's Hour*) and being shouted down when I suggested we were all on the same side was a salutary experience.

However that was nothing compared to what some others have had to endure. While the bad blood now flows from both sides of the debate (R.E. Dobash *et al.* 2004; D.G. Dutton and Nicholls 2005), the first recorded vitriolic attacks were against Steinmetz for suggesting that women might be violent towards men. The outcome was horrendous:

> when Steinmetz revealed that women are often as violent as their husbands, the fem-fascists started a whispering campaign designed to block her promotion at the University of Delaware. When that didn't work, they phoned in a bomb threat at her daughter's wedding. Cowed by the threats, Steinmetz soon suspended her pioneering research.
>
> Erin Pizzey of England had impeccable credentials – she was the founder of the first abuse shelter for women. So a few years later she published *Prone to Violence*, a book that revealed these women are often as physically aggressive as their mates.
>
> That provoked threats of violence by the women who said women can never be violent. Pizzey was forced to seek police protection as she travelled around to promote her book. She was met by jeering protesters with placards that read, 'All men are bastards.'
>
> Dr. Lynette Feder planned to do a study to find out whether batterer intervention programs work. But then the Broward County, Florida district attorney tried to block the study since, he claimed, everyone 'already knew' such programs work. Interestingly, other researchers later found such programs are often ineffective.[7]

What is worrying is how this polarisation of views has become formally politicised so that it is mainly 'right wing' commentators who take the side of Steinmetz, Pizzey and others of similar view (see the Renew America campaign by following the links on the website). The researchers and writers on domestic violence themselves (probably) do not have an overt political agenda other than to present evidence as they see it albeit that it contradicts the pro-feminist 'mainstream' and generally challenges the validity of qualitative research (D.G. Dutton and Nicholls 2005). Despite the increase in awareness and research on all aspects of domestic violence and abuse, we are far from an unequivocal understanding of its origins, causes in general and in individual cases, deciding who is responsible, the significance of evidence about women's violence, the effectiveness of programmes to alter the behaviour of batterers, the long-term impact of growing up in violent households on girls/women and boys/men, and a range of other matters which continue to be contentious. Overall, though, for women living in western democracies throughout which domestic violence is a crime, why do women stay?

Epistemology and thinking about domestic abuse

There are ethical issues to consider if publishing information that seems to show vulnerable women in a bad light is going to reduce funding to support them. It does seem that almost any attempt to explore the *psychology* of abusive relationships and those who take part in them, even for a brief period in their lives, is anathema and identified as politically reactionary, at least on the British side of the Atlantic. However many of the psychological studies in North America tend to be large-scale and quantitative, not taking account of issues such as gender-power relationships or contradictions and the meaning of women's experiences.

It is easy from a pro-feminist perspective to think that those approaching the study of violence to women from a sociological perspective already have all the answers. Indeed since the late 1980s an impressive and persuasive body of work has emerged, particularly from sociologists whose work began at Warwick, Bristol and Manchester universities, especially Audrey Mullender, the Dobashes, Gill Hague and Cathy Humphreys, as well as others like Jill Radford, Sue Lees, Liz Kelly (from London Metropolitan University) and Betsy Stanko (while at Royal Holloway). The sociological analysis posits gender-power relations as central to the causes and potential solutions for violence in heterosexual relationships.

This model is persuasive and to an extent proven. Chapter 1 above for instance documented the abuse to women by their male partners across the world and across the lifespan, and the sanctioning of these abuses of women's human rights frequently is provided through the state or religious institutions (as in the case of the Taliban or the Sudanese government as discussed in Chapter 1). The abuse of male power to gain control over women is horrific and strongly reinforces the credibility of the sociological gender-power analysis.

However that is not, and cannot ever be, the end to women's stories. Particularly in free societies such as western democracies, lives progress, evolve, change for the better and the worse. The need is to gain insights into these more detailed emotional and intimate experiences of living with domestic violence and abuse, where psychology has much to offer. Psychology's contribution to date has been overshadowed by the rhetoric of sociological feminism which takes exception to 'individualist' explanations of women's experiences (Mullender and Morley 2001). Women in abusive relationships find ways of coping to survive and live with terror (Loseke 2005; Green 2008). Women find ways to protect their children from abuse (Pizzey 1974/1977; Edleson 1999). Women find the strength to leave (Pahl 1985). However all of that comes with a *psychological* price to pay. Women experience loss of self-esteem during and after leaving abusive relationships (Mullender 1996; Wilcox 2000; Peckover 2003). Women may suffer trauma and depression and self-harm on leaving abusive relationships (Humphreys and Thiara 2003; Chew-Graham, Bashir, Chantler, Burman and Batsleer 2002). Women may have *entered* a particular relationship because of low self-esteem related to neglect in childhood (Andrews and Brown 1988).

These are all issues that have important and complex psychological dimensions which have not been fully explored, not least by many psychologists working in this area. Unless these issues are taken seriously women will continue to experience psychological trauma, as will their children, and supporting them and identifying couples at risk will continue to be hard (Herman 1992a, 1992b; S.L. Miller 1994; Jones, Hughes and Unterstaller 2001; Humphreys and Thiara 2003; Briere and Jordan 2004; DeJonghe, Bogat, Levendosky and von Eye 2008). Much has been written about women's reluctance to seek help for fear of exacerbating violence (R.E. Dobash and Dobash 1984), or having children taken into care and discrimination (see for example Peckover 2003). These fears may be put aside to act to save the children or themselves but that leads to the kind of chronic fear described by Green (2008) above.

While psychological dimensions of abusive relationships are frequently cited as evidence of patriarchal culture and male oppression (Hattendorf and Tollerud 1997; Banks-Wallace 1998; Bettman 2009), the use of even pro-feminist psychological methods to investigate and proffer a theoretical 'take' on the experience of living with domestic violence is disdained. For instance it is argued that women who leave their violent partners suffer isolation and loneliness (Pahl 1985). As Kirkwood summarises:

> The pain associated with these [loneliness, poverty and boredom] are products of a culture which is based economically and socially on married couples or two-parent families.
>
> (Kirkwood 1993: 31)

This is clearly true. 'Married' mothers are the acceptable face of young middle age for women. They don't breach any social norms. However there are other *individual differences* apparent across all studies of women's experiences of both staying and leaving their abusive partners, which need to be taken seriously. There is also evidence that some women, unsurprisingly, have difficulties in forming new relationships after leaving an abusive partner (Binney, Harkell and Nixon 1981; Kirkwood 1993). Again there will be individual differences in the ways in which women engage with support systems and build upon their prior experiences, which may be based on the qualities of their early relationships, which may result in vulnerabilities and psychiatric diagnoses (see for example Andrews and Brown 1988; Bifulco and Moran 1998; Bifulco, Moran, Baines, Bunn and Stanford 2002). Furthermore if the use of a medical model *exacerbates* distress through blaming the victim and offering medication rather than counselling (Humphreys and Thiara 2003), it is still important to examine the reasons why and how the 'condition' arose and also whether counselling might help. The deployment of a psychiatric label may be a convention of patriarchy but this does not deny the possibility of intergenerational transmission of vulnerability or remove the need to consider individual experiences.

Conclusions

Domestic abuse and violence by men towards their 'wives' has been taken for granted as a product of patriarchal societies across time and place. For at least twenty years feminist campaigns and academics have ensured that this is no longer an acceptable form of behaviour, and as shown in Chapter 1 there are now high-profile international organisations collecting data and launching campaigns to stop abuse and violence towards women.

Over the past ten years research on interpersonal violence of all kinds has burgeoned, along with equal emphasis on the study of domestic violence. It has become clear that women suffer psychologically from living *with* abusers in fear, isolation and vigilance for their own and their children's well-being. It is also clear that women also suffer psychologically during and after *leaving* abusers. What appear to be absent are psychological accounts of the experience of surviving domestic abuse that attend to gender-power relationships and individual differences in biographies.

Further the very process of naming domestic violence has produced difficulties. This is true for academics, practitioners and those who both suffer and perpetrate violence between intimate partners. The terminology debates themselves provide insights into the ideological complexities surrounding contemporary understandings of domestic abuse and the material, discursive and intra-psychic contexts in which it occurs. The passion with which beliefs about the causes, consequences and solutions are held by the various stakeholders (academic, policy makers and practitioners as well as those involved in the abuse and violence and the general public) is reflected in the debates about what to call violence between intimate partners and also how to name the person who is at the receiving end of the abuse and violence.

3

PSYCHOLOGY, FEMINISM AND IDEOLOGY: WHERE DO WE GO FROM HERE?

Introduction

Feminist discourses on domestic violence have been relatively successful. Public attitudes have shifted from tolerating wife beating to condemning domestic violence as unacceptable. . . . State policy and practice has become increasingly receptive to feminist concerns, with considerable shifts in the police response to domestic violence. . . . In the US and UK refuges for women have been continuously provided since the early seventies, though often with meagre financial support.

(Featherstone and Trinder 1997: 148)

Feminist campaigns to bring domestic abuse and violence to the fore over the past twenty years have been highly influential in explaining the causes and consequences of domestic violence and abuse. Activists in the USA, Canada, Britain and the rest of the EU have effectively ensured that domestic violence and men's abuse of women is clearly identified by both government and non-government agencies as socially and morally unacceptable (Goldner 1999; Skinner et al. 2005; van Wormer 2009), as a crime and recognised as a world-wide problem of women's human rights, public and physical health and community welfare (Walker 1999; Smith 2001; Sullivan, Bhuyan, Senturia, Shiu-Thornton and Ciske 2005a; Steinmetz and Tabenkin 2008). However domestic violence has not stopped. According to a British Home Office Report (2006):[1]

- Police need to be more aware of the connection between sport and domestic abuse when they make their plans before major events such as World Cup and Championship matches.
- Nearly half (40 per cent) of all suspects in domestic abuse cases were drunk at the time of the crime.
- Reports of domestic abuse increase by nearly a third (30 per cent) on England match days.

It would appear that men cannot help themselves – when they are excited or drunk they will take it out, violently, at home on their partner. Or, similarly, if they become frustrated, stressed or depressed for other reasons, as suggested most recently as a consequence of redundancies in the global recession. In Britain government agencies have warned that among other things 'social problems such as domestic violence and mental ill-health are expected to follow as the recession deepens' (Audit Commission 2009).

The implication of these relatively informal but serious risk assessments is that various stressors and (probably) alcohol are triggers for (male) violent episodes in many families (R.N. Parker 1993; White and Chen 2002). This raises important questions for activists and researchers, once again bringing the debate about how psychology sits with/against feminism into sharp focus. It seems that when you scratch the surface of violent heterosexual relationships for explanations you get the clear message that violence is intrinsically linked to gender-power relations. However to change behaviours and support women (and you cannot do this unless men are also supported) you have to turn to psychology for answers to the question 'so what are we going to do next?'

Do warnings about the exacerbation of violence under particular social conditions mean that alcohol brings about domestic abuse? Does stress, disappointment or upset cause domestic violence? Is it when masculine power is threatened at any level that patriarchal authority is exercised maliciously in the home? Do vulnerable and violent men come from across the social spectrum or are there particular cultural, ethnic, psychological, economic and/or social factors that lead to this kind of behaviour? How much nearer are we to being able to prevent domestic violence than we were thirty years ago? How influential are the individual circumstances of both or either of the partners complicit in violent and abusive relationships? For feminists these questions are irrelevant. For psychologists they are central if we are to understand how to support women living with and surviving domestic violence.

There are no excuses: feminism versus psychology

That the study of domestic violence is controversial must now be self-evident. Since at least the mid-1990s there have been 'rancorous debates' (K.L. Anderson 2005) between those who identify gender and power as the cause of domestic abuse and violence and those who view gender as only part of the story. There are no compromises in this particular struggle. Mullender and Morley (2001) have reiterated their position first taken in 1994:

> Work by feminist activists and researchers has produced strong evidence that the roots of domestic violence lie not in pathology,

stress, or family conflicts but in men's domination and control over women. . . . The abusive characteristics of men in violent relationships are best described as control tactics, ways of instilling fear and coercing compliance.

(Mullender and Morley 2001: 7)

This may be a coherent argument but it does not move us towards understanding what can be done to help women and families, particularly if women are unable or unwilling to leave their partners. Psychologists have argued for risk factors and correlates of domestic violence to be taken into account in considering the punishment and treatment of violent men (K.L. Anderson 1997; Yllö 1998; McFarlane *et al.* 2005; McCarroll *et al.* 2008), with a focus on the relationship and family circumstances. Are they right to do so? What do we know about the violent relationship?

The 'battered woman syndrome': pathologising women?

The work of Lenore Walker (1979) in the USA brought the 'battered woman syndrome' into the clinical academic arena just as Erin Pizzey's pioneering work in the 1970s had brought the issue into the public policy domain. Walker based her theory on her study of over 400 women who had experienced abuse from their partners. She developed a model which focused upon violent and abusive heterosexual relationships, identifying a 'cycle' of escalating violent behaviours to describe and explain how violence happens, why women don't immediately leave and from this what might be done to support the women and possibly the relationship.

Walker, as a psychologist, was concerned to show how abused women *think*, *feel* and *behave* as a result of their relationship with an abuser (Walker 1977). Her conclusion demonstrated functional *deficit* in the women and that along with her somewhat 'objective' approach to her subject matter (as is the habit of academic psychology) has led in part to her vilification by feminists amid criticism that she failed to identify the wider social implications of women's oppression under patriarchy and men's power over women (R.E. Dobash and Dobash 1984; Mullender and Morley 2001; Downs and Fisher 2005).

Walker's own accounts of her work though are harrowing by any standards. She clearly demonstrated that men indeed do control and terrorise their partners but she also provided evidence that this knowledge, even in the detailed manner she provided it, could not provide a solution in itself. The criminalisation of men *per se* was not going to make the abused women's lives turn around. Removing women and children from the scene was not the solution because lives and relationships were complex and for many reasons, ill and possibly good, women make choices to continue in particular relationships despite abuse. Her interviews with the women led her to propose the following (now (in)famous) three-stage model known as the 'cycle of violence':

Stage One: The build up: At this stage there is a slow steady increase in tension between the partners including petty arguments, complaining and possibly slapping or pushing. The batterer may enjoy provoking their partner or picking a fight or embarrass the partner in front of others. The abused partner tries to placate the partner hoping things will blow over.

Stage Two: The explosion: The tension reaches breaking point and the abused partner acts in a way that the batterer uses as an excuse to explode into a rage and let go of his self-control. He claims he wants to make a point or teach the victim a lesson. The abuse continues until the tension has been relieved and the batterer is exhausted or the police intervene or something else happens to break this behaviour.

After this episode both partners are shocked and may feel disbelief and denial. The abused partner may rationalise the episode and minimise her injuries. The abused partner may then isolate herself and retreat into listlessness and depression and feelings of helplessness.

Stage Three: The 'honeymoon': During this stage the batterer expresses remorse and guilt and tries to make it up to the abused partner. The abused partner is likely to fall into the trap of feeling encouraged that the behaviour will change and that the abuser really loves her.

Coping strategies and learned helplessness

The 'battered woman syndrome', as Walker presented it, included sophisticated and complex coping strategies on the women's part, to avoid, prevent or control the violence. Walker demonstrated the heightened level of alertness women reported in being sensitive to the violent abuser's likely actions. 'Like firefighters dealing with a brush fire, many women have learned to catch these little outbursts and calm their men down for a short period of time; this gives the women a feeling that they really have control over the batterers' behaviour' (Walker 1977: 53).

She went on to suggest the following horrific scenario:

Provocative behaviour that is sometimes observed in battered women can be more easily explained through this concept of cyclical behaviour. If the period of tension gets too painful for the woman to live with – and she has learned that she will be abused no matter what she does – then she may allow an acute battering incident to occur in order to experience a reduction in anxiety and the loving contrition that occurs after the incident.

(Walker 1977: 53)

It is perhaps this somewhat objective style of description, and the classification itself, that has so angered some feminist commentators, including feminist psychologists who would take another more discursive approach to the analysis of the evidence she collected. However other studies (including my own) indicate that Walker's findings still carry some weight and need to be taken seriously and reconsidered if appropriate support is to be offered to women.

Walker proposed that as violence in a heterosexual relationship was neither random nor constant it was necessary to examine the *details of violent episodes*.

She then went on to draw on Martin Seligman's (1975) work, originally based on animal learning, but extended later to apply to humans, particularly in relation to depression. His theory of 'learned helplessness' proposed that prior exposure to an 'inescapable shock', that is when the violence someone experiences is out of their control, interferes with the ability to learn later even in a situation where avoidance or escape was possible. So a woman who is battered by her partner without any warning, bearing no relationship to anything she has done (or might avoid doing), is likely after time to 'learn' she has no control over the rewards and/or punishments in her life. She consequently learns she is *helpless in the relationship*.

Thus the woman who had previously been beaten and traumatised would probably find it difficult not to expect the same to happen any time. A person undergoing this experience would become very depressed and suffer low self-esteem which in turn would impact on their motivation and abilities to alter their situation (Seligman 1972). Walker hypothesised that over time a woman exposed to violence and abuse by her partner would exhibit symptoms of depression and reduced self-esteem and 'learn' to be in a state of subordination. It was this state of learned helplessness, Walker argued, that prevented women from leaving abusive relationships.

Why won't she leave?

If a woman manages to leave an abusive partner for good and avoid getting into future abusive relationships then at least some of the battle for preventing domestic violence and abuse has been 'won'. However, there is increasingly psychological evidence to show that it is not simply learned helplessness and depression that prevent women leaving. Some women weigh up the costs and benefits of staying in or leaving their relationships (Peled *et al.* 2000) and find the thought of being alone more distressing than living with the abusive man, as with Mary whose experience is discussed above in Chapter 2. Mary decided both for the sake of her children and because she had put so much into the domestic unit (emotionally and materially) that she was not prepared to leave until the children had left home (Hendy *et al.* 2003). In spite of everything many women remain with the man because they love him (Goldner *et al.* 1990; Henderson *et al.* 1997; Wood 2001; Henderson, Bartholomew, Trinke and Kwong 2005; Shurman and Rodriguez 2006; Allison *et al.* 2008).

Henderson and colleagues (1997) developed a psychological model of attachment style to assist the explanation of why some women stay with an abuser, indicating that the degree to which the woman holds a positive view of the other person, a preoccupied attachment style and negative view of themselves influences whether or not they will stay with a persistent abuser (Bifulco *et al.* 2000; Doumas, Pearson, Elgin and McKinley 2008) (see Chapters 6 and 7 for further discussion of this). This suggests that simple categories of abusive patterns in relationships fail to explain the depth of the emotional problems women bring to a relationship (in addition to those which come from living with abuse). It suggests limitations on the psychological models of domestic abuse as well as the feminist ones – neither 'side' paying full attention to the emotional and psychosocial complexities in relationships (Coker *et al.* 2000; Essex, Petras and Massat 2007). There is relatively little research that focuses in-depth upon women's experience of continuing to live with domestic abuse (Kearney 2001; R.E. Davis 2002; M.E. Smith 2003) rather than the experience of those who leave (Kirkwood 1993). Part of the DASH study (discussed in the later chapters of this book) involved qualitative interviews, with the initial objective of examining the experience of help-seeking and leaving violent and abusive men. However the study provided more evidence to support the view that many women decide to stay with violent men, at least in the medium term, for many different reasons; and these reasons need further investigation from an individual psychological perspective over and above criticism of scarce resources and a blunt attribution to patriarchal power.

Whose voices?

Feminists and activists on the other hand have argued that *they* listen to women's voices and take their position from hearing what women survivors say. Their argument is that psychologists take the perspective of patriarchal society and blame the woman for what has happened (Humphreys and Thiara 2003). Psychologists however take a variety of pragmatic views with possibly more emphasis upon the role, backgrounds and circumstances of *men* (Corvo and Johnson 2003). This has reinforced the rejection by feminists of anything whatsoever psychology might contribute (Dutton and Corvo 2006). It has also been proposed that because psychological theories take an *individualistic* view by definition they *blame women* for the man's violence or at least for the consequences of it on the mental health and the care and safety of their children (Humphreys 1999; Humphreys and Thiara 2003). But there is a world of difference between focusing on women's experiences of domestic abuse and *blaming* women for living with violence and abuse.

Criminal behaviour

Despite a plea from at least one sociologist to support an integration of feminist and 'family violence' approaches (K.L. Anderson 1997), the barriers to integration or discussion between the opposing 'camps' have become entrenched and inflexible. Feminists and activists also operationalise a *criminal* discourse to support their case against patriarchy (Ferraro 1996).

The traditional feminist (sociological) activist position on domestic abuse and violence makes no concessions to any man. Violence and abuse of women, perpetrated by men, is socially, culturally and historically a product of patriarchy (Dobash and Dobash 1979; Dobash *et al.* 1992; Murray and Powell 2009). This is the case regardless of individual circumstances, family dysfunction, alcohol or substance abuse, mental health problems, stress on the family, the quality of the intimate relationship, culture, or the emotional or psychological history of the man (or woman); the man, as an agent of patriarchy, is responsible for the violence and abuse because it is a means of controlling his female partner (Kurz 1989; Dekeseredy and Dragiewicz 2007).

Walker re-visited

Lenore Walker's approach to her research and her consequent theoretical position have been challenged both by pro-feminist activists and by some psychologists. The former have taken the view that she is focusing upon individual relationships and suggesting women are complicit in maintaining the violence (Hague and Mullender 2006). The latter have challenged her stereotyping of the batterer as manipulative, out of control and malicious (Harrison and Esqueda 1999; Esqueda and Harrison 2005).

Walker's model of the escalating cycle of violence needs to be seen in the context of 1970s 'second-wave' feminism whereby the idea that middle-class women could be victims of abuse was 'shocking'. Second-wave feminism emerged from a mixture of resistance to post-war family patterns (Friedan 1963; French 1979) and the '(hetero)sexual' liberation of the 1960s which unsettled thinking about (mostly middle-class) women's experiences (Faludi 1991; Wolf 1991).

From a radical feminist standpoint twenty years on it was easy to criticise the 'cycle of violence' model and the idea of 'learned helplessness' for abused women. Walker had paid little heed to the social context of patriarchal oppression and control of women through fear and violence. But then that ideological framework had not been part of the dominant discourse at the time. In the aftermath of the Second World War, with increased affluence and women returning to 'the home' (Riley 1983; Ehrenreich and English 1989), to marry a man who was going to provide material comfort was seen as the be-all and end-all of most women's aspirations. To be married and a mother was the ultimate dream of living happily ever after. Domestic violence was the aberration and the exception – it certainly had not been theorised.

Domestic abuse was creeping into awareness in implicit ways, though, as Marilyn French demonstrated in her novel *The Women's Room* (1979), it had not been 'named' or identified as an important social problem by then. French's account of the 'ordinary' 1950/1960s family life in middle-class America included tales of intimate partner abuse and violence which implicated professional educated men. Most were tales of neglect and objectification of the woman who was expected to serve the man's every 'need'. There is though a current of anxiety running through the accounts of many couples' interactions. The women in the story have to be careful not to upset or anger their husbands which includes maintaining their youthful and attractive personal appearance.

One of the characters, Lily, told the story of Sandra who lived with a violent husband:

> Lily was full of sorrow for Sandra: imagine what her life was like, she said.
>
> 'One night me and her went to a Tupperware party. Oh, it was nothing, stupid, for the stupid housewives, you know, but it was a chance to get out, so I asked her if she wanted to go, and she worked on Tom and finally, she came. I picked her up and drove to my friend Betty's, and they had the party, and when it was over and everyone else had gone home, Betty brought out a bottle and we had some drinks. Oh, we had so much fun! We talked and laughed. It felt so good. Anyway, we stayed sort of late; I guess it was around midnight when I took Sandra home. We walked in the house – we were having so much fun we didn't want to stop, so Sandra said I had to come in for coffee because I was too drunk to drive – and Tom is sitting there on the couch in front of the TV, and he takes one look at her and leaps up and smacks her across the face so hard he knocked her down. Then he started for me. I ran.'
>
> (French 1979: 228–229)

A fantasy violation perhaps in a work of fiction but there is no doubting the resonance. Fun and women having a good time are juxtaposed with male anger lurking in wait to exact punishment on the woman who had chosen to have an evening with friends rather than with him.

This brief account of a domestic assault was a departure from contemporary thinking because it emphasised that women were really enjoying each others' company but it also drew the stark contrast with the price that Sandra was made to pay. From this extract we wonder how much Sandra had expected his reaction. Did she ask Lily in for coffee because she thought it would prevent an attack from Tom? Was this only the first time she had come home (and come home late) so that she was unaware of how he would react? We are not told about other aspects of the relationship and Sandra and Tom are never heard from again in the novel. In the 1970s it would have been unclear what the outcome of such a relationship might (or should) be. The novel itself provided examples of women who left their husbands or who never married but not of having to find a place of safety and the stigma to both the woman and man of parting for such a reason.

French's fictional account of women's lives in post-war North America was hailed generally as shocking and revolutionary. The back cover claims the novel was the most important of its time to be written about the 'realities' of women's life in the 1970s. The book characterises: 'the varied nightmares of rape, madness and loneliness to the dawning awareness of the exhilaration of liberation'. Women's lives were represented as a complex mixture of extreme pain and extreme hope and possibly anticipated pro-feminist challenges to the patriarchy. Not all the women in the story lived successful independent lives, along with women in general. Walker's 'cycle of violence' had provided a hitherto unavailable insight into why Sandra might have stayed with her violent partner and how she would have coped in the relationship.

'Psychologising'

> Some who have held a feminist position have minimised the emotional complexity of abusive relationships. There are a multitude of factors, other than the abuse of power, that operate to keep partners attached to and embroiled with each other.
>
> (Goldner 1999: 325)

As shown above and also in Chapter 2, there has increasingly been a mismatch between feminists' and psychologists' views on the causes, consequences and focus for research (Schechter 1982; K.L Anderson 1997; D.G. Dutton and Corvo 2006; Sandis 2006; Seave 2006). To summarise: the feminist position (broadly) is that masculinity is served by oppressing women and that when certain circumstances prevail that threaten his power and authority and his masculinity, the man acts violently towards his female partner. The psychologists' position (broadly) is that individualised explanations are important, and types of violence vary (Johnson and Ferraro 2000), and that if particular factors trigger domestic violence then it is essential to examine (as a therapist, clinician or researcher) how these might be understood and therefore changed. However while both sides present as 'ideal types', with the pro-feminists not brooking psychological theory and the psychologists minimising the value of in-depth qualitative research (and feminism), the stand-off remains.

It has seemed easy for many pro-feminists to typify psychology (and thus psychologists) as simplistic reactionaries who see the woman involved in the abuse as 'aggressive, provocative or masochistic' and the man as 'frustrated, depressed, with low self-esteem and unhappy' (Romito 2008: 70).

> More generally, psychologising consists of interpreting a problem in individualistic and psychological rather than political, economic or social terms and consequently responding in these terms. . . . Psychologising is therefore essentially a depoliticising tactic for supporting the status quo and dominant power relationships.
>
> (Romito 2008: 69)

Romito goes on to assert that psychology ensures that the problem resides with the woman (who is pathologised) and diffuses responsibility, thus removing the onus from the perpetrator. This caricature of psychology does no good to either feminism or women living with violence and abuse (Martin 2009; Nicolson 2009).

Psychology focuses on behaviour, thoughts and feelings and takes account of *individual differences* between women and between relationships that are apparent when talking about domestic abuse (Ferraro 1997; Hattendorf and Tollerud 1997; A. Smith 2001; Johnson 2006). There are good reasons to take individual differences seriously as some women stay with abusive partners and some women leave (Johnson and Ferraro 2000; Breckenridge and Mulroney 2007), although it is argued that not leaving is more to do with lack of resources (Garriga 2007) and fears for personal safety than psychological differences (Kirkwood 1993). It may be that it is simply the relative availability of material resources that determines women's actions, but evidence from women's accounts in the DASH study and many others indicates this is unlikely to be the only reason for many women (Riger 2001).

Surely failure to take women's *individual* accounts seriously is to deny women their agency (Kasturirangan *et al.* 2004). In other words, even though a woman might be locked in a relationship with a controlling, aggressive bully who has no excuse for his behaviour other than that he chooses violence as a means of controlling her, this doesn't mean that if she says she loves him, if she wants to have counselling to support their relationship, as feminists we should deny her this option (Jacobson 1994; Stuart 1997; Kurri and Wahlstrom 2001). We are all imbued with values from the dominant social discourses, and men have and wish to maintain their power. But leaving that as the end-point of the analysis and blaming psychologists for colluding in order to ensure violence(s) against women are invisible does not effectively support survivors of abuse (D.G. Dutton and Corvo 2006; Ellsberg 2006a; Gondolf 2007). As psychologists in Britain (and Europe) do not appear to have taken on the challenge of the sociological pro-feminist discourse, psychologists have been positioned as fair (and easy) game because there is little chance of a counter-attack.

There is though a world of difference between the pro-feminist analysis of activists and the experiences of many women (Peled *et al.* 2000). The opportunities for integration of feminism and psychology for the benefit of women who live with abuse are absent from the anti-individual/anti-psychology perspective despite evidence that structural inequalities impact on heterosexual couples to exacerbate violence (K.L. Anderson 1997) and that in many cases couple or family therapy has a greater impact on reducing violence than programmes directed at (criminalised) men (McConaghy and Cottone 1998; Arias, Dankwort, Douglas, Dutton and Stein 2002; Fisher and Oransky 2008).

The pro-feminist/non-feminist divide has evolved into a chasm (Mann 2000; Moe 2007). The split revolves around some of the issues reviewed above and in Chapter 2. These include hostility to those engaged in consideration of women's violence to men, but there also remains an antagonism to those thinking about the individual *characteristics* of women who have experienced and survived domestic violence or the nature of the particular relationship with their abusive partner. In other words psychological dimensions of domestic abuse are absent from the contemporary feminist standpoint research and activist agendas.

While acknowledging the value of pro-feminist scholarship and activism in the 1970s in giving domestic violence a name, Fraser (1989) argued that feminism ensured that domestic abuse was seen as political more than personal and linked to male power rather than individual pathology (in Featherstone and Trinder 1997). This was undeniably valuable and timely in the 1970s but the strategy now has to move on towards an understanding of the impact of gender and power relationships across and within generations, which takes account of individual experiences.

Is there anything about the quality of certain relationships that makes a man violent in ways that would not happen if that same man were to be with another woman? Are there particular conditions in a relationship that aggravate violence? These questions are taboo in most feminist contexts and yet, scientifically, they are very important.

Although the debate is about violence *to* women, in feminist analysis, with its emphasis on the role of patriarchy, aiming to secure that the burden of responsibility for violence and abuse in heterosexual relationships lies with the man, *women's roles are neglected beyond their experience as victim/survivors*. The feminist discourse, while calling for women's voices to be heard (Mullender and Hague 2005; Hague and Mullender 2006), focuses upon women as service users or their experiences of seeking help (Moe 2007) and trying or managing to leave their violent partner (Kirkwood 1993; Breckenridge and Mulroney 2007). What is absent is women's *experience* of living in and sometimes staying in the relationship (Johnson and Ferraro 2000; Wood 2001).

At the heart of these bitter controversies on domestic violence are matters of psychological epistemology and the status of its knowledge claims. Psychology as a discipline focuses on the *individual, or the interaction between individuals and groups* and the nature of the violent and abusive *relationship* (Ferraro and Johnson 1983; Ferraro 1996; Johnson and Ferraro 2000) as well as specific *circumstances* (personal and/or situational) that are impacting upon the couple (Martin 2002; Bacchus *et al.* 2006; Swan and Snow 2006).

These basic premises seem to go against the grain for those arguing that patriarchal relationships make domestic abuse in heterosexual relationships both possible and likely, so much so that to consider the individual, *whatever the context*, is positioned as a further abuse of women's rights (Hanmer, Griffiths and Jerwood 1998).

But psychologists, as clinicians and researchers, have made vital contributions to understanding abusive relationships, pointing the way to effective treatment and punishment for the abuser and eventual understanding and peace to live their lives for the victim/survivor. Psychologists however are not all in agreement with each other and the possibility of a critical, feminist and psychological approach to research and clinical work with those women living with domestic violence and abuse will be set out more specifically in Part 3 of this volume (Chapters 6 to 8).

The traumas of living with abuse over time

The socio-legal system, lack of support and lack of material resources have been cited as major reasons for women's failure to leave (Humphreys and Joseph 2004; J.R. Gillis *et al.* 2006). Women who stay with abusers suffer psychological and emotional damage not only from living with the abuse but also from the trauma of dealing with the systems to help them leave (Jones *et al.* 2001; J.R. Gillis *et al.* 2006). There is also evidence to show that women experience symptoms (similar to those of PTSD – post-traumatic stress disorder) even after they have left and have become safe (remembering of course that leaving does not necessarily guarantee safety) (Humphreys and Thiara 2003; Seave 2006; Breckenridge and Mulroney 2007).

PTSD is characterised by hyper-vigilance, flashbacks, disturbing dreams, reduced self-esteem and depression in the medium to long term. There is also evidence that PTSD exacerbates a lack of self-confidence in the ability to make decisions (including of course any decision regarding a change in circumstances) (Herman 1992a, 1992b). PTSD, first identified in shell-shocked soldiers, is now recognised as a syndrome that can develop following a traumatic event that threatens a person's safety or makes them feel helpless and vulnerable. Any overwhelming life experience can trigger

PTSD, especially if the event is perceived as unpredictable and uncontrollable, as in the experience of rape or a violent assault as well as exposure to domestic violence (Jones *et al.* 2001). PTSD symptoms can affect those who personally experience the event(s), those who witness it, and those who pick up the pieces afterwards (Herman 1992a, 1992b). Herman specifically argues that the psychological effects of living with domestic violence and abuse have to be understood as distinct from the experience of one traumatic event. Domestic violence is the outcome of *prolonged and repeated trauma where the victim is in a state of captivity and under the control of the perpetrator* (Herman 1992a, 1992b, 2004). Herman proposed that captivity (and the context of living with an abuser in the majority of cases *is* captivity) instils psychological *changes* in the victim that may reduce the sympathy of witnesses such as friends and family who have known her over time, which increases distress in the survivor/victim.

> The chronically abused person's apparent helplessness and passivity, her entrapment in the past, her intractable depression and somatic complaints, and her smouldering anger often frustrate the people closest to her. Moreover, if she has been coerced into betrayal of relationships, community loyalties, or moral values, she is frequently subjected to furious condemnation.
>
> (Herman 2004: 368)

The long-term traumatic stress experienced by some survivors of domestic abuse, which is caused by repeated trauma causing 'deformations of personality' (as with anyone who has been in captivity such as survivors of concentration camps, adherents of some religious cultures and hostages), is distinct from PTSD. Herman has identified a pattern of symptoms which reflect the extreme experience that some women have had.

These include:

- **Alterations in affect regulation** manifested in persistent dysphoria, chronic suicidal preoccupation, self injury, explosive or extremely inhibited anger and inhibited sexuality.
- **Alterations in consciousness** including amnesia or hyperamnesia for traumatic events, transient dissociative episodes, depersonalisation and reliving experiences in the form of intrusive symptoms or ruminative contemplation.
- **Alterations in self-perception** including a sense of helplessness or paralysis of initiative, shame, guilt and self-blame, sense of defilement or stigma and a sense of difference that no-one else could reach.
- **Alterations in the perception of the perpetrator** including a pre-occupation with the relationship which includes a pre-occupation with revenge, unrealistic attribution of total power (although Herman argues this needs to be understood with caution as it might reflect

reality), idealisation and/or paradoxical gratitude, a sense of a special or a supernatural relationship and an acceptance of the belief system of the perpetrator.

- **Alterations in relations with others** including isolation and withdrawal, disruption in intimate relationships, repeated searching for rescuers, persistent distrust and repeated failures of self-protection. This latter point was also picked up by Perez and Johnson (Perez and Johnson 2008) who found that symptoms of PTSD (or similar) predict that abused women's future safety is more likely to be compromised than those women who do not experience such symptoms.
- **Alterations in systems of meaning** including a loss of sustaining faith and a sense of helplessness and despair. (Herman 2004: 370)

Further implications of living with abuse and violence

Briere and Jordan (2004) in reviewing previous research on the complexity of the outcome of violence against women (and the associated clinical implications) support Herman's thesis in that they consider a PTSD diagnosis to be a blunt instrument and they argue that interventions need to be customised to take in a larger proportion of the person's symptoms and circumstances than would be the case through the response to PTSD alone. Their argument is based on the view that violence to women is endemic and it may be that women who seek treatment for the outcome of violence may have experienced prior trauma history of abuse (see below in Chapter 7 in particular). They draw upon the concept of the battered woman syndrome (BWS) as being more conducive to women's experience of domestic violence and abuse but stress that some responses of survivors are less obviously trauma-related and less specific but relate to their background situations which could include structural disadvantage. They conclude that the PTSD diagnosis is not necessarily useful because the

> effects of interpersonal violence vary substantially from person to person. . . . This is not to say that some effects are not relatively common among women who are victimised, such as depression, anxiety, or posttraumatic stress. Even these sequelae, however, are not inevitable, nor are they specific to a given type of assault.
>
> (Briere and Jordan 2004: 1267)

Mechanic (2004), responding to Briere and Jordan's overall thesis, suggests that the psychological traumatic symptoms of domestic violence are not always 'post'/in the past and that it is important

> not only to reconceptualise the nature of traumatic stress reactions experienced in the context of IPV/stalking from *post* to *peri* or

some other appropriate designation but also to develop therapeutic strategies to manage symptoms and help women deploy effective coping strategies in the face of continued harassment or threatened harm that often persist even after existing abusive relationships.

(Mechanic 2004: 1285)

To summarise, there is no doubting the impact of long-term abuse on psychology. Affect, self-esteem, anxiety, depression and many other symptoms are present in women who have survived or continue to live with violence. The symptoms may be exacerbated by previous traumatic experiences and other social disadvantages. It is also argued strongly that personality changes may occur in some women and that also women's experiences and degree of morbidity vary to a great extent.

Women who live with abusers therefore don't only suffer from the psychological symptoms of learned helplessness, for the reasons argued by Walker (2000), but the aftermath of leaving is also traumatic with medium- to long-term repercussions. Walker was trying to show that violent episodes are complex and form part of a long-term relationship whereby there is not only the 'event' but an accumulation and shared knowledge within the relationship about the abuser's behaviour, and the abused (the woman probably) begins to build up a sense of themselves within that framework. That person is not a powerful one perhaps but one who is able to survive. Walker's model has resonance in many stories of abuse. However from a different perspective Walker's work has been positioned as vilifying men because she has focused both upon some of the most violent perpetrators and upon the escalation of violence, which is not necessarily characteristic (Corvo and Johnson 2003).

Challenging men's control

Patriarchy has meant historically that men have controlled women's lives in heterosexual relationships (R.E. Dobash and Dobash 1984; Gordon 1988; Kelly 1988; Hague, Malos and Dear 1996), in organisations (Nicolson 1996) and across cultures and societies (Daly 1984). For the most part those working as activists in the area of domestic violence employ (a version of) a pro-feminist 'take' on the problem.

The point of disagreement between individualistic (psychological) explanations of violence and abuse and societal/structural (feminist) ones focuses upon the role of the man/perpetrator *in the context of the relationship*. The former, psychological approach highlights the difficulties faced by a particular family, couple or individual in the context of a violent relationship. This lies in stark contrast to the latter pro-feminist approach, which emphasises men's power and control over women (and children) as being the overarching problem.

Women's Aid, on their website, argue against the validity of Walker's (2000) 'cycle of violence' model as an approach to helping women break out of violent relationships. They make a case that the 'honeymoon' stage of Walker's cycle theory is in fact part of the operationalising of a continuing pattern of power and control whereby the perpetrator uses his expressions of remorse to absolve himself of responsibility.[2] But does the knowledge that you are being controlled/are controlling support women in being able to leave? Does it underpin permanent changes in men's behaviour?

The Duluth Domestic Abuse Intervention Project (DAIP), established in 1981, is identified as the gold standard by most pro-feminist commentators for confronting and changing the behaviours of abusive men. Women's Aid declares itself in favour of the Duluth model, using the 'Power and Control Wheel', which highlights the linked variety of ways in which men (or women if they are the abusive partner) use various forms of coercion and control to abuse their partners. The project aim is for the participant to move his behaviour (and attitudes) from power and control to non-violence and equality through becoming aware of male privilege and the need to change. The approach is generally speaking a CBT (cognitive behavioural therapy) take on behaviour change[3] including role play and 'psycho-education' about how women might feel and experience the abuse. Any pleas of extenuating circumstances are shown to be excuses (see D.G. Dutton and Corvo 2006).

Not all researchers give the Duluth model equal acclaim however (Jennings 1987; Babcock, Green and Robie 2004; D.G. Dutton and Corvo 2006; Gondolf 2007; Taft and Murphy 2007). The Duluth project was developed as a 'psycho-educational' one for court-sanctioned male perpetrators (Pence, Paymar and Ritmeester 1993) – i.e. mostly their partners would have had to press charges against them. An important component of the Duluth project is that it brooks no psychological 'mitigation'. Men's violent and abusive behaviour is positioned as unequivocally the result of patriarchy and not because men were brought up in violent, abusive families that were socially excluded, or had stresses in their lives, or succumbed to alcohol or other substance abuse.

Dutton and Corvo (2006), who oppose the Duluth approach, cite evidence from a number of sources demonstrating its flaws as a consequence of excluding psychology. Dutton (2003) also believes there are clinical limitations to the Duluth model that are not being acknowledged, but Dutton too is challenged in turn (Gondolf 2007) in the evidence he employs to make his assertions.

There has been increasing concern about the vilification of the (male) perpetrator (Corvo and Johnson 2003), with the plea that it should not be confused with advocacy for victims. Further, it is proposed that the stereotyping of perpetrators does not help either individual women or perpetrators, and neither can society learn from those who have perpetrated violence (Gerber 1991).

Questions of gender symmetry

There has been increasing awareness and acceptance by some of women's violence and the possibility that women engage in domestic violence and abuse (Johnson 2006; Straus 2008). There have been equally spirited challenges to this assertion (R.P. Dobash *et al.* 1992; R.E. Dobash *et al.* 2004). The psychology/feminist stand-off about the prevalence, causes and consequences of *women's* violence to men represents another ongoing battle (S. Steinmetz 1978; Tjaden and Thoennes 2000; Straus 2008). These opposing positions on whether violence is 'symmetrical' or 'asymmetrical' appear to be firmly entrenched, with (some of) the 'psychologists' arguing for symmetry using their treasured 'weapon' of evidence, based on quantitative methods, to show the frequency of violent and abusive behaviours (Straus 1979; Gelles 1980, 2000); and the 'feminists' focusing more theoretically, seeking evidence from activists and women survivors on the severity and repetitive nature of male violence compared with the violences perpetrated by women (R.P. Dobash *et al.* 1992; Hanmer *et al.* 1998).

Domestic violence continues to be positioned by pro-feminists as asymmetrical (Mullender 1996). Despite evidence that women *do* perpetrate violence towards men (D.G. Dutton and Nicholls 2005; Straus 2008) it remains true that in the majority (in around two-thirds at least) of cases men perpetrate the violence (Hamberger 1997; Saunders 2002) and when women do attack their male partners it seems to be context-specific so that these violent women are not a risk outside that situation or relationship (Henning and Feder 2004) and on the whole are violent in self-defence (O'Donovan 1991).

Despite Gelles's (1997) conviction that women are equally guilty of perpetrating violence to male partners, and [as Loseke and Kurz (2005) contend] his effort to take the moral high ground in condemning violence *per se*, the evidence is overwhelming that most violence perpetrated by men towards women is more damaging (emotionally as well as physically) than that perpetrated by women towards men. While there is some evidence that *rates* of violence between the sexes may be similar (Gelles 1997) women's violence to men tends to be at the less severe end of the violence spectrum such as slapping or pushing (other than in severe and highly unusual cases where 'weapons' are used). There is also strong evidence that women's violence to men is often in self-defence (Dasgupta 2002).

Re-stating this as a clear pro-feminist position has exacerbated claims to the contrary, including for example Straus (2005) whose (controversial) work is based upon identifying the prevalence and types of women's violence to men. He argues that women's violence in a relationship escalates violence by men towards women, and a violent woman in the family 'models' violence for children. He also appears to suggest that if women stopped being violent to men (or did not retaliate to male violence in kind)

71

then the violence from the man would extinguish itself. This assertion would fly in the face of all knowledge of social learning and behaviourist theories (Bandura 1977) and has not been supported by evidence even though Straus and Gelles constantly claim their work relies on scientific methods of data collection.

Straus further contends that most social scientists adopt the position that it is male violence that is most problematic because:

> One of the reasons social scientists and the public at large are willing to accept a single-cause approach advocated by feminists is the recognition of and indignation by most social scientists over past and continuing oppression and discrimination against women. As a result there is a tendency to accept almost anything that will change this aspect of society. . . . Thus avowedly feminist scholars have suppressed data on violence by women.
>
> (2005: 70)

This argument seems somewhat disingenuous. By making the point in this way, Straus does nothing to further thinking on the causes and consequences of domestic violence for women, men or children but expands the 'blame game'.

From another but equally controversial perspective, Felson argues that male violence against women has 'little or nothing to do with the oppression of women. . . . Physical advantage encourages men to use violence against women and discourages women from using violence against men' (2002: 4–5). His argument being that misogyny plays very little part in male violence to women but domestic abusers are 'versatile offenders' (2002: 5).

Even so, the view that patriarchy is the core of male domination, control and violence to women does not conflict with the possibility that perpetrators of domestic abuse are also violent in other contexts rather than misogynist *per se*. Accepting either this or a pro-feminist standpoint explanation should not be the end-point of enquiry and thinking about a problem that clearly persists despite changes in the law and the increased levels of public awareness.

As Featherstone and Trinder (1997) identified several years previously, the pro-feminist standpoint potentially conceals the complexities within violent intimate relationships. In doing so the needs of many vulnerable women and children may be neglected. However to claim that women's violence to men is covered up for ideological reasons does little to stimulate debate, conversely ensuring continued polarisation.

Critical approaches to psychology

Psychology is not a unified discipline by any means (Good 2007; Ouellette 2008; Papadopoulos 2008). Psychologists (particularly feminist and social psychologists) have long eschewed the dominance of positivism because of the de-contextualisation and reductionism of the human condition which, despite the critiques, in the early twenty-first century seems to have come firmly of age in the mainstream academic discipline through the use of modern technologies focusing on 'brain science'. However, psychology is not a moribund area of enquiry. As long as the discipline has existed, there has been resistance and alternative ways of conceptualising psychological epistemologies. This even applied to some degree to William James,[4] the 'founding father', who foresaw conceptual difficulties in understanding the idea of 'self'. In the end, though, he opted for 'science' over the more complex problems of exploring lived experience and identity.

Several 'crises' in the discipline over the past forty years, particularly in social psychology, have mostly revolved around questions of 'substance' and 'method' (see for instance Armistead 1974; Squire 1990). Is the 'subject' of psychology the biological basis of behaviour or social relations? What is the relationship between the 'social' and the 'individual' and what mediates this relationship? Are psychologists looking at 'behaviour' or are they looking at 'emotion' or 'experience' (among other possibilities). How should the substance of psychology be studied? Should methodology and the need to be 'scientific' outweigh the more philosophical or social questions which probe the essence of human experience?

These matters have variously been identified as the 'science' crisis, which came about because 'most of the troubles now facing psychology stem from the very fact of its claiming to be a science at all' (Westland 1978: 45). As a science psychology attempts to find causal relationships, as for example the predictive factors for domestic abuse. This might be achieved by trying to manipulate 'variables' and establish the effects. Thus a longitudinal study of a group of men whose fathers were violent might be compared with a group whose early family life was peaceful. It is not surprising that sociologists and feminists (whether or not their home discipline is psychology) are disdainful of this tradition in mainstream academic psychology. Positivist methods ensure that women's experiences are rendered invisible 'as a consequence of researchers' insistence of objectivity and the associated claim that the knowledge produced is therefore "value-free"' (Stoppard 2000: 15). However psychology is not a unitary discipline and this critique has been well rehearsed over the last twenty years.

Materialist approaches

There are several facets which underpin the potential for critique in psychology. For psychologists, consideration of the material world involves engagement with an 'observable' environment which *constrains* human action and behaviour (see Chapter 1). The environment includes the social and cultural context, the physical environment and corporality or the biological context. As human beings we can only act within the limits of our finances, gender, health, place and culture.

Traditional psychology typically prioritises some elements of the material world in its examination of 'cognition' and 'behaviour' (rather than more complex ideas such as 'subjectivity' and 'reflexivity'), but ignores it in that much of what is now taken to be the subject matter of mainstream academic psychology appears to be context-free. Thus most recently, as in cognitive neuroscience, mind, thought, emotions and even the unconscious have been reduced to brain functions and 'wiring' of synapses (Gallagher and Frith 2003). To take culture and social context into account in understanding human behaviour and emotions represents step one towards a critique of psychology as the measurement of mental mechanisms.

Discursive psychology

In response to the 'science' crisis in psychology in the 1970s and in parallel with developments of feminist critiques of the main discipline came the 'turn to language' (Harre and Secord 1972; I. Parker 1996). This development emphasised the ways in which language is used to socially construct subjectivity. That is, concepts, phenomena and ideas once taken to be unproblematic (e.g. the 'self') were opened up to reflexive questioning to make sense of action and experience (Byrne 2003).

The turn to language in social and feminist psychology has been so important and influential that the field of social constructionist psychology itself has a diverse epistemology. As Danziger (1997) is often quoted as saying, there is a 'dark' version which focuses on matters of power and subjectivity, which is rooted in the work of Foucault. There is also a 'light' version which focuses on conversation, speech and discourse analysis including ethnomethodology and deconstruction. However the two are not mutually exclusive (see for example Forrester and Ramsden 2000; Hepburn and Wiggins 2007). However, as Nightingale and Cromby (1999) propose, there are conceptual problems with social constructionist and discursive approaches in psychology, one of which is the neglect of embodiment, and 'While all . . . things may appear in discourse . . . they are not reducible to it' (1999: 11). (See Chapter 6 in particular for a more detailed discussion.)

'Doing' the 'material' in a discursive context

The resolute position held by pro-feminist activists is that material conditions under patriarchy, whatever the individual circumstances, make women's lives vulnerable to abusers. The solution to domestic abuse, it is argued, therefore, is to increase financial and human resources available to enable the victim to leave, be safe and prosecute her abuser.

Typically from this position it is the *material constraints* on women living with abuse, combined with parallel ones which materially constrain support and law enforcement, that are in the forefront of contemporary political discourse. The British Government for instance (typically) calls and claims credit for more investment for support services, new legislation to protect victims and manage perpetrators, and specialist training for members of law enforcement, health and social care and the criminal justice system (e.g. Home Office 2009). This position is reflected across Europe and North America.

As is clear, over the last thirty years domestic violence and abuse have come to be identified as a *crime* and rhetorically presented as legally and morally repugnant in western capitalist democracies (see Chapter 5). A contemporary example of these shifts in attitudes is reflected in the western response to the Afghan President Hamid Karzai signing legislation to curb women's rights (see Chapter 1). This legislation includes a clause to support rape in marriage and prevent women leaving their house without the permission of their husband. However, at a time when President Obama and the NATO alliance were promising an increase in military support for the Afghan government, Karzai's action sparked discussion in the western media about whether military and other resources might be withheld from Afghanistan to demonstrate objection to the destruction of hard-won human rights for women and the legalisation of domestic abuse.

This rhetoric of distaste reflects the general frame of mind of government and non-government agencies around the world who express the need to combat and prevent domestic violence and abuse, and other violences to women. This in itself has been a marked triumph for feminist campaigners and academics, *many of whom, in both categories, are psychologists*. No longer is men's violence to women seen as 'rare' or only something that happens to those who 'deserve' it (see Chapters 4 and 5). It has become recognised as a social and public health problem as well as a crime that bears costs in both human and financial terms (Walby/Department of Trade and Industry 2004).

Ussher (1997) suggests there is typically an epistemological divide between those who identify the body as 'corporality' and those who see the body as the product of 'talk' symbols and signs. Thus, for example, on the one side (the material) domestic violence is conceptualised as an observable set of actions, i.e. a physical assault by a man upon a woman causing her bodily harm. On the other (the discursive) domestic violence is socially constructed, a product of discourse which names a set of practices as domestic violence. Thus a woman may see her relationship as one in which she lives with a man who hits her or she sees herself as a survivor of domestic violence.

A material-discursive approach to psychology (Ussher 1997; Yardley 1997) facilitates links across the disciplinary divides of psychology, biology and sociology. It is particularly useful to explore complex areas where social constructions and rhetorical conventions employed to understand matters such as 'gender' or 'power' link with 'real' lived experience. The 'material' dimension represents the constraining elements in the lives of the participants, and the discursive represents the meanings given to those lives and experiences. The stories of Laila and Mariam outlined at the start of this book demonstrate such a juxtaposition.

A material-discursive approach stresses that bodily processes, emotions, cognitions and social relations are intricately intertwined and it is through the lived body that both discursive and material reality can be achieved (Luyt 2003). This approach takes account of the structural social relations (e.g. gender and power relations) and active agency (Burkitt 1999 in Luyt 2003) as well as dynamic social and historical contexts (Watson 2000 in Luyt 2003).

Conclusions

Psychological explanations of domestic violence and abuse which describe the context and content of violent relationships have traditionally been positioned as contravening the pro-feminist sociological position that domestic violence is a means of controlling and oppressing women. It is suggested that psychology is not a unified discipline, and a critical approach to understanding the psychology of abusive relationships and their impact upon those involved can only be helpful in trying to prevent, care for and emotionally liberate those surviving violence.

What is needed now is the careful and systematic re-consideration of women's *relational* actions and lived experience within and around violent and abusive relationships.

Part 2

DISCURSIVE CONSTRUCTIONS OF DOMESTIC VIOLENCE AND ABUSE

4

THE SOCIAL CONSTRUCTION OF DOMESTIC ABUSE: MYTHS, LEGENDS AND FORMULA STORIES

Introduction

What appears to be clear then is that 'domestic violence' is not a given, its meaning or even its existence, is not transparent. Rather 'domestic violence' is discursively constructed. Violence between spouses/intimates is a physical phenomenon, but whether or not it is recognised as significant or aberrant, or even what falls within its parameters, is subject to a range of discursive processes. The recognition and naming of a phenomenon as 'domestic violence' is by no means constant or consistent.

(Featherstone and Trinder 1997: 148)

Psychology as a discipline is diverse and dynamic and social psychology is well able to engage with feminism and sociology (Walsh and Nicolson 1997). Discursive, or social constructionist, psychology has shifted the emphasis of the discipline from consideration only of 'observable' behaviours such as those posited by Walker in her exposition of the battered woman syndrome, towards examination of the meanings and practices surrounding human interaction (S.D. Brown 2001). Social constructionist psychology has therefore confronted taken-for-granted, common-sense assumptions as to what counts as 'real' (I. Parker 2003). The concern in discursive psychology with how relationships between people and institutions are described and understood via language used to give them meaning provides a means of experiencing social relations that are not static or set phenomena but dynamic constructions (I. Parker 2002). This has been employed in feminist psychology for example to take apart (or deconstruct) the relationship between 'deficit' accounts of women's embodied reproductive status and mental health in for example the medicalisation of the premenstrual syndrome (P. Choi 1995; Ussher 1989, 2006), the menopause (Hunter 1990; Gannon 1999), postnatal depression (Nicolson 1998) and depression and mental health overall (Ussher 1989; Stoppard 2000). However, this enterprise becomes particularly sensitive, and important, when used to challenge taken-for-granted assumptions by feminists themselves.

Social constructionist and discursive psychology

Social constructionism, while increasingly influential in psychology, has faced internal challenges – the main one being the question of materiality in relation to discourse (see Chapter 3). The material-discursive approach provides some reparation (Nightingale and Cromby 1999; Edley 2001). Important to note though is the distinction made by Danziger (1997) between 'light' and 'dark' social constructionism (see Chapter 3). The former (light) refers to acknowledgement of the multiplicity of meanings which illuminate and potentially liberate. For example, following S. Brown's (2001) discussion of the social construction of child abuse by Hacking (1999), the concepts 'domestic violence' and 'domestic abuse' enable a meaning to be given to certain actions which become *understood* in a particular way – that is, as 'domestic violence' or 'domestic abuse'. It then follows that these concepts can operate as a *resource* for people to re-evaluate their lives and their relationships with others. So, a woman who has (previously) identified her partner as being 'controlling', with a 'terrible temper', who may sometimes hit her, will (now) be able to draw upon the *discourse of domestic abuse* to place her experience in a broader context.

Deidre for instance, interviewed in the DASH study, had only understood herself to be living with domestic abuse when her next door neighbour confessed to her that she herself had been re-housed after living in a refuge. Deidre also told us: 'I didn't think I were a victim of abuse to begin with and then one day I was watching Kilroy or something and they were labelling these women as battered wives and I thought "that's me" and that's when it dawned on me.' This was potentially liberating for Deidre and other women who had hitherto been unable to 'name' their experiences, not only intellectually and emotionally but in supporting action to leave the abuser or develop other means of stopping the abuse.

The latter (dark) version of social constructionism however, influenced by Michel Foucault, involves the regulation of conduct through discourse. Foucault claimed that power and knowledge are linked and discourses are created to *regulate* the everyday lives of individuals, operating as forms of constraint and norms (Hyman and Chez 1995; Peckover 2002). Thus, for Foucault, discourses on mental illness, criminality and sexuality are as much aimed at the regulation of conduct as they are at the liberation of individuals from mental illness, crime or sexual repression (Burkitt 1999). Taking this Foucauldian approach, a woman recognising she is living with domestic abuse may hold the 'formula' story to explain and constrain her experience and motivation. It would follow that on recognition of her plight as being one of living with the experience of domestic abuse, a woman *should begin a process of leaving*. Other implications, including how she makes sense of her *self* and how she *ought to behave* as a victim/survivor, follow too. Indeed the discourse in which 'victim' is replaced by 'survivor' places responsibilities upon abused women which were not available when the dominant discourses were around 'battered women' rather than 'domestic abuse' (Ferraro and Johnson 1983). Recent policy-directed research in the UK for instance indicates the responsibility authorities have for including survivors as 'service users', which potentially places a further formal burden on the survivors of abuse, impelling them to contribute to develop future policy and services (Mullender and Hague 2005; Hague and Mullender 2006).

It is not only the woman survivor who is regulated by discourses of domestic abuse. Policy makers, law enforcers and health and social care professionals around the world have now come under surveillance *themselves* about their practices in relation to domestic violence and abuse (Fanslow and Norton 1994; Rodriguez, McLoughlin, Nah and Campbell 2001; Ellsberg 2006b; J.S. Smith, Rainey, Smith, Alamares and Grogg 2008; Sully 2008). The power of discourse to regulate is thus achieved through the power of social norms, and as it is now 'accepted' that domestic abuse and violence are socially and politically intolerable, so tolerating or ignoring goes against normative behaviours, risking ostracism.

Armstrong (1995), following Foucault (1976), had identified the impact of surveillance medicine as the attempt to bring everyone within its networks of visibility whereby the medical 'gaze' problematises what is normal. In other words, medical power is achieved through discursive practices whereby *power is the knowledge of the discipline* of medicine and doctors identify what is 'health' and what is 'health-related' behaviour. Using that analogy as a template then it follows that women who experience abuse and seek help do so under the gaze of the relevant experts. Knowledge-claims about what counts as suitable behaviour towards an intimate partner are grounded in discursive practices, so that the police or health visitors for instance will judge claims of those who might be victims/survivors of abuse or who wish to deny it (Bacchus, Mezey and Bewley 2002; Rodriguez, Sheldon and Rao 2002; J.R. Gillis *et al.* 2006). Maggie made this point well.

> It's like they would not take it seriously . . . your heart, emotionally, you know, mentally you know you feel like you are really beginning to struggle. But they don't see . . . as long as he hasn't touched you they say 'oh you haven't got bruises' or something. They can't do anything about it, even if you have got bruises you still have to go to court and prove it, so all that is like . . . and you keep going back to the same problems, and you feel like, 'no I am losing, there's no point, I might as well stay here and take it'.

The power of the experts here is used to regulate who might be identified as abused, overriding the account from the woman herself. More so Maggie herself is aware of how she might be seen based both on past experience and knowledge of discursive practices around domestic abuse.

It has therefore been further proposed that the gaze of the expert would involve a survivor in simultaneous self-surveillance, 'usually understood as the attention one pays to one's behaviour when facing the actuality or virtuality of an immediate or mediated observation by others whose opinion he or she deems as relevant – usually observers of the same or superior social position' (Vaz and Bruno 2003: 273).

Thus women, aware of feminist and activist discourses around abuse and violence, will pay attention to their own 'failings' if they are not wanting to take the line of choosing to leave (Shurman and Rodriguez 2006). Like Maggie, if they do want to leave they will attend to the apparent merits of their 'case' as they might be viewed by those with expert power (Loseke and Cahill 1984).

This regulation, surveillance and self-surveillance also applies to academics writing about and researching domestic abuse, regulated by the knowledge-claims of feminist sociologists who deride psychology (Romito 2008; see Chapter 3). As a pro-feminist academic psychologist concerned about domestic abuse and violence I remain aware of the activist/anti-psychology discourses, the feminist 'gaze' and potential denunciation.

Regulatory discourses operate on a number of levels. Several women interviewed in the DASH study for instance said that they were wary of contacting the police or social services because they knew that their claims would be dealt with cynically (by the police) and possibly punitively by social services who might challenge their ability to care for their children. This links with the common belief that women who seek help for domestic violence are 'unreliable' witnesses and unfit mothers. However it may be that these women are also drawing on the formula stories of agencies they think might be able to help them such as Refuge or other voluntary sector organisations.

However, as will be clear in Chapters 6 onwards, pressure to submit to expectations and norms about domestic abuse is problematic for many women survivors over and above the material level of resources and support agencies.

Myths and the regulation of men (and women)

Discourses of domestic violence and abuse have been constructed as a series of regulatory mechanisms serving to reveal abusive behaviours to the abuser and victim/survivor and to the agencies of law enforcement, health care, social services and specialist domestic abuse organisations. Claims to knowledge(s) and the construction of knowledge(s) about what constitutes domestic abuse have been practised by professional and advocacy agencies.

A powerful discourse running through the text of websites from advocacy and activist agencies has been the identification and debunking of 'myths' (R.P. Dobash *et al.* 1992; Haaken 2010). A myth or unsubstantiated story has been described as leading to attitudes and beliefs which encourage acts *as if* that story were indeed the reality or *'an unproved or false collective belief that is used to justify a social institution'*.[1] The myths, which I call here 'primary' myths, resonate with the general theme that domestic violence and abuse are rare events targeted at the 'deserving'. This was the general publicly accepted view (or mass denial) before it was debunked by the pioneering work of Erin Pizzey at the Chiswick refuge. However the process of debunking these primary myths has led to ideologically laden formula stories which have fixed public knowledge about the causes and impact of domestic violence.

Constructing the survivor: myth or lived experience?

The list below is common across all campaigning websites. The intention is to dispel primary myths that undermine women's survival and it is on the whole aimed at heterosexual women living with abuse. These primary myths are:

- She could just leave.
- It mainly happens to poor women on council estates.
- It's alcohol that causes men to be violent.
- Abused women must have done something to deserve it.
- Certain women attract violent men.
- Abusers were abused themselves.
- Domestic violence is quite rare.
- Domestic violence does not affect older women.
- Women are not violent to their male (or female) partners other than in self-defence.

The message has been very powerful and has altered the public landscape making more people than ever before aware that domestic abuse is common and that it can happen to anyone (Borg 2003; Nicolson and Wilson 2004). Debunking these myths for ideological reasons, to support women who are experiencing violence but who may have been too afraid, ashamed or emotionally reduced to seek help, has been invaluable for campaigns against domestic violence (Featherstone and Trinder 1997). Abused women may feel isolated or even 'to blame' for what is happening to them. It may be that they fail to recognise the experience as abuse and see it as normal in their particular relationship.

The primary myth about domestic violence, which was challenged by campaigners, went something like this:

Domestic violence happens infrequently but when it does, it happens equally between men and women, to young and middle-aged women in particular who won't leave their partner because they are somehow natural victims or even masochists, who come from underprivileged backgrounds, deserve the abuse and who intentionally or unintentionally attract violent men.

However, such myth-breaking, challenging 'defensive' public perceptions of domestic abuse (i.e. defences that people might use to deny the prevalence and severity of domestic violence for emotional protection or more practical reasons), has in itself perpetuated a further set of immutable 'truths' that cannot, it seems, be questioned further. Thus it becomes difficult to say as an academic, policy maker, manager or practitioner that, for instance, some women *do* attract violent men, that *most* women who experience domestic violence *are* underprivileged and that men raised by violent families may well perpetuate that behaviour in adulthood (Pizzey and Shapiro 1982; Markowitz 2001; Ehrensaft *et al.* 2003). Being prepared to take these more complex issues on board intellectually and deal with their social implications requires effort, particularly because it makes action more difficult. The picture of what really happens in abusive relationships and why abuse occurs is far more complex than most popular notions of myths and myth-breaking indicate (Ferraro and Johnson 1983; A. Smith 2001; Worden and Carlson 2005).

For campaigners and feminists these primary myths have now been effectively dismissed. It is mostly 'accepted' that domestic violence and abuse can and does happen across the social spectrum, to anyone, albeit some groups are more vulnerable than others (Humphreys 2007), and that it is influenced by men's need to control, not by stress or related or unrelated substance abuse (Bettman 2009). It is also clearly stated by activists and campaigners that women are the survivors not the perpetrators and should ask for help.

The very fact that domestic abuse is hidden from public view means that evidence used to demystify it has been supportive to women (and their advocates) who may have felt they were the only ones living with abuse. Thus for example:

There are many popular myths and prejudices about domestic violence. Not only do these myths lead to many women feeling unable to seek help, but they can cause unnecessary suffering. They may come to believe these myths in an attempt to justify, minimise or deny the violence they are experiencing. Acknowledging these cultural barriers can be an important part of coming to terms with what is really happening.[2]

84

Some of these knowledge-claims will be discussed more fully below in this chapter because despite the effectiveness of these feminist campaigns in changing public perceptions and enabling women to seek help, these anti-myths themselves are not always backed up by empirical evidence. The enthusiasm of activists trying to ensure that they make their point persuasively has inevitably meant that some important distinctions have not been made and some contradictory evidence has been ignored. In making it clear that women are on the whole the ones who experience abuse from men, though, lesbians', and gay and heterosexual men's survival has been ignored (Hammond 1989; Letellier 1994; Renzetti 1998; Ristock 2003). Men too who have been victims of domestic violence, even though in a minority, have been marginalised by the rhetoric of campaigners (Brush 1990; Johnson and Ferraro 2000; Dasgupta 2002). Thus a second generation of 'debunking' has occurred (albeit subtly), usually from non-activist public service sites and information leaflets. An example is as follows:

> Domestic violence occurs in heterosexual, lesbian, gay, bisexual, and transgender relationships. Whether the victim is male or female, violence of any kind in relationships is unacceptable. Domestic violence affects people from every age, racial or ethnic background, religious group, neighbourhood, and income level.[3]

In making their point, this group use the idea that the experience of domestic abuse can happen to *absolutely* anyone including men and thus it subtly clarifies that women too can perpetrate abuse to female and male partners. This 'blandness' unintentionally I suspect negates the primacy of heterosexual male violence, undermining the pro-feminist position.

Men's resistance

Not so subtly, though, the idea of the myth is also employed by men's campaigning groups who seek to challenge the idea that domestic violence is mostly perpetrated by men towards women. So:

> The myths are statements of ideology, not based on any scientific research. In fact, domestic violence is an issue of power and control in a relationship, and women can also be what Erin Pizzey, author of *Prone to Violence*, calls 'family terrorists.' In fact, domestic violence is committed by men and women with identi-fiable psychological pathologies, sometimes exacerbated by use of alcohol or drugs.[4]

The latter debunking is rather 'shrill' in its (incorrect) assertion that ideology has replaced science for advocates of women survivors. It conflates issues of power and control by (mis)using Pizzey's work as its only evidence (Pizzey and Shapiro 1982), and it follows this with the allegation that it is only psychologically disturbed people who are violent to their partners.

Highlighting websites focusing specifically on this part of Pizzey's work indicates that the majority of commentators are 'bloggers' or radical men's groups who *selectively* seek support from her arguments. They identify with anything that appears to show women in a bad light, and emphasise female aggression with the aim of bolstering men's image but also implicitly and sometimes explicitly justifying male violence. For example one blogger suggests:

> The contempt for males is everywhere, from the unsubtle brain-washing into appropriate (read 'female') behaviour in pre-schools, through to the corruption of the judiciary, with male judges being sent to re-education camps to purge them of alleged sexism. In universities, what were once academic disciplines – such as history and literature – have been transformed into courses which 'deconstruct' history and literature for 'evidence' of oppression of women and minorities.[5]

This 'rant' serves to fuel not only misogyny but racism too, being an attempt to undermine liberal-humanist attitudes across the board in the guise of attacking the 'politically correct' lobby. The following text, although more restrained in its surface approach, selectively exploits the work of Straus and Gelles (Gelles 2000; Straus 2008) to indicate that men can also be victims of violence. It then proceeds to claim that *women* are the main abusers in the family, particularly of children.

> So, in summary, it is clear that women are involved in inflicting violence on men, and to a degree not far different from the level at which men inflict violence. This rings true with anyone who has an experience of troubled families, whereas the focus on men alone denies the reality. It would be preferable to see interpersonal violence in all its forms stopped, and all perpetrators, men and women, treated in a way that carries a clear message that violence is unacceptable in our community.
>
> In addition, if we were to broaden the concept of DV to include child abuse, we would find that the discourse on men as batterers, women and children as victims, is erroneous. Most physical and emotional abuse of children is perpetrated by women, with the single largest group of child abusers being mothers.[6]

The polarisation between 'men's groups' and their *versions* of feminism is unhelpful in the extreme as a means of understanding and preventing domestic violence. Men may indeed become victims of violence from both male and female partners. But this does not exonerate men who are violent and abusive to their partners and children. Nor does it in any sense imply that it is no longer important to take violence towards women seriously.

The reason why all these messages are in the public domain however is because there is so much at stake and so many vested interests claiming the moral high ground. Research evidence and theoretical development have been hijacked because of the sensitivities reviewed in Chapter 3.

From myth to formula story

Formula stories, as regulatory discourses, as described by Loseke (2001), reinforce certain myths because the myths themselves are pragmatic. They become 'interpretive resources' and thus 'widely acknowledged ways of interpreting and conveying experience, they become virtual templates for how lived experience may be defined' (2001: 107). In the case of women's experiences of domestic abuse, Loseke observed that accounts reflected contemporary discourses of gender-power relations and men's controlling behaviours. In this way the narrative obscures the *'mundane complications of everyday social relations and interpretation may virtually disappear as the formula story presents troubles in bold relief'* (Loseke 2001: 107). Loseke's study, with groups of women discussing their experiences, contrasted in both method and content with the individual data collected in the DASH study. Many of the DASH participants were from underachieving, uneducated backgrounds. Their narratives contrasted strongly with the expectations of some abused women's advocates. The narratives frequently contravened the stance taken by, for example, Women's Aid,[7] on how women who had survived domestic abuse and left the abuser might account for themselves. As extracts from interviews demonstrate, several of the women were ambivalent about leaving their abusers and certainly did not offer anything even resembling a formula story or feminist analysis of their situation, although they did talk about the lack of sympathy and/or resources from various agencies. As stated in Chapter 2, this left me in a quandary similar to that reported by Buchbinder and Eisikovits (2003) who identified an ethical dilemma for those who engage in research *for* women but end up presenting research findings which *may* cast women survivors in a negative light.

Evidence about the prevalence of domestic abuse by men towards women is clear (see Chapter 1) but evidence of women's violence is less so because of the near embargo on feminist research into women's violence (Campbell 2002; Archer and Coyne 2005).

In the remainder of this chapter I will examine some of the evidence that both supports and challenges claims about the primary myths identified by feminist activists. The intention is to show the extent to which the naming of these primary myths *simplifies* a complex set of circumstances, desires and motivations and thus serves to *regulate* women and impact on the way they account for themselves in ways which may not always be to the material or emotional advantage of those women.

Staying in or leaving abusive relationships

The most commonly expressed primary 'myth' is that an abused woman should be motivated to 'just leave' her partner (see Chapter 3). The counterpoint is that it is not such an easy decision to make because of the multiple barriers presented by the emotional aspects of the abusive relationship and the practicalities of leaving, particularly if the women are mothers. There is a lack of safe housing, a lack of help from and trust for the law enforcement and social work agencies, and health care workers; and there is not enough funding to support a woman who may have no independent income, or who may have to leave her job in order to be safe, who has the responsibility for her children and other matters related to seeking safety from a violent partner (Haaken and Yragui 2003; Breckenridge and Mulroney 2007) (see Chapter 1). Tricia for example, who eventually left her partner, and was on a council housing list, showed just how unsafe women can be *after* leaving a violent man:

> I went to look at it [a house]. One of his best friends lives four doors away so I refused it. I said 'I'm sorry but I have got to refuse' and basically she just says 'well that's your lot then, you've been offered a place and you won't take it . . . we've got nothing else to offer you so we'll send out a letter saying we are taking you off our list'.

This was clearly both devastating for Tricia and a serious indictment of the lack of understanding by the housing services in that area. Safety for women and children escaping abuse should be paramount. Tricia had left her partner once before three years earlier because 'he beat me up pretty bad', only to return because once she left him she realised that with three small children it was impossible to find somewhere safe and affordable to live. Prior to her interview she had been offered support through a local specialist project which enabled her to finally move away from him.

Not everyone *wants* to leave the abuser however and even though this may appear irrational, and the reasons given may not ring true to the outside observer, there are individualistic explanations that women draw on to support themselves in such relationships. Ferraro and Johnson (1983) explored the psychology of living with and returning to an abuser through interviews with 100 women. The notion that women stay in violent relationships because of masochism was challenged and replaced with a theory that suggested coping strategies which attempt to 'neutralise' men's abusive behaviours. What is valuable about this work, which has largely been overlooked by feminist standpoint commentators, is that not only do the authors propose that systems (e.g. psychiatric, justice and law enforcement) neglect the material and cultural problems abused women experience when trying to leave a violent man, but they suggest that women themselves operate within the same culture and *make sense of their worlds in the same contexts*. That is, self-surveillance accords with dominant knowledge-claims.

Ferraro and Johnson suggest following the typology originally developed by Sykes and Matza (1957) to analyse the 'techniques of neutralisation' employed by young people who had committed criminal acts. This framework was adapted to identify six techniques of 'rationalisation' used by battered women. These were:

- an appeal to the salvation ethic
- denial of injury
- denial of victimiser
- denial of victimisation
- denial of options
- an appeal to higher loyalties

The argument was that using these psychological rationalisations helped women cope with the sense of their lives in a relationship with the abusive man.

An appeal to the salvation ethic: Connie proposed some personal salvation through taking part in the study because, 'for me it's taking something out of what he's done to me and being able to give something back so something good has come out of it rather than just being a victim all the time'. As discussed further in Chapter 5, many women take a moral stance on their commitment to their relationship as well as commitment to the man himself.

Denial of injury: Deidre felt she wanted to share her experiences to help other women. She had at the time of being abused survived the experience by denying the abuse was taking place and hiding her injuries from others. 'In the beginning I never talked to anyone about it. I used to like, hide it.'

Such denial is both a conscious and unconscious process (see Chapter 6).

Denial of the victimiser and victimisation: Catherine denied both the victimiser and victimisation, and partly blamed the entire experience on her husband's family who were 'aware of the abuse but swept it under the carpet', but also said her divorce was 'an amicable separation' and 'it wasn't just abuse – it was a breakdown between us both, we both wanted different things'. Here it appears that she cannot face the fact that her husband had responsibility for perpetrating the abuse.

Denial of options: Many women in the study saw little opportunity for options other than continuing to live as they were with the abuser and his abuse. This was because most women who are in abusive relationships are trapped in some way. They may not be believed by law enforcement agencies, they fear their children may be taken into care, they fear their partner will find them if they leave and be even more violent; they thus fear for their lives and the future of their children, they have nowhere to go, they see no opportunities for a reasonable life if they leave. R.E. Dobash and Dobash (1977/1978) identify these same phenomena not as women's rationalisations and coping strategies but as a material reality.

An appeal to higher loyalties: Finally there is evidence that women from South Asian backgrounds in particular were frequently denied the opportunity to leave their abusers on the grounds that their families expected them to remain for the sake of family honour.

It is clear that women *do* develop strategies for explaining their actions and motivations for staying with abusive men, to themselves and others.

The conundrum is in explaining women's *agency* in staying, contrasted with men's *agency* in controlling and abusing women. Thus, should we focus attention on *women's experiences* and how to interpret them and whether as 'rationalisations' or 'victimhood', or should we focus on men's behaviours and the influence of patriarchy?

Kirkwood (1993) in a summary and critique of psychological approaches to understanding women's experience of domestic abuse cites NiCarthy's (1987) book, based on a study of thirty-three women's stories of their thoughts, feelings, social situations, and personal histories, as the exemplary shift away from the development of a predictive model, the stuff of traditional psychology. NiCarthy's work is optimistic in that it is about escape and *survival*, providing data on context as well as individual experience (Kirkwood 1993). Kirkwood herself describes women's experiences of leaving rather than their rationalisations for staying, showing that awareness leads to empowerment and gaining control over their lives. However women who stay are once again neglected. Their stories do not appear to empower women.

Domestic abuse can happen to anyone regardless of economic and social status

Domestic violence most definitely happens to women from all social, economic, ethnic and religious groups across all social strata (Humphreys 2007). However, many women from affluent, educated backgrounds, such as Mary, whose case is outlined in previous chapters, have greater choice, although Mary herself was concerned for reputation and lifestyle particularly because of the investment that she had made into their domestic and social world. She did not know of others in her social circle who had lived with domestic abuse (which of course did not mean that they hadn't).

In cases where better educated, middle-class men abuse their wives, the disclosure is sometimes treated more sensationally, particularly when the revelation is about someone in the public eye.

In 2002 Dominic Carman, the son of a highly successful barrister, wrote a book about his father George Carman whom he accused of being a 'wife beater and a drunk'. Dominic said his father made him watch as he humiliated and beat his mother. He also said his father drank and gambled heavily. In the book, *No Ordinary Man*, he wrote: 'From the age of four or five, I was made to watch each punishing performance as he degraded her [Dominic's mother, Celia] with violent, caustic language and blows from his fists.'[8]

Domestic violence knows no boundaries of class, race or religion. However, one group of women who are particularly liable to suffer prolonged abuse are those from ethnic and religious minorities where women are not valued (Wilson 2006). For instance one respondent, Batz (an educated South Asian woman), reported that she could not go to her family for help, even though they loved each other, because they would tell her to 'stick with him'. She managed to leave her violent husband eventually because there was a special project for Asian women survivors to support her. However it meant isolation from her family. Talking of her cultural background she said:

They [men] think you're like dirt. They marry the women and they clean the house and cook the food and bear children for them. That's all. They don't think about qualifications or how capable she is they only worry about whether she's capable of looking after the family. The only thing they ask is 'can she cook?', not how many years she spent in college because they know if she is working that as soon as she's married it has to be stopped and she has to be in the house looking after the kids and the in-laws as well. Some women have never been to a post office in their lives, have never handled money even 'cos when they are young their parents look after them and as soon as they get married the husband takes control of them. Even those women born in this country they haven't got a clue what their rights are.

Domestic violence can happen to anyone but strategies for survival and the impact of the abuse vary.

Debunking the myths about alcohol (and substance abuse)

Refuge and other agencies all propose that it is a *myth* that alcohol causes men to be violent. This claim is aimed at ensuring that responsibility for violence resides with the man himself and that being drunk is no excuse for crossing the line towards violence. There is evidence that in fact alcohol *is* frequently a component of domestic abuse (Parker 1993; Quigley and Leonard 2000; White and Chen 2002; Galvani 2006). The Gascoigne family for example (see Chapter 5) were a high-profile case where Paul Gascoigne was violent when drunk, but this story is typical of many, as there is plenty of evidence that alcohol exacerbates violence. While it is unlikely that alcohol alone will *cause* otherwise well-adjusted and well-intentioned men (or women) to be violent, it does play a part in pushing some potential perpetrators over the edge. It also plays its part in violent relationships when the woman begins drinking in order to stave off the physical and emotional pain. Drinking (and other substance abuse (Rosenbaum and Leisring 2001; Yeager and Seid 2002)) by either or both partners is a common pattern in long- to medium-term abusive relationships. A report produced by the British Government summarising key studies identified that alcohol does contribute to violence in the home in a number of ways (http://www.homeoffice.gov.uk/rds/pdfs04/r216.pdf). Around a third of all cases of domestic violence are committed while the perpetrator is under the influence of alcohol. 'Problem drinking' over time is an indicator of intimate partner abuse. Heavy drinkers are also at risk of victimisation and heavy drinking exacerbates existing conflict (Martin and Bachman 1997; Mirrlees-Black 1999; O'Farrell, Van Hutton and Murphy 1999; Quigley and Leonard 2000; White and Chen 2002).

'Abusers were abused themselves': myth or reality?

It is clearly the case that some abusers were abused themselves. This does not mean that every abused man is going to abuse his partner and/or children. Dryden *et al.* (2010) have shown that some boys brought up with violent fathers eschew such behaviour while others show signs that they might mirror the violence. However almost every woman interviewed for the DASH study reported that the man had come from an abusive family background (aspects of this are discussed in Chapter 7 (Stith *et al.* 2000; Ehrensaft *et al.* 2003)).

Women are not violent to their male (or female) partners

Increasingly there is acknowledgement in policy documents and websites that women are violent, and there is evidence that women may well be violent and abusive to their partners, although the debate about how that compares with male violence remains ongoing (see Chapters 2 and 3; Straus 2005; Pizzey and Shapiro 1982).

The example below of a woman who killed her husband gratuitously rather than in revenge for his abuse is newsworthy and as such unusual. It also happened in Russia, which 'distances' the story twofold.

Woman kills husband with folding couch
Wed Jul 9, 2008 12:17pm EDT
By Denis Pinchuk
ST PETERSBURG (Reuters) – A Russian woman in St Petersburg killed her drunk husband with a folding couch, Russian media reported on Wednesday.

St Petersburg's Channel Five said the man's wife, upset with her husband for being drunk and refusing to get up, kicked a handle after an argument, activating a mechanism that folds the couch up against a wall.

The couch, which doubles as a bed, folds up automatically in order to save space. 'The man fell between the mattress and the back of the couch, Channel Five quoted emergency workers as saying.

The woman then walked out of the room and returned three hours later to check on what she thought was an unusually quiet sleeping husband.

Police refused to comment.

The St Petersburg Emergency Services Ministry said a private rescue service removed the man's body.

Video on the television channel's website showed emergency workers sawing away the side panels of a couch to remove a man in his underwear lying headfirst between the cushions.

Emergency workers said the man died instantly.[9]

The woman's aggression here was reported as being fuelled by an argument after he returned home drunk and it is therefore possible (or indeed likely) that he was so drunk he could not defend himself. Even so, her intention was to do harm, but we do not know whether or not his drunken behaviour had been violent in the past or even on this occasion or even whether she feared violence once he had sobered up.

Women on women violence is a difficult issue to face. Kelly (1996), in a thoughtful and provocative article about feminism and violence by women, concedes that it is painful to discuss because the issue would be used to undermine the grudging acceptance of the extent of men's use of violence towards women and children, and/or reinforce negative stereotypes of lesbians. She makes the point that it is important to move from silence about female violence to consideration of the reasons for it, and to support the survivors. I believe a similar argument holds true when considering women who have more than one abusive partner and/or choose to stay with an abuser, as they are likely to be particularly vulnerable women and it is important to identify how they might be supported. This cannot happen if it remains a taboo subject for research or if there are problems in 'reporting' information about these women.

Conclusions

Common myths and stereotypes about domestic violence abound. Evidence indicates that advocates and survivors frequently buy into, and in turn reproduce, formula stories. Myths about domestic violence from the perspective of some advocates and survivors are, at least in part, *psychological defence mechanisms* used to defend themselves against the anxieties, sense of helplessness and distress that awareness of domestic violence and abuse causes. They also defend against 'thinking' which might reduce the impact of advocacy. This is not only true for those who experience it (as victim/survivors and perpetrators), but it is also the case for the various levels of community and professional groups who face its existence and have to act.

5

PUBLIC PERCEPTIONS AND MORAL TALES

Introduction

The construction of domestic violence discourse between 1970 and 1996 is an example of the deployment of power within liberatory discourses. As a challenge to male violence, it exemplifies the potential for resistance through recasting the meanings of gender relationships. The ascendance of crime and control strategies within the discourse, however, tends to replicate gendered as well as racialised and class-based hierarchies. The domestic violence discourse is not outside of, but is constituted by the power dynamics it confronts.

(Ferarro 1996: 88)

Researchers and therapists working with perpetrators and survivors of domestic violence are engaged in a complex, multi-faceted task that involves not only the analysis of gender-power relations but an acknowledgement of meanings from 'moral', legal, social and psychological perspectives (Goldner *et al.* 1990; Goldner 1999; Vetere and Cooper 2003). Activists and women's advocates have been highly successful in raising political and academic awareness of domestic abuse, bringing about key legal changes particularly in North America and Europe (Morley and Mullender 1992; Sully 2002; J.R. Gillis *et al.* 2006; Camacho and Alarid 2008; van Wormer 2009) where domestic violence is now an indictable offence. Even so, recent studies have identified a gap between policy and evidence-based knowledge, particularly about *public perceptions* of causes, prevalence and the seriousness of domestic abuse (Markowitz 2001; Muhlbauer 2006; Worden and Carlson 2005).

It is apparent, anecdotally, that there is a 'morality' implicit in lay thinking about domestic violence and abuse which is present in the press coverage which frequently implicates the survivors as well as the perpetrators (McConaghy and Cottone 1998; Goldner 1999; Kurri and Wahlstrom 2001). In other words there seems to be an everyday understanding of domestic violence and abuse that does not mesh with the messages that have emerged from the campaigners and women's advocates about gender-power relations, i.e. that men are wholly responsible for their violence in hetero-sexual relationships. Why should this be? What are the differences between these understandings?

In this chapter I outline the results of research on public perceptions of domestic violence and abuse as well as high-profile media stories, showing the ways these relate to some of the myths and stereotypes outlined in Chapter 4.

Lay perceptions and public awareness of domestic violence

E. Klein, Campbell, Soler and Ghez (1997) considered that in the USA domestic violence had become increasingly a matter of public concern, which represented a shift from the view that it was a 'private matter' which persisted until the 1980s. This change, they argue, was as a direct result of public awareness and education campaigns which have had 'a tremendous impact in changing behaviour, particularly in arenas where individuals need to be given permission and encouragement to challenge other people's actions that were once thought to be "none of their business"' (E. Klein et al. 1997: 6).

From a series of three vignettes testing this, Klein and colleagues asked participants if they would intervene to stop a person smoking in a non-smoking restaurant, prevent a friend who had had too much to drink at a party from driving home, or stop a friend hitting his wife (even though she had been behaving very badly towards him).

The results indicated that 57 per cent said they would intervene in the smoking scenario, 95 per cent in the drink-driving one and 83 per cent in the domestic abuse one. Men's and women's responses were effectively equal in all three cases. Similarly a British Home Office survey for England and Wales (2009) identified that 87 per cent of the public believed they would take action if a female friend or female family member (93 per cent) were to be a victim of violent abuse from her partner, although this pro-portion dropped to 81 per cent if the victim were (only) a female neighbour.

This all suggests that, at the least, campaigns have established that *domestic violence is socially unacceptable*. Most members of the public consider that domestic violence is wrong and that individual incidents can be stopped or even prevented (Worden and Carlson 2005).

However the results of the surveys reported here (Klein et al. 1997; Home Office 2009) also indicate that many people are naïve and perhaps unaware of what it is like actually to *witness* violence. In violent situations the protagonists are usually out of control. Like most people, I have heard and seen couples shouting abuse at each other in a public place, or a man (usually) dragging a woman down the street while shouting at her. It is frightening. I was once having a drink at lunchtime with a male colleague who was pulled to his feet and punched by a man for no reason other than the stranger claimed my friend had taken his seat. I was terrified, screamed at the assailant to stop and ran to ask the barman to call the police – everyone's head went down – no one wanted to know, but luckily the stranger stormed out of the bar.

It is unusual for 'uninvolved' people going about their everyday business to intervene in a situation which is *already violent*, although they might decide to call the police. Classic social psychological studies have clearly demonstrated that in many cases it is unlikely that anyone will intervene on behalf of a stranger, not only because of apathy but when other people are around there is a 'diffusion of responsibility' and the belief that someone else will do something to stop the violence or will call the police (Latané and Darley 1969; Banyard, Plante and Moynihan 2004). Even so there have been seriously disturbing anecdotal accounts of individual members of the public taking a stranger to task for smoking or getting into a car to drive when obviously over the alcohol limit, particularly in cases where the 'offence' takes place near to home or involves a family member or friend (A.R. Gillis and John 1983).

So even though these types of scenarios (smoking and drink-driving) do not start out violently, and the protagonists in Klein *et al.*'s last two examples were meant to be 'friends' of the respondents, predictions about behaviour in these circumstances still need to be treated with caution.

A vignette study

For part of the DASH project we conducted a study using the following vignette to assess attitudes:

Peter is a 56-year-old consultant surgeon who has worked for many years in a District General Hospital. His current partner, Isobel, is a 40-year-old divorcee with three children from a previous marriage. They live together as a family and the children are looked after by a nanny whilst Isobel pursues her very successful career as a Member of the European Parliament.

They return from a night out with friends in a local wine bar, having both consumed a large amount of alcohol. A row breaks out between them when Peter mentions his dissatisfaction at Isobel's increasingly long working hours. Isobel replies by claiming that her career is going well and it's not fair of him to try and spoil it. Peter grabs her by the arm and forces her up against the wall where he continues to shout

97

at her. Peter then slaps Isobel's face causing her to fall backwards onto the settee. Isobel attempts to get away and during the noise of the scuffle, the youngest child wakes up and sits at the top of the stairs, observing what is going on downstairs.

Isobel gets up and runs up the stairs. Peter runs after her shouting. The child at the top of the stairs begins to cry and shouts for them to stop fighting. They both run towards their bedroom. Isobel gets there first and locks herself in. She calls the police asking them to come out as her partner has attacked her. This kind of incident has happened several times during the course of their relationship.

Randomly selected participants from a university staff list were e-mailed with the vignette and given a number of seven-point Likert scales (see below).

The Likert statements were:

- I can understand why Peter behaved like that
- Peter's behaviour was reasonable
- I cannot sympathise with Peter
- I cannot sympathise with Isobel
- Isobel could not have prevented the behaviour
- Isobel was right to call the police

Table 5.1 Characteristics of the sample (*n* = 454)*

Sex of respondents	
Female (*n* = 314)	69%
Male (*n* = 140)	31%
Mean age of respondents	Overall = 38 yrs
	Female = 37.8 yrs
	Male = 38.5 yrs
Age ranges by sex	
Female	
18–33 (*n* = 121)	38.5%
34–49 (*n* = 146)	46.5%
50–63 (*n* = 47)	15.0%
Male	
18–33 (*n* = 47)	33.6%
34–49 (*n* = 68)	48.6%
50–63 (*n* = 25)	17.9%

* It should be noted that the characteristics of this sample cannot be said to be representative of the general population; in particular the older age group (50–63 years) are under-represented.

- Peter has not committed a criminal offence
- Peter should not be arrested
- Isobel should end the relationship

Nearly 500 replies were received, indicating that this was an area that interested people; 69 per cent of the replies were from women.

The general view was that the violence was unacceptable (97.1 per cent), but more men expressed negative attitudes towards Isobel than did women. So for example while there was general disagreement with the statement that 'Peter's behaviour was reasonable' and agreement that he had committed a criminal offence, almost a quarter of the men (compared with 18.2 per cent of the women) agreed with the statement that 'Peter should not be arrested' (see Table 5.2). Also the majority of both sexes agreed that Isobel was right to call the police. It seems that there is ambivalence about what should be done about the violence.

Furthermore a fifth of the women and over a quarter of the men disagreed with the statement 'I cannot sympathise with Peter' (Table 5.2). This indicates that many people will cite mitigating circumstances to defend men's violence and abuse. In this case the protagonists were drunk, but Peter continued in his aggression even in the presence of a young child. The focus of his aggression seemed to be his jealousy about Isobel's priorities and perhaps a general frustration about his life circumstances. How could his attack be excused in any way? Clearly several of our respondents were not persuaded that Peter should take responsibility for his controlling, abusive and violent behaviour.

It is also noteworthy that just over a quarter of the women and almost a third of the men who responded disagreed with the statement that 'Isobel could not have prevented the behaviour', which places an obligation on the female partner to take the edge off an altercation to prevent an attack. Over a third of the men and nearly a quarter of the women were uncertain about whether Isobel should end the relationship.

Of the age group surveyed above the age of 50 (Table 5.3) a fifth could not sympathise with the woman but 76.8 per cent disagreed with the statement that 'Peter has not committed a criminal offence'. A quarter of this older age group agreed that he should not be arrested although 72.2 per cent agreed that Isobel was right to call the police. Nearly half of this group agreed that Isobel should end the relationship, with a third of them not knowing whether or not she should, and nearly half disagreed with the statement that 'Isobel could not have prevented the behaviour'.

This study indicates a reasonable degree of success of awareness and 'zero tolerance' campaigns. However it also indicates that more focused attention should be paid to the views of middle-aged and older people, who may have missed the messages from these campaigns. This is not simply to influence their attitudes but because there is no doubt that some will be

99

Table 5.2 Responses to attitudes towards domestic violence vignette by sex*

Negative statements

Peter's behaviour was reasonable

	Agree	*Disagree*	*Don't know*	χ^2	*df*	*p*
Female	0.3%	99.7%	0.0%	4.94	1	0.03
Male	2.1%	97.1%	0.7%			

I cannot sympathise with Isobel

	Agree	*Disagree*	*Don't know*	χ^2	*df*	*p*
Female	9.6%	87.5%	2.9%	3.52	1	0.06
Male	14.7%	80.1%	5.1%			

Peter has not committed a criminal offence

	Agree	*Disagree*	*Don't know*	χ^2	*df*	*p*
Female	6.1%	80.3%	13.7%	0.688	1	0.41
Male	9.3%	78.6%	12.1%			

Peter should not be arrested

	Agree	*Disagree*	*Don't know*	χ^2	*df*	*p*
Female	18.2%	63.7%	18.2%	3.66	1	0.05
Male	23.6%	53.6%	22.9%			

Positive statements

I cannot sympathise with Peter

	Agree	*Disagree*	*Don't know*	χ^2	*df*	*p*
Female	78.0%	20.4%	1.6%	4.97	1	0.03
Male	67.1%	28.6%	4.3%			

Isobel could not have prevented the behaviour

	Agree	*Disagree*	*Don't know*	χ^2	*df*	*p*
Female	59.1%	25.9%	15.0%	3.33	1	0.07
Male	47.9%	30.7%	21.4%			

Isobel was right to call the police

	Agree	*Disagree*	*Don't know*	χ^2	*df*	*p*
Female	83.0%	6.7%	10.3%	0.75	1	0.39
Male	78.4%	7.2%	14.4%			

Isobel should end the relationship

	Agree	*Disagree*	*Don't know*	χ^2	*df*	*p*
Female	67.1%	9.3%	23.6%	18.97	1	0.01
Male	45.3%	18.7%	36.0%			

---

* For presentation purposes these results are split into two categories – those statements which indicate endorsement of violence against women (negative) and those statements which indicate a condemnation of violence towards women (positive).

Table 5.3 Responses to attitudes towards domestic violence vignette by age

---

Negative statements

Peter's behaviour was reasonable

	Agree	Disagree	Don't know	χ^2	df	p
18–33	0.6%	99.4%	0.0%	1.5	4	0.8
34–49	0.9%	98.6%	0.5%			
50–63	1.4%	98.6%	0.0%			

I cannot sympathise with Isobel

	Agree	Disagree	Don't know	χ^2	df	p
18–33	6.0%	88.6%	5.4%	12.8	4	0.01
34–49	12.6%	85.1%	2.3%			
50–63	20.3%	76.8%	2.9%			

Peter has not committed a criminal offence

	Agree	Disagree	Don't know	χ^2	df	p
18–33	7.1%	76.9%	16.0%	5.0	4	0.29
34–49	7.4%	82.9%	9.7%			
50–63	5.6%	76.4%	18.1%			

Peter should not be arrested

	Agree	Disagree	Don't know	χ^2	df	p
18–33	17.2%	59.2%	23.7%	4.9	4	0.30
34–49	20.4%	62.0%	17.6%			
50–63	26.4%	58.3%	15.3%			

Positive statements

I cannot sympathise with Peter

	Agree	Disagree	Don't know	χ^2	df	p
18–33	71.0%	24.9%	4.1%	5.1	4	0.27
34–49	76.9%	21.3%	1.9%			
50–63	76.4%	23.6%	0.0%			

Isobel could not have prevented the behaviour

	Agree	Disagree	Don't know	χ^2	df	p
18–33	66.7%	17.9%	15.5%	23.3	4	0.01
34–49	52.1%	28.8%	19.1%			
50–63	38.9%	45.8%	15.3%			

Isobel was right to call the police

	Agree	Disagree	Don't know	χ^2	df	p
18–33	81.5%	5.4%	13.1%	9.5	4	0.05
34–49	84.1%	6.1%	9.8%			
50–63	72.2%	15.3%	12.5%			

Isobel should end the relationship

	Agree	Disagree	Don't know	χ^2	df	p
18–33	63.9%	13.0%	23.1%	9.9	4	0.04
34–49	62.3%	9.3%	28.4%			
50–63	46.5%	19.7%	33.8%			

Table 5.4 What is domestic violence?

Action	Rank order	N (%) agreeing	Men agreeing N (%) of total respondents agreeing N (%) of men agreeing	Women agreeing N (%) of total respondents agreeing (%) of women agreeing	χ^2	p
Punching	1	1,253 (95%)	501 (40%) (95.2%)	752 (60%) (94.8%)	0.116	0.734
Sex without consent	2	1,151 (87.3%)	447 (38.8%) (85%)	704 (61.2%) (88.8%)	4.099	0.043
Slapping	3	1,087 (82.4%)	433 (39.8%) (82.3%)	654 (60.2%) (82.5%)	0.005	0.943
Threats of violence	4	1,056 (80.1%)	417 (39.5%) (79.3%)	639 (60.5%) (80.6%)	0.336	0.562
Verbal aggression	5	936 (71.2%)	337 (36%) (64.6%)	599 (64%) (75.5%)	18.488	0.000
Controlling social life	6	733 (55.7%)	260 (35.5%) (49.5%)	473 (64.5%) (59.7%)	13.305	0.000

living with domestic abuse themselves and not know what to do to gain support (Richardson *et al.* 2002; Gracia 2004).

Defining domestic abuse

Following on from the vignette study we conducted a more extensive community survey of a random sample of 1 per cent of registered voters in one British city. We asked a broad question about how they would define domestic violence[1] using the following question (for detailed results and discussion see Nicolson and Wilson 2004):[2]

4. Which of the following do you consider to be acts of domestic violence? (Please tick *as many as you think apply*)

The acts we provided were ranked according to the number of ticks they received, with the outcome as follows, from one to six respectively: *punching, sex without consent, slapping, threats of violence, verbal aggression* and *controlling social life*. The high response rate to the survey reinforced the emerging pattern that members of the public take the issue of domestic violence seriously.

In a similar study funded by the Maltese Government (Borg 2003), around two-thirds of the respondents identified *psychological* violence (equivalent to our categories of 'controlling social life', 'verbal aggression' and 'threats of violence') as 'very serious', with an additional 19.7 per cent identifying it as 'fairly serious'. Similar proportions unsurprisingly agreed that physical and sexual violence were serious events, and only slightly fewer agreed that 'threats of violence' were also serious. However, only 54 per cent of the Maltese sample considered 'restricted freedom' to be 'very serious', which corresponded with the DASH study results.

It also suggests once again that in Malta as in England there is a sense that *domestic violence is about what is happening in the relationship, not about cultural values or gender politics.* In other words there is not an irrefutable belief that domestic abuse by men towards women is solely the responsibility of the man, and an understanding that men use violence and abuse to control women. It indicates ambivalence despite increased public awareness and a general acknowledgement that domestic violence is wrong. There also appear to be some uncertainties about condoning or condemning the protagonist. What does this mean for the campaigns by organisations such as Refuge? Why have some of the messages fallen on such apparently stony ground?

A similar trajectory of severity appears to be related to similar acts. Borg also reported further on the outcome of an EU-wide survey, demonstrating that across the EU 63.7 per cent (compared with 54.1 per cent in Malta) considered 'restricted freedom' of victims to be 'very serious', with 86.6 per cent (cf. Malta 77.3 per cent) and 90.1 per cent (cf. Malta 75.1 per cent) considering physical and sexual violence respectively to be 'very serious'. In the Home Office survey of England and Wales 88 per cent of the public did not consider it acceptable for a man to hit or slap his wife or girlfriend in response to her not treating him with respect (cf. how Isobel's husband in the DASH vignette experienced her), although as many as 11 per cent still considered that it was acceptable (2 per cent) or acceptable under some circumstances (9 per cent) (Home Office 2009).

It seems that for many across Europe violence is widely condemned (although not exclusively), and constraining women's lives is condemned but not considered to be the worst thing that could happen to women. Generally speaking, domestic violence is in the public domain in terms of consciousness and condemnation, but relatively significant proportions of onlookers do not roundly condemn the male protagonist, and the woman's behaviour is 'taken into account' when judgements are made. The implications of this include the possibility that misogyny remains rife (including female misogyny), which is a consequence of patriarchy in which women are still the forgotten 'second' sex (R. Dobash and Dobash 1979; Bettman 2009).

What causes domestic violence?

We also asked the DASH community survey respondents (Nicolson and Wilson 2004) about the *causes* of domestic violence:

5. Why do you think men are violent towards their partners? (Please choose the *3* main reasons from those listed below)

- He saw it at home when growing up
- Stress
- He has mental health problems
- Drugs or alcohol abuse
- Woman provokes him
- Because society accepts it
- To be in control
- Because he can get away with it

Ranking of reasons

In this case respondents were asked to choose three possible reasons. As shown in Table 5.5, 'drugs or alcohol abuse' was selected over 10 per cent more times than the next choice, 'to be in control', which in turn was selected 10 per cent more times than 'he saw it at home when growing up', which was chosen over 10 per cent more times than 'because he can get away with it' and 'stress', which again in turn were chosen by 10 per cent more people than 'he has mental health problems' and 'woman provokes him'.

Around half the men surveyed and over half of the women believed that drug or alcohol abuse caused men's violence. The Malta study also indicated that 87 per cent believed that 'drug addiction' could be a cause of domestic violence.

It is important to recall (see Chapter 4) that there is empirical evidence to demonstrate a link between alcohol and domestic violence (Martin and Bachman 1997; Mirrlees-Black 1999; O'Farrell *et al.* 1999; Quigley and Leonard 2000; White and Chen 2002) despite the pro-feminist campaigns which categorically deny that alcohol and substance abuse cause domestic violence.

Gender differences

Beyond attributing causation to substance and alcohol abuse and 'stress', there were significant gender differences in responses across all other reasons given for men's violence. For example only a third of the men, in contrast to two-thirds of the women (all statistically significant at the .005 level), attributed men's violence to being in control, with similar

Table 5.5 Reasons given for men's violence

Reasons (rank order)	N (% of sample)	Men N (%) of all those who ticked 'yes' (%) of men who ticked 'yes'	Women N (%) of all those who ticked 'yes' (%) of women who ticked 'yes'	χ^2	p
Drugs or alcohol abuse (1)	948 (73.2%)	385 (40.6%) (74.3%)	563 (59.4%) (72.5%)	0.552	0.458
To be in control (2)	769 (59.5%)	264 (34.3%) (51%)	505 (65.7%) (65.2%)	26.265	0.000
He saw it at home when growing up (3)	645 (49.8%)	226 (35%) (43.6%)	419 (65%) (53.9%)	13.179	0.000
Because he can get away with it (4)	478 (36.9%)	167 (34.9%) (32.2%)	311 (65.1%) (40%)	8.092	0.004
Stress (5)	444 (34.3%)	218 (49.1%) (42.1%)	226 (50.9%) (29.1%)	23.308	0.000
He has mental health problems (= 6)	263 (20.3%)	118 (44.9%) (22.8%)	145 (55.1%) (18.7%)	3.257	0.071
Woman provokes him (= 6)	263 (20.3%)	148 (56.3%) (28.6%)	115 (43.7%) (14.8%)	36.558	0.000
Society accepts it (8)	99 (7.6%)	29 (29.3%) (5.6%)	70 (70.7%) (9%)	5.120	0.024

proportions citing 'he saw it at home when growing up' and 'because he can get away with it'.

This suggests that women were more likely than men to see domestic violence as representing abusive male power (Hearn 1998; K.L. Anderson and Umberson 2001; Edley 2001), a view which extends to the impact of male domestic violence on boys' views (Dryden *et al.* 2010).

However by way of contrast E. Klein *et al.*'s (1997) North American survey had demonstrated significant gender differences in how people explain why a man would beat a woman, with male respondents more likely to say it was because he was drunk and out of control (25 per cent of men compared to 16 per cent of women), while women were more likely to say he learned it when he was young.

Individualised explanations

Worden and Carlson's (2005) survey of public perceptions in the USA however concluded that most people saw domestic violence in the context of individual relationships and family problems rather than seeing it as caused by social or structural issues (Cody 1996; Featherstone and Trinder 1997; Johnson and Ferraro 2000; McCarroll *et al.* 2008). The majority of their respondents' explanations indicated that financial stress, alcohol and anger were major exacerbating factors (Gelles 1980; Rosenbaum and Leisring 2001).

The public perception still holds to more complex and differentiated explanations although there has been major success in raising levels of awareness and approbation for the services that challenge domestic abuse (Carlson 2005).

Questions of morality?

From a feminist perspective, intimate violence is a criminal act, the effort by a male perpetrator to control, intimidate, and inflict harm on his partner-victim. Given this framework, it seems obvious that such behaviour should be punished within the criminal justice system and mental health professionals should position themselves as advocates for the female victim.

(Goldner 1999: 325)

Despite this inherent logic the results of the surveys reported above suggest that for the general public decisions about the treatment (in every sense) of those involved with domestic abuse (perpetrators and victims, men and women) do not necessarily arise from such clarity of thought.

Public perceptions of domestic violence demonstrate a set of underlying *moral values* that are complex, not necessarily influenced so much by the feminist arguments as such but by a sense of justice applied to individual circumstances (Gondolf 1987; Kearney 2001; Nienhuis 2005). One well publicised finding from the Home Office (2009) survey of attitudes for instance was that 20 per cent of men *and* women believed that it was acceptable (6 per cent) or acceptable in some circumstances (14 per cent) for a man to hit or slap his female partner if she dressed in sexy or revealing clothes in public, although only 8 per cent believed that such violence was acceptable if she were having an affair. What are the implications of this for understanding public perceptions of sexuality and gender relations? While across the same Home Office survey the majority of respondents found all 'reasons' for abuse to a partner unacceptable, a significant minority still thought nagging (16 per cent) or flirting with other men (13 per cent) might justify hitting or slapping. It would seem therefore that an undercurrent of misogyny and the view that men have the right to control women, particularly their sexuality but also their rights within a relationship,[3] remains.

Who should take *responsibility* within a violent heterosexual relationship? Did the woman 'provoke' or 'deserve' the abuse? Should the woman take responsibility for 'choosing' a violent man? Where should the shame and embarrassment lie? Are the social and criminal justice services to blame for not supporting victim/survivors appropriately? Should a man who is violent be punished or 'cured'?

Domestic violence and abuse are firmly in the public domain as unresolved 'problems' which means there is still a serious mismatch between feminist campaigners' and lay understandings (Erlick Robinson 2003; Worden and Carlson 2005). There is also a disparity between the views of many professionals working in the area of domestic abuse such as therapists, social workers and health care workers and campaigners and advocates (Goldner 1999; Vetere and Cooper 2003; see Chapter 7).

As Vetere and Cooper (2003) propose, it is important to identify the *responsibility* for the abuse as belonging to the abuser, but that is the beginning rather than the end-point of the road that those who want to prevent domestic violence need to take. Goldner (1999) likewise argues that although domestic violence is a criminal act, if people come to professional services to seek help *as a couple* then condemnation and retribution and 'taking sides' with the (usually) female partner is not helpful. A neutral rather than moral stance enables both partners to struggle with the 'overwhelming emotional process' (Goldner 1999: 325).

Psychologists and anthropologists have shown that human thinking, emotions and behaviours indicate an intrinsic 'morality' which comes into play in responses to domestic abuse and violence.

Studies of human development have shown that we continuously make judgements about who is right and wrong in all types of situations and our reasoning behind these judgements is both biologically developmental and contextual. Thus as we mature physically/biologically we become more sophisticated thinkers. As we develop through childhood and adolescence we take complexities and ambiguities into account in our judgements (Piaget 1932; Kohlberg 1973). It has also been argued that women's and men's moral judgements vary, so that although both sexes can make sophisticated judgements about a range of issues, men and women frequently come to different conclusions (C. Gilligan 1993). Following Freud (1926/1921) Gilligan attests from her evidence of research on boys' and girls' moral judgements that women's development arises from their experiences in relationships that differ from those of men. While boys/men focus on 'logic', girls/women focus on the complexities in relationships and essentially seek to maintain links. One development of men's 'logical' stance can be seen in a study of batterers' explanations (Gondolf 1987). In examining the type of moral dilemma presented in Kohlberg's (1973) studies a girl/

woman is likely to seek a way around taking account of everyone's needs (see C. Gilligan 1993; see Chapters 6 to 8 for further discussion).

Social learning theorists (such as Bandura (1977)) have shown that girls and boys are influenced by the behaviours of role models in their understanding of what is good and what is bad behaviour, and role models are mostly of the same sex as themselves. Together these theories present a complicated picture of how we develop a sense of morality both in relation to our own behaviours and when sitting in judgement over others. Boys/ men and girls/women have very different experiences while growing up, including different experiences of embodiment, and the two genders make different sense of their worlds. Understanding these differences goes some way to explaining the gender differences in public opinion surveys on domestic abuse, particularly when a vignette with any degree of ambiguity is presented about a relationship (see Chapter 7).

Deserving and undeserving wives

In 1998 Sheryl Gascoigne, the wife of former England international footballer Paul Gascoigne, was granted a divorce on the grounds of his unreasonable behaviour (domestic violence). In 2009 Sheryl collaborated in a 'fly on the wall' television documentary to record her ex-husband's return to *her* family home following his discharge from alcohol addiction rehabilitation. The *News of the World*[4] reported:

> **TEARS AND FEARS: Sheryl invited Gazza back into her life but he let her down**
> By Dan Wootton, 04/01/2009
> In a tragic replay of the long abusive relationship that climaxed in their bitter 1998 divorce, 41-year-old alcoholic Paul let down his ex and their three kids again – storming out because she refused to have sex with him.
>
> Shocked Sheryl told him: 'I haven't seen you for five years and you just think you can jump straight into my bed. It's not going to happen.'
>
> Nevertheless, in an explosive Channel 4 documentary to be screened tomorrow at 10pm she tearfully admits she STILL loves Gazza despite all they've been through.

The documentary confirmed that she had visited him while he was in an alcohol rehabilitation unit and from the documentary it appeared that she and the three children (two of whom were not biologically his) did care for Gascoigne. Gascoigne though could not keep away from alcohol. Perhaps it was his vulnerability that Sheryl loved? As with Walker's stage three ('honeymoon') of the 'cycle of violence' we saw Gascoigne begging forgiveness, although we also saw equal amounts of his aggression and repudiation towards Sheryl on the occasions when she demonstrated that she had had enough of his drinking and abuse. Her graphic descriptions of his violence towards her and public humiliations during their married life, which had made her divorce him ten years previously, were atrocious and distressing to hear about. Despite her love for him she was clear that she had become stronger since they had parted and was not prepared to let that happen again.

The commentaries that preceded and followed this documentary ranged from slightly through to highly cynical of her motives (attempting to hold on to a celebrity status) but also acknowledged her affection for the man and his inability to help himself. There was never any question that 'Gazza' had been, and probably still was, a violent man, nor was there any doubt expressed in the popular media that Sheryl had tried all she could to save her marriage and that she and Gascoigne had loved each other. The BBC website reported the account of the divorce (which had happened in 1998) from the story in the *Sun* newspaper in the following way:

> The 33-year-old former model was granted a decree nisi on the grounds of the Middlesbrough and England star's unreasonable behaviour last August. Gazza, 31, met Sheryl in 1991, and the couple got married shortly after he played a starring role in England's Euro 96 campaign. But the marriage was soon in trouble, with the midfielder admitting beating his wife. Last year he acknowledged he had a drink problem, and checked into the exclusive The Priory Clinic in Roehampton, south-west London, for treatment. The *Sun* said Gazza was being generous to his former wife with the divorce settlement because he still loves her.[5]

In this report Gascoigne 'admitted' what he had done and was seen to be 'generous' to her and the children because of his 'love'. Thus (for the most part) coming under the media gaze 'exonerated' them both. There was little or no publicly expressed antipathy towards Sheryl at the time or afterwards for gaining a financial settlement (even though it was seen to be generous) because she had tried to keep the family together and the money would be used to support her children.

A very different public discourse surrounded Sir Paul McCartney and Heather Mills's recent (very public) divorce after about six or seven years of their relationship (the time they were together was disputed), which was conducted, among other things, under the spotlight of accusations of domestic violence by his second wife Heather. She reported that Paul:

- forced her to cancel an essential operation because it clashed with holiday plans.
- drunkenly grabbed her by the neck and pushed her over a coffee table.
- became angry and pushed her into a bath, causing her 'shock and distress' when she was four months pregnant.
- yelled at her and then 'grabbed her neck and started choking her' when she asked if he had been smoking marijuana.
- hurled abuse and called her an 'ungrateful b***h'.
- refused to let her breastfeed after their daughter Beatrice was born, saying, 'They are my breasts. I don't want a mouthful of breast milk.'
- threw a bottle of red wine over her, then 'lunged at her with the broken, sharp stem of the wine glass, which pierced her arm and left a scar', shortly before they split up.

These claims describe serious physical and mental abuse.[6] However, in the public statement she made after the twenty-five-million-pound divorce settlement (about ten million more than McCartney had originally offered) she no longer talked of his abusive behaviour, only about the fact that she had 'won' financially. The formal judgement paid minimal attention to her accusations of abuse and the judge himself was, it seemed, firmly on McCartney's side.[7] There was very little sympathy for Mills in any media account either (see websites in note 6 and many others including accompanying 'blogs'). It was possible that her use of domestic abuse in this way might have served to diminish her settlement claim because the judgement was highly critical of her as a person compared with McCartney and she herself said she should have been entitled to more money. The accusation of domestic violence and the financial settlement itself certainly made her a target for media and public scorn. Whether or not her account bears any truth, Paul was portrayed as being beyond reproach as he was still grieving for Linda his first wife and had 'mistakenly' married on the rebound (albeit six years after Linda's death). There were a number of media and internet articles in April 2008 following the McCartney–Mills divorce settlement, with Paul talking about his relationship with Linda and how he felt when she was dying.[8] His 'love' for Linda and the children they had had together was presented in these media accounts as more important (to McCartney and the public) than any 'trivialities' of his relationship (violent and abusive or not) with this woman, Heather, who was not loved or loving.

These two high-profile 'celeb' depictions of domestic abuse underline key contemporary discourses. The Gascoigne case was depicted as one of the vulnerable abuser suffering from stress and alcohol addiction who nevertheless in between (inexcusable, albeit helpless) episodes of violence was a 'good' father and lovable husband. Sheryl was seen as a good wife standing by her man. The McCartney–Mills case by contrast was depicted as one in which the 'gold-digger' wife was accusing the 'loving family man' (even though that love was for his former family) of behaviours that she allegedly exaggerated or lied about.

In the first case both parties had agreed about the fact that violence had occurred. This enabled retribution, forgiveness and reparation and particularly enabled Sheryl to gain public support, enhanced by her caring about Gascoigne's attempts at recovering from his addiction to alcohol. However in the second, the McCartney–Mills case, the violence was only alleged by the woman and the accusation was not accepted by the man. Neither McCartney nor his supporters ever agreed that it had happened and the court judgement failed to take the allegations into account.

So what was the difference between these images of domestic abuse? Do we judge the *facts* of abuse by our value judgement of the merits of each of the protagonists? How far do the general public see gender-power relations as the cause of domestic abuse? How far does public opinion rest on stereotypes of the kind of person who would perpetrate violence (Harrison and Esqueda 1999)? There seems to be an implicit set of moral rules underpinning public judgements which rely on stereotypical views on what makes a 'good' wife and what makes a 'good' husband. These have been reflected in several of the studies which have focused on attributions in stranger- and date-rape cases (Kopper 1996; I. Anderson, Beathe and Spencer 2001). One characteristic appears to be that women who abuse their male partners may be judged more harshly than abusive men (R.J. Harris and Cook 1994) because that goes against the stereotyped judgement that a 'normal' woman is passive and nurturant (Broverman, Broverman, Clarkson, Rosentrantz and Vogel 1970; A. Brown and Testa 2008). A man's aggression is considered more 'normal' and therefore, perhaps, he is judged less harshly, although there is disagreement about how far stereotypes of gender are used in judgements in post-feminist societies (Broverman *et al.* 1970; Auster and Ohm 2000). Further the press coverage and public opinion of Heather Mills have been perceived as paralleling those of British serial killers Myra Hindley and Rose West (Storrs 2004; Anslow 2008). Why should this be the case? Mills's public image may have been damaged by her accusations but there was no evidence to make her comparable in any way to those vilified accomplices in murder.

Constructing the abuse: moral tales

There is evidence that news coverage of gender violence is framed in the context of family pathology (Meyers 1994, 1997) or individual isolated incidents (Bullock and Cubert 2002). Thus the Gascoigne family could be seen as having a 'domestic problem' (i.e. Paul's violence and his substance abuse). In the case of 'Gazza', from Sheryl's television documentary and newspaper reports about him over the years we see a vulnerable and damaged man who had failed in his attempts to combat his addictions. He himself admitted this publicly during the documentary. Press exposure of his vulnerabilities (and while they were still married Sheryl's injuries) enabled the public to believe that he was indeed violent and likely to continue to be.

The documentary indicated that he was possibly never going to be able to have a relationship with any woman (or child) that did not involve bouts of helplessness along with abusive behaviour exacerbated by his drinking. Sheryl as wife and mother was long-suffering but somehow that was a necessary prerequisite for *her* public salvation. She was both a victim and a survivor, for which she was given credibility, public support and acclaim. Her behaviour and public image accord with the feminine stereotype of the wife and mother.

On the other hand in accounts of the other couple, it is the man, McCartney, who is positioned as a long-term hero – much loved by his late first wife, his children and the public, providing a good 'fit' in terms of masculine achievements with the added value from his ability to be loving as well (Bem 1993). His friends[9] added to the public image of his vulnerability, saying how he had made a 'mistake' in marrying a much younger, 'unsuitable' woman while still grieving for Linda.

Gazza and Sheryl were socially and morally equals. Both were positioned as 'flawed'; they were of similar ages and thus appeared a 'normal' couple. McCartney and Mills were not. McCartney was nearly twice Mills's age and he was acknowledged as a talented musician whose work spanned many years. He is also a popular music 'royal'. Mills was a former model with no prior reputation for any particular skills although arguably ambitious to maintain a status as a celebrity. Heather herself claimed (probably correctly) during the court case that she had been 'independent' in her own right as a charity worker and model prior to meeting McCartney and thus neither a 'nobody' nor a 'gold-digger'.[10] Even the judge in the case said he could see that McCartney would find her attractive and in return how she would be swept off her feet with the fairy-tale relationship with such a figure as the ex-Beatle. Even though Mills was younger, a mother and a woman, she was positioned as the 'perpetrator' not the victim.

McCartney by contrast was the 'victim' (preyed upon and falsely accused), as one of the many reports of Mr Justice Bennett's judgement emphasised.

'I am driven to the conclusion that much of her evidence, both written and oral, was not just inconsistent and inaccurate but also less than candid,' the judge in the divorce, Mr Justice Bennett, ruled. 'Overall, she was a less than impressive witness.'

In his ruling, Bennett said there was no evidence of Mills's 'charitable giving' in her tax returns, ridiculed her claim to have been

McCartney's business partner as 'make believe' and said she was a 'volatile and explosive' personality who could be her 'own worst enemy'.

He also rejected her argument that she had rekindled McCartney's 'professional flame' after he had lost his first wife, Linda, to cancer.

The judge was complimentary about McCartney, saying 'the husband's evidence was, in my judgment, balanced. He expressed himself moderately, though at times with justifiable irritation, if not anger. He was consistent, accurate and honest.'[11]

McCartney was also the 'survivor' in that he has subsequently found a relationship elsewhere with a more suitable partner (Nancy Shevell) with whom he shares the care of Beatrice (his daughter with Mills), and he is not identified in any way as a violent or abusive man.

The people's princess

Another example of a public relationship where it appeared there was a more even split in the public assessment of who held the moral prerogative was that of Princess Diana. In 1995, two years before her death, Martin Bashir interviewed Princess Diana on a BBC TV current affairs documentary programme (*Panorama*). Diana was giving 'her side' of the Charles/ Diana relationship following publication of Charles's authorised account and various 'leaks' from each side. In no way does Diana talk directly about domestic violence and abuse. In fact she focuses more upon self-harm brought about by her depression. However it is clear from her 'third person' account that she believed Charles was jealous and failed to support her when she most needed it. Also she emphasised how she had been hurt by the public sexual betrayal by Charles and the lack of support, and even censure, she received from the rest of the royal family. For instance:

Bashir: At this early stage, would you say that you were happily married?

Diana: Very much so. But, the pressure on us both as a couple with the media was phenomenal, and misunderstood by a great many people. We'd be going round Australia, for instance, and all you could hear was, 'oh, she's on the other side'. Now, if you're a man, like my husband a proud man, you mind about that if you hear it every day for four weeks. And you feel low about it, instead of feeling happy and sharing it.

Bashir: When you say 'she's on the other side', what do you mean?

Diana: Well, they weren't on the right side to wave at me or to touch me.

Bashir: So they were expressing a preference even then for you rather than your husband?

Diana: Yes – which I felt very uncomfortable with, and I felt it was unfair, because I wanted to share.

Bashir: But were you flattered by the media attention particularly?

Diana: No, not particularly, because with the media attention came a lot of jealousy, a great deal of complicated situations arose because of that.[12]

Diana teased her audience by taking the blame for being a little naïve and inadequate as a royal partner while casting her husband as rather unreasonable, cold and even cruel. She described the ways in which the royal household marginalised and pathologised her, and confessed to her own sexual transgressions albeit in the context of being forced into a troubled and isolated life. She took a gamble in terms of her public image which she obviously valued. Diana, despite being positioned as having self-confessed failings, had been seen to 'do good' (unlike Mills whose lucrative divorce appeared to eclipse any public sense of her charitable works). As a result of the various relationship scandals, the marriage break-up and the interview, and (probably) because Charles had not been seen as a particularly sympathetic figure, Diana probably 'won' the public relations game 'on points' although there was (and probably still is) a long-running newspaper campaign taking 'his' or 'her' side.

Perceptions of gender and morality: the return of the hero versus the 'Madonna'/whore

The news media still has power to 'subtly shape our perceptions' (Anastasio and Costa 2004: 535) and newspaper coverage of gender violence(s) frequently ends up blaming the woman (Hill and Ly 2004), because of the anonymity and depersonalisation of the woman (often for legal reasons) and the detail provided about the man which might show him as desperate or stressed or in some way human (e.g. Meyers 1994). The greater the information about the woman's life circumstances, the more likely the public are to understand and be sympathetic (Carll 2003; Ryan, Anastario and DaCunha 2006; Vives-Cases, Torrubiano-Dominguez and Alvarez-Dardet 2009).

However it is also possible to depersonalise, demonise or vilify a woman even in cases where names and faces are known as with Heather Mills-McCartney. Reports and photographs of her during and after the divorce hearing for example show her with twisted features, noting that her trouser suit worn in court was 'bizarre' (although giving no evidence for this assertion) and positioning her as aggressive (visually with the twisted features and behaviourally because she had thrown water over McCartney's lawyer). Additionally there were frequent allusions to Mr Justice Bennett's negative perception of her. All of this reinforced Mills's portrayal as a one-dimensional harridan.[13]

However it is not always the case that women are portrayed unsympathetically in high-profile domestic violence cases. The 1995 trial of O.J. Simpson (former American football star and actor) for the murder of Nicole Brown Simpson (found with a bruised face, multiple stab wounds and severed vertebrae around the neck), mother of his two children, who had divorced Simpson two years prior to her murder (and that of her friend Ronald Goldman), led to much media interest and sympathy for Nicole. Simpson however declared himself distraught and suicidal because she was dead. The trial was televised across the world and was apparently the most viewed trial ever. Even though Simpson was found not guilty in the criminal trial, in 1997 a civil court judgement brought about by the Brown and Goldman families went against him, finding him liable for the wrongful deaths of Nicole and Goldman.

The Simpson case has become something of a legend, with polarised views, frequently on an ethnic black/white basis. In 2008 however Simpson was sentenced to serve at least nine years in prison for various felonies.[14] Despite his celebrity status Simpson became a fallen hero with that hint of intimate partner murder following him from Nicole's death to his arrest and imprisonment for a completely different crime.

There appears to be an attempt to make 'celebrity' domestic violence cases into moral tales to serve as lessons. The violence that ended the relationship between showbiz couple Chris Brown and Rhianna in 2009 for instance has been used to support young people (women in particular) in coming forward if they consider they are being abused.[15] Chris Brown himself had been open about the abuse his mother had allegedly suffered at the hands of his stepfather and how he himself had witnessed it as a young boy.

In 2007, Brown also spoke about his family's past with *Giant* magazine. 'He used to hit my mom,' the singer told the magazine. 'He made me terrified all the time, terrified like I had to pee on myself. I remember one night he made her nose bleed. I was crying and thinking, "I'm just gonna go crazy on him one day." . . . I hate him to this day.'[16]

What is interesting here though is how Brown portrays himself as a potential hero (Dryden *et al.* 2010) rather than as (it would appear to be the case) having followed in his stepfather's footsteps. A programme that came out on MTV shortly after Brown's arrest for his alleged assault on Rhianna was titled: *Love in Trouble*. Brown's relationship with Rhianna was positioned as a love story. While there were many different responses from the public to the Brown/Rhianna story, Brown himself has not been universally blamed or held responsible, even though witnesses claim to have heard an argument between a man and a woman in a car escalate to the man's physical attack on the woman.

The first of two listed blogs,[17] both posted in February 2009, stated that the blogger was tired that 'America' always jumped to conclusions about celebrities' lives and actions. This first blogger argued that noone really knew what had taken place in the car but he (I assume) said that he was sure that Chris would not have hit Rhianna without a good reason. It might not have been the right thing to do, the blog continued, but the blogger urged the public to give some thought to why women can hit a man with impunity, thinking they should not be hit back in response. The writer imagined that Rhianna would have hit Chris as many times as he had hit her, and that if that were in fact the case, she deserved to have been hit.

The second listed blogger proposed that lots of people witness abuse or get abused as children and stated that he (again I presume) himself grew up with violence every day. He said he understood that it may take a long time to recover from such a childhood and remove violence from your life. He went on to say that it had indeed been wrong for Brown to hit his girlfriend, but that some people can 'snap' so easily and quickly that they don't have time to think about what they are doing. He indicated that he believed Chris Brown would want to make amends and suggested that the public give him a chance to do so and feel some sympathy for what he had gone through as a child and how it would have impacted upon him.

The moral discourses drawn on in these two examples potentially blame the woman for (probably) having done something wrong even though it is seen to be wrong for a man to hit a woman. However this position is juxtaposed with the idea that women can be as violent as they wish with impunity. Thus her (presumed) violence can justifiably be met by his.

The second example also positions violence as wrong but it is excused because through trying to overcome living with violence in childhood the man is vulnerable to flipping back and losing control. This blogger states adamantly that the man needs to be cut some slack.

Furthermore, it is impossible to escape the (unconscious, perhaps) collision between popular media and public versions of 'masculinity' and 'femininity' in the context of domestic violence, alongside the distinct moral positions pertaining to them. Men are supposed to be rational, strong, assertive and not particularly 'relational'. Women are expected to be kind, warm, loving and good at maintaining relationships. Women are expected to hold the family together – they are not expected to complain about male violence unless they have done all they can to repair the situation or are prepared to leave for good (Broverman *et al.* 1970; Bem 1993; Barzelatto 1998; Capezza and Arriaga 2008).

Sheryl Gascoigne fitted the criteria of the 'Madonna'. She was seen to be nurturing, caring and taking emotional responsibility for the family. Heather Mills-McCartney was not. Heather is positioned as the 'hard' unfeminine woman – the 'whore' exploiting male weakness and out to get what she can from this. Women, the arbiters of family morality, have to ensure that everyone is looked after, and that includes the errant man. A woman steers a straight moral pathway for her partner and the rest of the family. Rhianna is invisible in the early reports, which made it easy for the sympathy and interest initially to be with Brown. However there was a media frenzy of outrage when she returned to be with him, with fans' views shifting their positions from sympathy to disgust.[18]

Morality, conscience and the unconscious

Gilligan (1993), examining gendered moral development, asserts that psychological theorists have implicitly adopted the position of:

> male life as the norm. . . . It all goes back, of course, to Adam and Eve – a story which shows, among other things, that if you make a woman out of a man, you are bound to get into trouble. In the life cycle, as in the Garden of Eden, the woman has been the deviant.
>
> (C. Gilligan 1993: 6)

Eve, the temptress, corrupts Adam and brings about the moral downfall of humankind. Gilligan cites psychoanalytic theories, particularly Freud, on how men's and women's sense of right and wrong is constructed. Freud proposed that, 'for women the level of what is ethically normal is different from what it is in men' (Freud 1925: 257–258, cited in Gilligan 1993: 7).

Chodorow (1978) argues that Freud's 'case' about women's morality is at best 'condescension' if not simple misogyny. Freud argued that because women did not have so much to lose (i.e. a penis) they were less fearful of being judged and had a less developed super-ego (conscience) (Freud 1925). Freud also claimed that women have less sense of justice than do men. He concluded that women are more often influenced in their judgements by feelings of affection or hostility (see Chodorow 1978: 143).

This might suggest that *women's* judgements of domestic abuse in public perception surveys are swayed by whether or not they can identify with the woman or man in cases of domestic violence. Their more emotional and polarised judgements will also influence how people in the media spotlight are perceived, so that Sheryl Gascoigne's behaviour is perceived more sympathetically than that of Heather Mills whose decision to cry abuse might have been interpreted as intended only to denigrate Paul McCartney's persona and achieve some revenge. The the former woman's judgement was depicted as flawed and driven by affection, which is more acceptable than Heather's, which was perceived to be driven by envy and malice.

Conclusions

Popular discourses of gender relations shape the constructions of public moralities. However, constructions of domestic abuse change over time with growing awareness of its prevalence, its nature and through discourses surrounding high-profile cases. Initial feminist-led successes in bringing domestic abuse into public awareness secured its place on the public social care, health and human rights agendas. As awareness grows, it is becoming a criminal offence across the world, but this has meant that debates have moved closer towards an individualised case model.

As Ferraro (1996) points out, the feminist politics of the 1970s supporting women's freedom from male violence as a gender issue evolved into the criminalisation of domestic abuse, making it a law enforcement matter. Thus women became positioned as victims of *individual* male crimes and the onus was on them to seek legal redress if they suffered violence at the hands of a partner or ex-partner.

What seems to be at stake now is the discourse of the *agency* of women – individually and collectively. Are women victims with all the implications of 'deservedness', including interrogation of their conduct, motives and efforts to protect themselves and their children (Ferraro 1997)? Or have victims' rights movements 'breached the wall of patriarchy in the 1980s and eroded male authority' so that the myth that domestic violence is exceptional has evaporated (Wolfe 1994: 21)?

Part 3

(RE)TURNING TO INTRA-
PSYCHIC PSYCHOLOGY

6

LIVED EXPERIENCE AND THE 'MATERIAL-DISCURSIVE-INTRAPSYCHIC' 'SELF'

Introduction

You're frightened, you don't want to get out, you just want someone to be there for you and love you. And you think you've found the right partner and at the end of the day you're too ashamed to admit it, in case people keep saying 'oh it's your fault, it's your fault'. You don't want to get out. You're just scared to run.

(Chrissie)

I really wish I could sit him in a chair and ask him why. He always wanted some action, some war going off . . . anything that weren't peace and harmony. And after a while I knew that and I was still sleeping with him so I thought 'well I deserve whatever happens then'. I know he's the devil and I'm lying down with the devil. I saw it like that . . . the sex was getting me into trouble 'cos it was serious. I think I'm a spiritual person and I knew he was evil. I did.

(Sasha)

Living with domestic violence and abuse changes lives whatever the material context (Jones *et al.* 2001; Humphreys and Joseph 2004). Discourses of domestic violence and abuse have enabled women living with violent partners to identify and name their experiences and to realise they are not alone (Humphreys and Thiara 2003; Faramarzi *et al.* 2005). Discourses of domestic violence have regulated the behaviours of women, violent men and the health, social care and law enforcement professionals across the areas circumscribed within the regulatory discourses (Ferraro 1996; Bettman 2009; Murray and Powell 2009).

A material-discursive approach (Yardley 1996, 1997; Ussher 1997, 2006; Stoppard 2000) exploits both the perspectives of discursive psychology and the constraints of materiality to *describe* and *define* experience (see Chapters 2 and 3). That is, researchers, practitioners, policy makers and those involved in abusive relationships all have access to the linguistic, ethical/moral and material resources to contextualise and act (e.g. as an 'abusive man' or as an 'abused woman' or as a psychologist working with abuse). However from the extracts from the interviews with Chrissie and Sasha (above) it becomes clear that there is a further dimension to be considered in understanding lived experience. Both Chrissie and Sasha draw on moral discourses and position themselves as carrying shame and blame for staying with and sleeping with a man, and judge themselves and perceive others as judging them harshly. They also position the man as 'wanting' in some way. For Chrissie he didn't make it as the man she wanted to love. For Sasha he was 'evil'. Sasha also felt herself to be 'spiritual' and Chrissie positioned herself as 'loving' and fearful.

In both cases and throughout both short extracts they claim 'agency', reflecting on their 'performativity' as both story tellers and abused women (Butler 1988; K. Davis and Taylor 2002). If being a survivor of domestic violence and abuse does impact upon the whole of lived experience as suggested in Chapter 3 (Humphreys and Thiara 2003; Herman 2004; Humphreys and Joseph 2004) then a woman's identity/selfhood interacts in some relation to this at different stages of living with and recovering from the abuse (Bifulco *et al.* 2000).

Drawing on Butler's work on gender constitution and performance, and similarly following a phenomenological view, it becomes possible to see identity *per se* as a performance, with the lived experience of 'survival' as the 'object of belief' (Butler 1988: 520) that sustains the performance of the self. That is, the *material fact* of survival (which includes the act of continuing to live with the abuser in some cases) gets reconceived as distinct from the discursive as a process that gains a cultural meaning. Discursive practices enable the identification and regulation of domestic violence and abuse (see Chapter 4) and as such impact upon the materiality for women survivors, enabling them to act the lived experience of 'survivorhood'. As Reavey and Brown (2006) have shown in discussing adults' memories of abuse in childhood which link survivors' identity and agency, there is pressure to recall detailed events as 'evidence' of their memories, to bear witness to both the reality and the cause of ongoing trauma.

This means that memories have to be 'managed', and in the case of traumatic lived experience following abuse 'condensation' or 'simplification' takes place so that *'there is the conflation of multiple episodes of abuse in a singular image'* juxtaposed with *'the reduction of an ambiguous set of conflicting forces and an indeterminate set of motivations into a manageable, dramatic structure'* (Reavey and Brown 2006: 193).

As well as being performative and agentic we also have a history and memories which are managed by our being 'story tellers' with 'narrative intelligence' (Mateas and Sengers 2002). We 'furnish our worlds not just with data but with meaning . . . by telling stories we make sense of the

122

world. We order its events and find meaning in them by assimilating them to more-or-less familial narratives' (Mateas and Sengers 2002: 1).

The shift among many social psychologists towards a discursive approach (and more recently for some a material-discursive approach) lends impetus to the use of narrative to understand lived experience. A narrative approach to psychological research and analysis is particularly important for making sense of questions of 'self' and 'identity' problematised by the turn to language which prioritised discursive constructions of subjectivity. Crossley (2003), who has continued to focus on what she calls the methodology of self, takes the 'storied' nature of human life as a means of attributing a central role to language, *'but more specifically to "stories", in the process of self-construction'* (2003: 290).

Crossley proposes that narrative psychology goes beyond the idea that stories are simply used to make sense of unexpected events but that human psychology has 'an essentially narrative structure' (2003: 291). For Wood (2001) too, considering domestic violence, narratives offer 'insight into the cultural authorisation of violence and women's toleration of it in romantic relationships' (2001: 241). The three premises on which her paper operates are that humans rely on narratives to make sense of their lives, narratives are social in nature, and narratives are most urgently sought when experience does not make sense. For women living with domestic violence it is hard to make sense and 'story' of what is happening. How did the abuse begin? Whose fault is it? What should I do to survive (physically and emotionally)? And (perhaps) why couldn't I leave?

A further dimension to consider is not just the social nature of the story-telling and construction of the narrative but the relationship between 'performing' a narrative, in the context of a research project when the topic of the study is mutually recognised)[1] (Enosh and Buchbinder 2005) or during therapy where a patient/client might either want to reveal or conceal material. The latter two cases might set up the narrative with a particular purpose beyond simply constructing the story for the story-teller themselves (McLeod and Balamoutsou 1996; Iliffe and Steed 2000; Ferro and Basile 2009). Enosh and Buchbinder (2005) for instance in their research interviews with male perpetrators and female survivors identified four different styles of interaction. These were narrative as a struggle, as deflection, as negotiation, and as a self-observation process.

A similar process is demonstrated throughout all the DASH respondents' accounts of living with (and leaving) violent and abusive men. The respondents all knew they had been identified as survivors with a 'survivor' rather than a 'victim' tale to tell. Having loved, lived with and left or tried to leave an abusive man is complex and raises contradictory emotions so that women try to construct a 'sensible' story to explain these contradictions to themselves as well as others, in addition to providing the 'evidence' for their memories. When the 'love' has been romantically idealised the story is even harder to tell and respondents try to construct a scenario that enables them to make sense of their lived experience of abuse and its place in their sense of who they really are (Henderson *et al.* 1997; M. Harris, Fallot and Berley 2005).

Narratives of living with violence

Despite the pro-feminist rhetoric it is significant that the stories almost all show that at some level the women see their experience of living with violence as a private one (Berns 1999). Charlotte, whose childhood had been marred by her father who was an alcoholic and 'extremely abusive toward my mum' who herself 'wasn't the calmest of people', leaving Charlotte with 'a lot of childhood memories that were not very nice', talked about her second husband whom she had met through her church. She had joined this church after her first marriage to someone whom she had got on with but whom she had found to be very materialistic. When she met her abuser:

> I just thought 'my goodness me' you know it's, he believes, we have the same faith what a wonderful man. Charming. Just fell over himself to be charming and nice and absolutely swept me off my feet and then I thought 'well all my dreams have come true', you know. It's erm, I have got two wonderful children, he accepts them and I, although it all happened within three or four months, I just thought I had won the lottery you know.

She pins down her reasons for being in love in a highly romanticised way ('dreams come true'), using evidence of shared faith, his charm and particularly his acceptance of her children. But at the same time there is a subtext in which her life is positioned as already out of her control as she is 'swept off her feet'. In what follows there is more detail of events, acts and a chronology:

> Then erm we got married and the very day, the day after we had got married, the boys had gone to my mum's for a long weekend and the day after we had got married he erm we'd moved into a house into a hospital house, and because he was training to be a nurse and erm the girl next door to me had, the daughter had got married on the same day as me and erm for some reason they had got our milk. I can't remember why, but for some reason they had got our milk and so in the afternoon I popped round to the house to get erm to get the milk, pick the milk up and I'd said to him 'I'm just going round next door

you know they have got our milk' and erm and I must have been round there about twenty minutes, twenty-five minutes and when I came back you know we were talking about 'oh what a beautiful day it was', talking about weddings and things, how nice her daughter had looked and things and I came back and this man who I'd left you know our honeymoon period had just turned into this monster basically.

From Prince Charming her husband had 'turned' into a monster. The fairy-tale came to an end the day that ordinary life with this man began. Liter-ally, she described the honeymoon as over, with the ongoing relationship as cruel and controlling. She had two more children with him before even-tually they parted. She had remained optimistic and tried to make the relationship work. She talks of the contrast between the 'monster' and her former 'Prince Charming', trying to justify (to herself in the context of the narrative and to us the researchers who perform the moral/judgemental role) why she had fallen in love with him but also trying to make sense (in detail) of what happened when she went round to their neighbour.

She uses 'facts' in the account to anchor and manage both her mem-ories and the narrative. She actively 'remembers' herself as light-hearted, happy and looking to a future that matched her dreams. She positions herself also, and possibly by contrast, as 'deserving' in that her childhood was not described as happy nor was her first marriage.

Returning to Butler's (1988) phenomenological take on performance as constituting identity (the *appearance of substance*) this notion supports an understanding of the *telling* of lived experience so that one performs in the mode of belief constructed as self. Charlotte thus needed to account *for* herself and *to* herself for choosing a life with this man for herself and her two older children (and the two she later had with him perhaps).

Perspectives on 'self'

Living with domestic violence and abuse transcends many other experiences in that (mostly) corporeal damage is sustained which impacts on mental and physical health (Coker *et al.* 2000; Chrisler and Ferguson 2006). To consider domestic violence and abuse as a socially constructed linguistic device (whether it be one that liberates or regulates) fails to take account of lived experience, especially corporality (Nightingale and Cromby 1999; S. Brown 2001), and also the ways in which the survivors' narratives 'maintain a sense of the essentially personal, coherent and "real" nature of individual subjectivity' (Crossley 2003: 289).

Survivor accounts demonstrate that their sense of a 'material' self and consequent lived experience is fluid, complex and actively constructed through the stories of relationships (M.E. Smith 2003; Carlson 2005), as well as providing the narrator with a sense of a coherent embodied materiality (Loseke 2001; Stenius and Veysey 2005). The material and discursive 'selves' then are mediated by a sense of time and place. They are also driven by unconscious wishes and phantasies (the 'intra-psychic dimension').

A place for emotion

Potential for success or failure in acting as a 'survivor' (an autonomous and liberated human being) has implications for a woman's view of 'self' (M.A. Dutton, Burghardt, Perrin, Chrestman and Halle 1994; Gubrium and Holstein 1998). Domestic abuse practically/empirically results in physical and emotional *damage*, and the ability to leave, or not to leave, an abuser is bound up in the impact of that abuse upon the woman herself, the constraints of the material context, relationships and meanings both within and outside of that abusive relationship (Kirkwood 1993; Wood 2001).

Cindy's account for example (she was 26 years old at the time of the interview) described a context in which she had been warned by her parents and siblings about her prospective partner's potential violence, so that when it began within her relationship she was told, 'forget it. Forget him. It's not worth it.' But, as Cindy herself said, 'That makes me feel rejected. I get a lot of "I told you so". That's not nice to hear . . . the only thing my dad has said is "I don't know why you went for that violent relationship when you haven't been brought up like it".'

Cindy reported in her story that she was glad that they had now split up but she then continued to talk about her ex-partner's new relationship in such a way that she herself said she felt 'resentful'. She still seemed very involved in that man's life, and her sense of who she was, the object of her belief (Mead 1934; Butler 1988; Kimura 2008), was very much bound up with his fate (which she saw as being more successful than her own) and also seen in relation to her family, all of whom she felt had let her down. This extract from Cindy's narrative provides an emotional clue which parallels the 'facts', whereby what might be interpreted by one reader as support (i.e. giving guidance that the man was not going to be a good partner) was taken by Cindy to mean something 'rejecting'.

Molly, who was older than Cindy and had lived with violence and abuse for longer, had left her partner, who had beaten her up many times, about six months before the interview when she gave her story. She had initially moved to a refuge with her two teenage daughters, a few miles away from her former home. She felt the refuge workers had: 'put me on my feet. They showed me the roads I could go down and I went down that road and I didn't look back and I've never looked back since then' (Haaken and Yragui 2003; Hague and Mullender 2006).

As she spoke though she said she could feel tears welling up, and it seemed that finding the 'markers' to structure her story (unsurprisingly) reminded her of her previous life of living with abuse. Shortly after she had left her partner however she began to reflect on her 'self' and what she had become, not just as a woman living with abuse for so long but a woman who had found a place of safety:

> when I first went to the refuge I was bottling it up and I was being nasty to me kids. I were more or less pushing everyone away and then I went 'no. stop. It's not like you, this. You're getting the way *he* were. Don't go down that line.' And I just went to a worker and said 'I need help'. I'm taking it out on me children'. . . . I had to do that 'cos I could feel myself going really nasty and it's not me to be nasty.

Molly tells of behaviour not influenced by fearing the abuser but in which she seemed to mirror what she saw as his behaviour. Contrasting Cindy's and Molly's accounts there is already evidence of their constructions of different *ways of being* through the presence of a motivational, emotional and reflexive quality to each of their stories. Cindy resents that she does not feel able to talk to her family because they will (she believes) crow over her 'failed' relationship. Cindy also resents the ex-partner's new relationship.

Molly, despite years of suffering, was cognisant of what she, *herself*, was like (or rather what she was *not* like and did not want to become), and through that self-awareness was able to seek and cope with receiving help. In both cases there is a material quality to their lived experiences which they were able to reflect on discursively.

This storied sense of self as a survivor is constructed discursively through language, as Molly's account in particular makes clear. She actively constructs her self, objectively, as she both 'was' and 'is' and might have 'become' in the context and constraints of her new way of life.

Being in time/authentic memories

In the above examples that new way of life existed in contrast to a time when there had been a previous set of constraints – living through and with abuse and violence (P.J. Miller, Potts, Fung, Hoogstra and Mintz 1990; Peled *et al.* 2000; Kimura 2008).

Verity, similarly, is particularly clear in her account of how she engages with the concept of 'survivor', which has a present, past and future. She distinguishes herself materially and discursively from other women as being 'a proper battered wife', although it was in the past as she had left the abuser long before. What is interesting is how much this 'self' is constructed in the story as very much integral to the experience of living with the abuse and also how much the process of 'telling' is important to convey a meaning to the interlocutor:

Verity: I couldn't have come to talk to you about it when I was going through it.
Interviewer: Oh no?
Verity: I wouldn't have had the opportunity for a start, but I wouldn't even if I'd have had the opportunity, because then I was in a cleft stick and I were in an impossible situation and erm I, well I couldn't have come. Because I should have felt ashamed and I should have thought this woman thinks I'm daft for putting up with this and I don't, I'm sure I would have done. It's only now I can talk about it.

Telling the survivor story, it seems, requires not only the material/corporal sense of 'safety' but more so needs perspective or distance from 'going through it'. Verity continues telling the interviewer that she doesn't talk much about her experience so it must be that she volunteered to take part in the study to legitimate her story, and one aspect of her narrative was to persuade the interviewer that she herself was the object of her belief (Mead 1934; Butler 1988), that is, a 'real' version of a battered wife. In the extract below the interviewer tries to help Verity with her story which appeared to 'stick' around her effort to demonstrate 'authenticity'.

Verity: . . . a battered wife can mean anything can't it?
Interviewer: yes.
Verity: you know err . . .
Interviewer: what does it mean to you that, when you hear somebody say battered wife, what . . .?
Verity: well I think about me, I were definitely battered.
Interviewer: yes, yes.
Verity: I were definitely battered, but I know that people have said they're a battered wife, when they like, like fighting, they giving as good as they got, they've got and if they come off worse, then they're a battered wife, I'm not excusing it.

At this point Verity is emphasising her passivity in the face of the battering, making a moral judgement about women who 'like fighting', suggesting not just that some women fight back but she seems to be suggesting that some women begin the violence (perhaps) in order to claim the status of 'battered wife'. At this point in the narrative, it seems, far from surviving domestic violence being an experience for silence it is (almost) a badge of honour, an indication of inner strength (R.E. Davis 2002). There is also the possibility that the 'silence' has exacerbated symptoms of anxiety and even a sense of disbelief (Wood 2001; Usta, Farver and Zein 2008). Verity continued with what was almost now her 'declaration' of her status, which was only stilled when the interviewer 'gave in' and declared 'recognition'; at which point Verity moved on.

Verity: I still think it's wrong, but there's battered wives and battered wives and I were a proper battered wife.

Interviewer: certainly sounds like it.

Verity: I was yes, oh I were, mm, it were horrendous, it's lucky he didn't really er . . . [she does not say at this stage of the interview but the implication is that he might have killed her].

Her corporality and lived experience are revealed here through discourse which comprises a 'plot structure' (Crossley 2003) to both describe and reflexively organise the meaning of that lived experience which for Verity was that she was an authentic battered wife. The story Verity wanted to tell could only progress it seemed after the acknowledgement of her status, which for Verity (possibly unconsciously and certainly emotionally) had priority over the interviewer's own agenda.

As seen in Chapter 4, women survivors are well aware of what they are expected to be like (in the eyes of the public and the expert advocates) and are able to draw on formula stories to make sense of their experiences (Loseke 2001; Buchbinder and Eisikovits 2003). Verity wanted to make it clear to herself and others that she had had a terrible set of frightening physical experiences but that she was different from many other (if not all other) women who say they were abused. She also expresses her sense of shame for staying with this man and awareness that others would think she had been 'daft' (Buchbinder and Eisikovits 2003). She also says that she doesn't talk much about what happened – either in the present or back when she still lived with the man (Humphreys, Mullender, Thiara and Skamballis 2006; Moe 2007; Cohn 2008).

In a similar way other women draw on their material constraints to present their 'self' to themselves and to those who they know have helped, will help or want to help them leave their abusive partner. This presents complications for their stories of lived experience because leaving is complicated materially and *emotionally*. Making sense of one's own failure to leave, having made the fact of abuse (and abuse over time) public, requires hard work in the narrative context.

Unconscious drives

Verity had actually left her violent and abusive husband of nearly twenty years about twenty-five years before the interview. She volunteered following a short local newspaper article saying that we wanted to interview women who had left abusive partners to find out about their experiences of seeking help. It was interesting that she had chosen to speak because she had been apart from him for longer than she had been with him. Clearly living with an abuser becomes something in a life story that does not go away (Humphreys and Thiara 2003; Humphreys and Joseph 2004). It may also be though, as Verity's account suggests, a means of recalling the 'exciting' romantic life (Kearney 2001; Wood 2001; Henderson *et al.* 2005). She talked about her (first) husband and how much she had loved him and then about how he had humiliated her even before they were married:

> He was emotionally abusive towards me before we were married, because he once showed me up at the bus stop in town and a neighbour of my mother's saw us and I were crying and the neighbour of my mother's told my mother.

After her two children were born she discovered:

> I'd got this irresponsible drunkard selfish, drunkard of a husband who was utterly selfish and a hypochondriac and erm whose mother had absolutely ruined him, but who I loved desperately, I loved him desperately and he made me laugh and I worshipped him and erm I think I was too busy to really think much about it, but I can remember it [the violence] must have made an impression on me because I can remember it happened, where it happened, and everything you know.

Verity, in ways similar to the women in Wood's (2001) study, tells her story it seems both to make sense of her life and because there remained a desperate need to make sense of what happened to her marriage to a man she had been so in love with (Henderson *et al.* 1997, 2005). A sense of continuity of 'self' had been taken away from her through no longer living with the abuser and telling her story gave her another opportunity to construct that continuity. That she continues with the story-line struggling against the 'natural' flow of the interview (Enosh and Buchbinder 2005) and making it difficult for the interviewer to follow the story is in line with Henderson and colleagues' (1997, 2005) conclusions that preoccupation with a previous abusive relationship stems from a negative sense of self as an outcome of early poor attachments (see Chapter 7). Verity continues her story with an account of her background which was strict with parents who never drank or smoked. Verity said that she had been a Sunday School teacher who had had piano and ballet lessons, positioning herself as 'respectable'. Jonathan, her first husband, on the other hand used to drink and had many girlfriends. They had met when she was 17 and married when she was 19. She described herself as looking like Audrey Hepburn 'very thin and stylish'. Verity thought Jonathan had been particularly attracted by her 'girl next door innocent sort of thing'.

In a Foucauldian sense, the narrative was used to make sense of Verity's experience as a good girl who ended up in an inappropriate situation, as part of the regulatory gaze resulting in the narrative as self-surveillance, presented as confessions to a researcher as well as told to oneself. Verity's sense of the power and romance of being with this man, regardless of the early warning, was possibly reignited through taking part in the research. Later in her account she talks of her second husband: 'I don't think Malcolm has ever made me laugh once'. Verity it seemed had had a 'self' that had been stolen from her, not by her abusive ex-husband, but *by leaving him* and choosing the life that for her was different from that led by other more ordinary women – not the violence but the excitement that Jonathan otherwise provided. This contradiction was very much on the surface with Verity – but this narrative was also one of long-term reflection, in fact twenty-five years of thinking about and making sense of her experiences. This is in line with Reavey and Brown's (2006) examination of transformation of memories related to child abuse whereby 'memory resists immediate resolution because experience is, fundamentally, not easily resolved into clearly defined differences' so that the '"burden" of all past experience is continuously with us, "gnawing into the present"'. Furthermore Reavey and Brown propose that recollections are transformative and the place and meaning of memories are not as they were but managed to make sense of agency and action (2006: 179).

Contradictions and understanding

Camilla had had less time to look back over her life and her ambivalence was further beneath the surface than Verity's. Camilla, clearly desperate to stop the abuse, wanted the police or someone to help her, either to break her addiction to this man, or to find a way of changing his behaviour. For instance, having told the interviewer that the police don't understand women's situations she continues:

> It's just because they go to so many houses you know. Women suffering from the same problem and they kind of see it every day. They get used to it. It's like 'OK he does this to you – I'll ask him to leave'. But beyond that person leaving you need help to . . . it's like you're addicted to that person. OK that person isn't good for you but at the same time you want to get away but they don't give you that help. They just tell you to close the door. OK he's out of your door and

you sit there alone and you're thinking about it and the person will come back and knock on the door. You see yourself maybe they will say 'I want this. This is my hi-fi' or 'I want my phone back'. And you do something stupid like opening the door and that is it you know. They [the police] are not helping you to talk about this. 'What made you get involved with this person?' and other ways of helping you. All they can do is protect you from physical abuse. . . . They are not in the same situation to understand why I keep phoning them to get rid of this person that I keep bringing back. You have to understand the root of the problem.

Camilla herself may not have fully understood the root of the problem, but she certainly recognises that there *is* a psychological/emotional issue, and in the way she talks, she seems aware that this applies to some other women as well. This account provides insights into the multi-layered experiences being described. The telling of the story itself is clearly not only intended for the researcher but is part of a reflexive process within the active construction of a conflicted 'self'. Camilla appears to be reflecting on what she has done and what she is narrating to answer her own question: what sort of person calls the police after having been abused over time and then does 'something stupid' and re-engages with the abuser? This is a person who is 'addicted' to someone and the experience of being with that someone who is not good for them. Alongside her self-questioning is her *presentation* of someone not able to access suitable resources to ensure that she is able to do what she should do and is expected to do and make sure she separates from the abuser. She needs to know she is seen as conflicted, not only through her emotional 'weakness' expressed by her addiction, but as someone not getting the type of help that she needs and that other women would need. Goffman (1959/ 1990) showed that people both 'give' and 'give-off' signs/signals that enable an observer to make a judgement of them. This judgement involves the observer's understanding and interpretation of the intentional signals and also the unintended signals. According to Goffman the individual will provide both conscious and unconscious impressions that may or may not be understood by all parties concerned. Paula Heimann (1950), Melanie Klein (1959) and Herbert Rosenfeld (Tuckett 1989) from a psychoanalytic view have presented the idea of 'counter-transference' (see Chapter 8) as a similar phenomenon, at least on the surface.

Underlying this extract from Camilla's narrative is an unconscious demonstration of her *dependence* not only on the man, but on the police and any possible other opportunity to have someone with whom to talk through her problems. This is not only a clue into Camilla's conscious and unconscious needs but it also provides important insights into what many women would want to have in place to support their leaving. There is also a sense in this extract of the 'mundane' nature of her experience of abuse – him leaving and him coming back for some trivial reason, her letting him in and the cycle beginning once again.

Levels of consciousness

Anthony Giddens's (2003) theory of 'structuration' helps to explain both lived experience across time and ways of being and thinking that play a key part in understanding a material-discursive-intrapsychic approach to the relationships and 'selfhood' of survivors of domestic abuse. Simply put, his theory suggests that experience is constituted in time-space which is a 'banal and evident feature of human day-to-day life' (Giddens 2003: 35). The *durée*, or daily duration and flow of life, indicates both that time is constituted in repetition (as in 'day-to-day') and that for the human individual it is finite and irreversible. All social institutions (the material and the discursive) are expressed in the routines of daily life, mediating the physical and sensory properties of the human body, the latter being the 'locus' of the 'active self'. As was clear in the accounts above, the day-to-day passing of time could also be overshadowed by time passed in the past, and it is that ability to experience time passing that supports the ability to experience and 'know' self and others (Reavey and Brown 2006).

Giddens (2003) proposed that it is important to be able to test a theory empirically. Therefore from his social theory it is possible to draw out foundations of a material-discursive-intrapsychic *psychological* perspective that supports analysis of the stories of lived experience.

His stratification model of consciousness involves not only *durée* but three levels of consciousness: the *discursive*, the *practical* and the *unconscious*. As Giddens describes it:

> The reflexive monitoring of activity is a chronic feature of everyday action and involves the conduct not just of the individual but also of others. That is to say, actors not only monitor continuously the flow of their activities and expect others to do the same for their own; they routinely monitor aspects, social and physical of the contexts in which they move.
>
> (2003: 5)

Therefore an individual actor has a motivation (or drive), takes action, rationalises the action and reflexively monitors the consequences and conditions of that action. The survivors' accounts all demonstrate this acutely.

Giddens's sociological/philosophical understanding of human motivation and experience (as described thus) turns us towards the psychoanalysis of Freud and Erikson to examine how 'the psychological foundations of the interweaving of the conscious and unconscious can be represented'

(Giddens 2003: 41; see Chapter 7). While what Giddens calls 'competent actors' discursively report their intentions and reasons for acting as they do (as with, for instance, Camilla), they cannot necessarily do so about their motives which may be unconscious (see below).

Levels of consciousness

The discursive consciousness here refers to the level at which we reflect upon and account for our self to our 'self' and others. This is similar to Mead's (1934) 'I' as subject and 'me' as object (of belief), as again similar to Butler (1988), the 'I' reflexively, and continuously, making sense of the performative 'me'.

The practical consciousness, although different from discursive consciousness because it lacks the same degree of reflexivity, is the awareness of what is simply and practically done. For example, practical consciousness is the awareness that 'I am divorced' or 'I have left him' or 'he beat me'. However to become divorced or recognise that one has been abused requires the discursive level of consciousness. Giddens says that he does not intend 'the distinction between the discursive and practical consciousness to be a rigid and impermeable one. . . . Between discursive and practical consciousness there is no bar' (2003: 7). This makes sense in the context of all the accounts and approaches such as those of Ussher (1997) and Yardley (1997) as well as Crossley's (2003) exploration of narrative psychology.

Barriers *do* exist however between the unconscious (which contains material repressed and thus 'inaccessible' to consciousness) and the other two levels of consciousness.

Stories of leaving abusers for example rarely appear as examples of triumph as might be expected if adopting an unsophisticated materialist stand. Camilla, who had been in contact with the local refuge, accounted for constraints which not only involved lack of material resources (practical level) but also involved her in making sense of her life *as it might be* in the context of being a (potential) survivor (discursive):

> I just took my son. I couldn't take any more [abuse] and I just came with the intention of going back . . . probably having a break you know, knowing that I am not going to get help. But [Women's Aid] gave me the names of hostels and you know and the young women's project is the one I chose. The one I found that it's helping more than what the others are doing. Sometimes when you live in a house and then you move to a hostel you feel 'no I have got all this . . . I can't fit in here'. New people. And you tend to pull back and think 'no, I am going back to what I already know'. So it is like they gave me the chance to be independent. . . . In a hostel if you see someone who's

drinking, probably you feel you know I have got problems as well and you could start doing things you wouldn't because you are upset. You try to forget someone and not go back.

She was clearly conflicted about taking that step in her life to leave and was able to reflect upon it. She knew she had planned to return to her abusive partner but was justifying her exploitation of the refuge (because she was 'probably having a break') by 'knowing that I am not going to get help'. She was also both distancing herself from other survivors (she could not 'fit in here', they were drinking which was both abhorrent to her and somehow took others' attention away from her problems) while also identifying with them by the fact that she had chosen the young women's project.

Giddens's consideration of the unconscious is based largely on Freud's model (see Chapter 7) whereby the unconscious includes repressed material denied to consciousness (particularly *motivation*), and his concepts of the discursive, practical and unconscious structure of the individual are parallel to or in place of the ego, super-ego and the id.[2] Freud developed a model of human development and the human psyche which identified the role of the unconscious (psychosexual development), taking account of biology and psychology, later built upon by Erikson (psychosocial development) who focused specifically on the links between biology, culture and conscious and unconscious drives. Both theories explain the potential for a range of outcomes in psychological development including the sense of a secure, autonomous selfhood, and will be discussed further in Chapter 7 particularly in the context of attachment theories. The unconscious while important is also potentially controversial in the management of relationships and of memories and is frequently neglected by most mainstream psychologists.

Conclusions

Women living with domestic abuse account for their experiences in the context of their lived experience rather than a broader understanding of gender-power relationships. In telling their stories to the interviewer and to themselves across the course of their lives they draw upon discourses of romance, love and passion which, as Chodorow (1994) describes, are ever present in culture from earliest childhood in myths, fairy-tales and contemporary media. These tales are gendered and women have a part to play in these dramas. In order to understand how women live with abuse and make decisions about continuing, entering and ending relationships it is important to make sense of the multi-faceted way we each understand our lives consciously and unconsciously through the constraints of materiality, regulatory discourse and intra-psychic life. The unconscious is a highly complex concept and, as will be addressed in the next two chapters, is complicit in both 'taking in' patriarchal gender-power relations as part of the 'self' and communicating to other people, unconsciously, fears, anxieties and contradictions in the experience of a storied self.

7

DOMESTIC ABUSE ACROSS GENERATIONS: INTRA-PSYCHIC DIMENSIONS

Introduction

The use of violence as a means of resolving conflict between persons, groups and nations is a strategy we learn first at home. All our basic problem-solving, problem-exacerbating, and problem-creating strategies, for living and dying, are learned first at home.

(J. Gilligan 2000: 5)

Pro-feminists who eschew psychological explanations of domestic violence (Mullender and Hague 2005) and advocates for the contributions made by the discipline (D.G. Dutton and Corvo 2006) all emphasise the pervasive nature of domestic violence. Further, all sides of the debate consider violence and abuse to be aberrant rather than typical (Verhulst 2000). However until relatively recently there had been a division between those who examined the transmission of violence across generations (paying attention to 'cycles of violence'[1]) (J.P. Smith and Williams 1992; Dankoski et al. 2006) and those (Ehrensaft et al. 2003) who focused on how to care for child witnesses to violence through protection of both the children and their mothers (Humphreys 1999; Humphreys et al. 2001, 2006). Research to explore the transmission of violence across generations has been mostly focused on the impact of living with family violence during childhood on the (potential) *perpetrators* (Smith and Williams 1992; Chapple 2003; Stover 2005; Dankoski et al. 2006; Davhana-Maselesele 2007; Dryden et al. 2009).

Relatively little attention has been related to how *survivors'* early experiences of witnessing domestic violence and abuse have impacted on their relationships in adulthood. There is though an increasing interest in children's resilience following traumatic and violent events (including but not only domestic violence) (Caffo and Belaise 2003; Haight, Shim, Linn and Swinford 2007) and the long-term impact of childhood trauma on adult mental health *per se* (Street, Gibson and Holohan 2005; Anda et al. 2006, 2007; Simeon et al. 2007; Taft, Resick, Panuzio, Vogt and Mechanic 2007) and/or the risk of childhood trauma leading to substance and/or alcohol abuse in adolescence and adulthood (Fergusson and Horwood 1998; P. Choi and Ryan 2006).

In this chapter the emphasis is upon the intergenerational transmission of *vulnerability* (Holt, Buckley and Whelan 2008) to women who are survivors rather than perpetrators of violence. Following the ideas introduced in Chapter 6, particularly about the role of the unconscious in motivations, emotion, behaviour and 'story-ing' the self, I take up psychoanalytic ideas first from the work of Sigmund Freud and Erik Erikson. Then, more specifically, to development the intra-psychic dimension, I apply the work of object relations theorists, most particularly Melanie Klein, John Bowlby and Donald Winnicott, who (clinically and theoretically) examined the relationship between the infant and mother (or responsible adult and primary carer) which they showed to be crucial for shaping the adult's means of coping in the world.

From this evidence I make the case for girls whose early lives are characterised by negative attachments, witnessing or being the victims of family violence and/or whose parents cannot be 'good enough' to ensure emotional security, as being at a high risk of living with abuse and violence in adulthood.

From Freud to Erikson

One of the most important aspects of psychoanalytic thinking, which is also highly relevant to understanding the experiences of women who have lived with and survived domestic violence, is the role of *anxiety* (Sutherland, Bybee and Sullivan 1998; Shurman and Rodriguez 2006; Ludermir, Schraiber, D'Oliveira, Franca-Junior and Jansen 2008).

Both Freud's and Erikson's theories enable an explanation of how early development, in the multiple contexts of biology, psychology and environment, influences emotional life and the sense of 'self' in adulthood. The powerful unconscious which originates from the start of life through the *id* (containing the life/Eros, libidinal and death/Thanatos instincts) also becomes the repository for subsequently repressed feelings such as shame and guilt (Gay 2007[2]).

The ego is the mainly conscious part of the mind which develops gradually throughout infancy and beyond, and the super-ego (conscience) (mostly) unconscious develops around the age of 5. These parts of the personality are seen as being in conflict, and the result of this conflict is anxiety. Most people experience anxiety, which can often be directly handled by the ego (conscious 'self').

When there is too much anxiety to be handled by the ego, individuals resort to 'defence mechanisms', Freud's term for unconscious strategies for reducing anxiety. Because these mechanisms are unconscious they involve some self-deception, which is normally part of everyone's experience. The defences can take the form of denial, repression, rationalisation, projection or displacement (see Gay 2007). So for instance someone might repress the feelings surrounding domestic abuse and violence by insisting to themselves that nothing has gone wrong (denial). Deidre, for example, had initially only recognised her situation as living with domestic abuse when her next-door neighbour confessed to her that she herself had been re-housed after living in a refuge. Deidre went on:

> I didn't think I were a victim of abuse to begin with and then one day I was watching Kilroy[3] or something and they were labelling these women as battered wives and I thought 'that's me' and that's when it dawned on me.

Alternatively, a woman survivor may 'rationalise' that she never loved her partner anyway, and a break-up would be the sensible solution. More problematically a woman may rationalise that he only hits her because he loves her and is jealous of any attention she pays to herself or other people. Alternatively anxiety could be 'displaced' by having arguments at work or being irritable with the children, and thus focusing attention on these 'problems', and away from the abuse at home, the real source of the anxiety.

Erik Erikson's (1968/1977) work is particularly helpful to make sense of why so many of us fail to see our lived experience as a set of clear life choices. His work has been neglected by many psychoanalysts and only taken account of in its popularised form as a model of psychological development. But the process he identifies is more complex than usually credited and it is important for understanding ambiguities in the way we make sense of our lived experience.

Work by contemporary narrative psychologists has gone some way to reviving the importance of Erikson's work for explaining how we make sense of ourselves through ambivalence and contradiction pieced together in narrative construction (McAdams, Reynolds, Lewis, Patten and Bowman 2001).

Erikson maps his theory of psychosocial development onto Freud's psychosexual developmental model in that he sees us as having unconscious libidinal and aggressive desires and as going through developmental stages, and like Freud he sees the relationship between biology and psychology as immutable. Thus girls/women and boys/men are biologically and psychologically different from each other. He particularly emphasises that women being able to contain a foetus in pregnancy and give birth is something that men envy rather than, as Freud argued, that women envy men their penis. However he also identifies culture and context as impacting on conscious and unconscious life and here it is his 'eight ages of man' (*sic*) (see Table 7.1) that are important.

While there is great emphasis on experience in the first weeks of infancy and the relationship with the mother (or primary caretaker) Erikson follows

139

Table 7.1 The eight ages of 'man' (adapted from Erikson's model of psychosocial development)

Age*	Stage	Challenges
0–1	Basic Trust v. Mistrust	Will the infant trust their caretaker?
1–3/4	Autonomy v. Shame and Doubt	Will basic trust lead to a sense of autonomy and accomplishment?
4–5	Initiative v. Guilt	Will the child's new skills lead to failures? How will they feel about those failures?
6–12	Industry v. Inferiority	How will the child cope with the challenges of school? How will they manage the challenges of coping independently of their family? How do they match up to their peers?
13–18	Identity v. Role Confusion	Addressing the questions: who am I? who will I become?
19–25	Intimacy v. Isolation	Managing successful relationships
26–40	Generativity v. Stagnation	Coping and creativity at work and/or in family life and child rearing
41+	Ego Integrity v. Despair	What have I made of my life?

* These ages are approximate in the table and equivalent to those identified by Erikson to relate to stages of development, but the specific ages are not so appropriate in the twenty-first century when 60 is the 'new 40'.

on with how these experiences may be partially resolved or compounded across the lifespan. Erikson's work, relating to domestic violence and abuse, is particularly insightful through his theorisation of ambivalence in the formation and development of the ego (or conscious sense of selfhood).

> The infant's first social achievement, then, is his willingness to let the mother out of sight without undue anxiety or rage, because she has become an inner certainty as well as an outer predictability. Such consistency, continuity, and sameness of experience provide *a rudimentary sense of ego identity*[4] which depends, I think, on the recognition that there is an inner population of remembered and anticipated sensations and images which are firmly correlated with the outer population of familiar and predictable things and people.
> (Erikson 1968/1977: 222)

In other words if the infant is able to 'trust' those who care for her to be 'good enough' (Winnicott 1953) then *she will be able to trust in herself* and so will begin a developmental process which will build on this trust. This idea of 'trust' does not imply a naïve view of others. On the contrary it means that a woman will develop an ability to recognise and take responsibility for her own mistakes or to reject a man if he demonstrates abusive behaviour with a degree of self-confidence, rather than overlook or deny the abuse, or assume that she is only worthy of this type of man.

This trust is part of a dynamic – it doesn't just happen once and then become incorporated into identity. The infant/individual is in constant interaction with their social and biological environment and the meaning of experiences and their integration into the ego depends on the psychosocial context through which trust in the self and integration of the ego/selfhood become stronger or more fragile.

Each of the 'eight ages' or developmental stages described by Erikson (see Table 7.1) has the possibility for degrees of positive or negative psychoemotional outcomes. Thus the psychic possibilities arising from the first months of life, 'basic trust versus mistrust', lead to potentially different outcomes which vary by degree. As can be seen in the accounts of many of the women in the DASH study, some early experiences made them emotionally vulnerable although they also gained strength in other ways. Sandra for example (who is also discussed below in this chapter) was put into care as a 9-year-old child because her mother, whose own life had been traumatic, had a mental breakdown and could no longer cope. Taking Erikson's framework, Sandra would have been dealing with 'industry versus inferiority' at that point in her life when she went into care, although the circumstances she relates would imply possible earlier stresses and anxiety as well. Talking of her mother's breakdown she said:

> she just went, you know, mentally unstable and stuff and so they stuck me in a children's home. When I first went in they said they were taking me for a three week breather, do you know so my mum could have a break . . . and I ended up in the same children's home for two years so it weren't three weeks. I might have to go through my mum's life story a bit.

The acute anxiety and disruption to Sandra's life are palpable when listening to her story. The shock to a child of having the mother she relies on removed even for three weeks would be bad enough, especially after the child had experienced her mother's breakdown, but being in the children's home for two years must have been a major trauma from which it would have been difficult to ever recover without specialist support (Ogawa, Sroufe, Weinfield, Carlson and Egeland 1997). It is important therefore, regardless of pro-feminist anti-psychology sensibilities, that the question of what would happen to this woman as she reached adulthood should be addressed (Bifulco 2002).

There are a range of ambiguities and possibilities within each of Erikson's developmental phases which rely in part on biological development (influenced by corporality and health) and social context, with lived experience making 'psychological sense' which becomes part of identity. So the first post-infancy stage (autonomy versus shame and doubt) not only presents a dichotomy dependent on context but builds on the first stage and the sense of strength and confidence in the infant ego. The following six stages – 'initiative versus guilt', 'industry versus inferiority', 'identity versus role confusion', 'intimacy versus isolation', 'generativity versus stagnation' and 'ego integrity versus despair' – are all cumulative, so that in the latter stages of older age Erikson believed an individual would reflect on previous lived experience and if they felt that they had not lived up to their sense of who they should have been they would despair at the end of their life and fear death.

In summary, Erikson's work is relevant here for two reasons. First, for the sense that development involves integration of the psychological, social and biological contexts into the 'self'; second, for the account of the relationship between the strength of the 'self' and the ambiguities of experience and how that relationship develops throughout the lifespan. As Chodorow (1978: 59) recounts, achievement of basic trust constitutes, reflexively, a core beginning of self and identity. Erikson's model offers something potentially positive in that he shows how emotional growth continues through the lifespan. It is possible under the right conditions and with psychological support and (probably) therapy to strengthen the ego in adulthood even if early life phases have been characterised by negative experiences (see Chapter 8).

From biology and culture to relationships

The ideal for us all would be to have what psychoanalyst Winnicott (1953) calls 'good enough' mothering, with the adult managing to hold a sense of the 'good object' in themselves. In other words a good enough parent, by showing the child care and love, will have enabled the child to have a sense of self-worth and adequate self-esteem to withstand the impact of moral and physical abuse or other life stresses in *any* context. Part of that care and love is to make the infant feel that even if they have to withstand some frustration, the carer will come back and care will continue. Also the child will realise that the love will be there even if the carer is sometimes cross with the child. However well or badly a parent behaves towards them, though, most people have a 'loyalty' or attachment to that person, although

142

often it may be an idealised version with a hope that one day that ideal mother or father will 'emerge'.

A child whose early months have included good enough parenting will be able to understand and cope with the fact that the mother/parent is not perfect, and consequently the child will be able to deal with their own good and bad aspects as well as those of their own children, friends and future partners. Thus idealisation of another person is brought about because the child has not been enabled to tolerate uncertainty or to realise that good and bad can co-exist in a human being – their carer or themselves.

In seeking and establishing intimate heterosexual relationships, women whose sense of self is insecure are likely to idealise the prospective partner, and this idealisation may continue after evidence that the man is abusive, representing a major influence in preventing a woman from leaving. Charlotte's story of her 'Prince Charming' who turned into a monster and Verity's account of her first marriage to the handsome and romantic Jonathan reflect this (see Chapter 6).

The intra-psychic dimension

Object-relations theory, based on the work of Fairbairn (1944/1952) and later Klein[5] (see below), focuses upon the nature and origin of unconscious phantasies of anxiety, their impact on adult life, and how *defences against anxiety* characterise an individual's inner world and their experience of social and emotional relationships (M. Klein 1959; H. Segal 1964).

Klein (e.g. 1959) considered that the ego and id develop from the start of life, which is in contrast (although not in contradiction) to Freud. She suggested that the ego, the *manager* of the conscious, defends against unconscious impulses in a number of ways – some helpful to mental well-being and others not. Through meticulous observations of infants she hypothesised that from birth we experience anxiety of a 'persecutory nature', and without being able to grasp it intellectually the infant, unconsciously, feels every discomfort as if it were being inflicted by hostile forces.

Frustration, discomfort and pain in infancy are experienced as persecution and their concomitants (frustration and hate) become destructive impulses which *are still operative in later life* (Klein 1959: 248–249). We unconsciously take in the world around us (our experience of others, i.e. objects and how we relate to them) and expel impulses we cannot tolerate (e.g. extremes of anxiety and hatred) onto others as a means of defending the ego. This process is called splitting. The ego splits off the bad, intolerable feelings of frustration and badness which produce feelings of persecutory anxiety and we *project* them into others. Early infancy and the primitive as yet unarticulated feelings that arise are brought to the surface again in adulthood, particularly when individuals go through stressful situations such as living with or leaving an abusive partner.

If the woman's mother/carer during infancy has been good enough at containing the persecutory anxieties during what Klein terms the *paranoid-schizoid position*, the woman will grow up with a sense of autonomy and the ability to care to a great extent for herself. This meshes with Erikson's early stages as described above. In this position the infant, and at times the adult,[6] fears retaliation for their aggressive and phantasy envious attacks on the mother figure. When the baby is about 3 months old the baby becomes able to tolerate frustrations and integrate their experiences rather than split them off. This is what Klein called the *depressive position*. If the baby has experienced enough good care and containment for their persecutory anxieties in the paranoid-schizoid position then it is likely that the individual will be able to hold within herself some representation of good objects. In so doing the woman will be able to see herself as worthwhile, strong and autonomous and able to deal with her anxieties (see Chapter 8 for a development of Klein's work in a clinical setting).

Attachment, love and neglect

Bowlby (1979) and Winnicott (1969), both psychoanalytic practitioners and theoreticians, following both Freud and Klein have made it clear that early relationships have a profound and enduring impact on those that follow throughout life. Marris (1996) summarises part of this work by examining the importance of a good attachment relationship and the ways in which an individual becomes able to organise the meaning of subsequent relationships and events. 'Whether we tend to see order as natural and secure, something to learn about and respond to, or as the fragile imposition of human will on chaos and destructive impulses will be determined . . . largely by our childhood experience of attachment' (Marris 1996: 79).

Attachment studies have been central in experimental developmental psychology (Ainsworth 1996), psychoanalysis (Bowlby 1979) and most recently cognitive neuroscience (Schore 2005), with all studies pointing to the basic human experience of attachment in early infancy and, in different ways, throughout life.

As attachment quality and style in infancy is demonstrably a predictor of attachment quality in adulthood (Bifulco *et al.* 2002) there is a clear link to how a woman will experience and manage a future intimate relationship. While much developmental psychology research has focused on mother–infant bonding and the impact of poor attachment on relationships over the life course, childhood neglect as a specific focus has largely been overlooked as a risk factor for psychological well-being in later life and a factor that will also influence relationship quality. Childhood neglect has been poorly defined because definitions of neglect are actually about *things that didn't happen* rather than things that did (Bifulco and Moran 1998), so it may be that risk factors for vulnerability in adulthood do not get identified because no specific traumatic event had taken place, although neglect for a child is insidiously traumatising in itself.

Is there evidence of intergenerational transmission of abuse?

Catherine, one of the DASH respondents, raises important issues about transmission of vulnerabilities in her own words during the course of her story. Catherine's violent father left the home when she was 8. Catherine split up from her violent husband when her daughters were of a similar age. How should a mother look after her children who witness the violence? Can a mother develop her daughters' resilience so that they are not so likely to be at risk of living with violence in adulthood?

Catherine had left her violent husband, the father of her children, and in this part of her story she talked about how her children (girls aged 6 and 7), having both seen and heard his violent attacks on her, were protective of her.

> It's stayed with them . . . they are very protective of me. I mean he didn't really hit me a lot in front of them but the last time that he hit me, before he left it was in front of them. I would be really calm and you know quiet and keep the fact that I was really hurt from them but it didn't matter. It was just how they perceived it you know.

She believed that her children were giving meaning to their own experiences as witnesses of their father's violence, so that 'they don't like anybody shouting, they have become quite traumatised by it, because obviously they know well, they think, you know violence comes after the shouting'.

Catherine had decided not to talk to her daughters about their father's violence because, 'I don't really want to make a big thing of it with them, I mean if they ask me anything then I am quite honest with them. I think it's something that I will talk to them about you know when they are older.' But of course domestic violence is a 'big thing' and cannot be disguised despite Catherine's efforts to remain calm and almost 'pretend' it away.

Given Catherine's awareness of her daughters' distress this seemed at first a little surprising. It looked as if she was both acknowledging and denying their pain and her own agency in offering them emotional support. However, she went on to qualify her reasons for not opening the discussion with her daughters:

> because I know where they are coming from. I *was* actually that child, I was them because my dad was an alcoholic, and my dad was horribly abusive to my mum and you know he did everything in front of us. So I know what it's like to be them and not to understand what

145

daddy's doing to mummy and wanting to protect mummy. You know I know where they are coming from but I just don't think, at the moment they are old enough to handle it.

Catherine, justifying this position, recalled how when she herself was about 8 years old her mother told her that her father was moving out:

and I was just like 'yeah great but will he?' and I used to think to myself 'I'll *never* when I grow up'. I just attributed it all to the alcohol, and I thought, 'when I grow up I am never going to marry a man that drinks'. My husband doesn't, he is not really a drinker.

Despite recognising the similarities across the three generations of women and two generations of men, Catherine hints at the end of this extract that somehow even though she was vigilant when finding a partner, his violence was masked by the fact that he didn't drink while she herself had attributed violence to alcohol.

There are unsurprisingly gender differences in family relationships, conflicts, love, loss and attachments across and among generations that contribute to shaping intergenerational transmission of family culture, which stem from the fact that women 'mother' (see for example Chodorow 1978) and, as Catherine's story shows, even in the direst circumstances women try to mother in the best way they can. Women's mothering is a key feature of family life and crucial to the way culture and values (at the micro family level and wider societal level) are transmitted. Mothering is about gender too and 'does not exist in isolation. It is a fundamental constituting feature of the sexual division of labour', and as such it is 'structurally and causally related to other institutional arrangements' (Chodorow 1978: 32). Mothering produces gendered capacities in children within mother–child relationships, 'an interactive base of expectations of continuity of relationship' (Chodorow 1978: 34).

For witnesses of parental violence, there is the question of whether they might become a perpetrator, or victim or protector (Stith *et al.* 2000; Dryden *et al.* 2010), and evidence indicates the possibility of both outcomes. A female child witness might be more likely to live with a perpetrator of domestic violence, as in Catherine's case, than a child from a non-abusive background, and a boy might be more likely to become violent to his partner.

It is likely that the experience and meaning given to intergenerational transmission of violence differs for girls/women and boys/men and in particular the *gender of the violent parent* interacts with the gender of the child. However listing even these levels of complexity ignores the wider familial context of grandparents, aunts, uncles, previous partners and siblings, of which little is as yet understood (Ragin *et al.* 2002).

Feminist concessions?

Kelly (2001), a pro-feminist sociological researcher, states that no study has yet demonstrated that there is an immutable 'cycle' of abuse, i.e. that abuse is inevitably transmitted from one generation to the next and that children who witness abuse of their mothers by their fathers will re-enact this kind of scenario in adulthood. She continues to stress that

> Disputing this model does not mean, however, that there are no cases where experiences of abuse are present in generations of families. Rather, it means questioning simplistic ideas about repeating behaviour as if it were the same as learning a nursery rhyme. Human beings are not machines – we make sense of, place ourselves in relation to, events and actions. A thinking and decision-making process is involved before we act similarly or differently to events we have witnessed or experienced.
>
> (Kelly 2001: 50–51)

She maintains that the *idea* of a cycle of abuse is a common-sense one that appeals to the public as well as academics and health and social care professionals, her point being that perhaps it is easier to see domestic abuse and violence as something that is specific to certain families and types of child-rearing practices than something endemic in gender relations. It is that 'breaking cycles is much easier and safer to discuss than changing the structure of social relations' (Kelly 2001: 51).

Lay understanding is in fact more sophisticated and alert to nuances of knowledge-claims than Kelly supposes (see Chapter 5). In the same volume as Kelly, Morley and Mullender (2001) reiterate that same message. They claim that the assertion of an intergenerational transmission of violence is accepted as a received truth to justify professional intervention to break the cycle of violence (Morley and Mullender 2001: 33). They decry studies that have pointed to children growing up in abusive homes being either abusers or victims of abuse in adulthood. They go on to say: 'A large literature (much of it North American) exists addressing the cycle of violence in some fashion: many writers simply assert its existence with no support at all; some make reference to authority' (2001: 34). However Morley and Mullender do accept that there 'may be some merit in the cycle of violence hypothesis, though clearly in a muted form; transmission is in no way absolute' (2001: 34–35).

As with other researchers in this area they acknowledge the difficulties of designing and conducting a relevant study to test this hypothesis for certain.

They save their crushing antagonism however for the work of Straus (1980), discussed in Chapter 3, conclusions from which most commentators would find difficult to support without question.

Following Kelly (2001) – i.e. that we all make different and varied decisions about how to lead our lives despite our backgrounds – it may be there is a useful link to be made here between the *sociological feminist* discourse, and a material-discursive-intrapsychic *psychological* position which has not been apparent previously (see Chapter 3) in the literature. Paradoxically a feminist sociological position that vilifies violent and abusive men's influence on their children is nearer to the classical psychoanalytic perspective which gives importance to the relationship between the infant/ child and their mother over all. Kelly drew attention specifically to the way that for some women, 'bearing and caring for their children is so connected to their own abuse, that it is extremely difficult if not impossible, to disconnect them' (2001: 53).

Women in the DASH study showed they could in fact withstand a great deal but were concerned about how their abusive relationship impacted on their children. For instance, 'the relationship was just totally, it was just disastrous it were just awful and I just thought "I have got these beautiful children and they just deserve better"' (Charlotte). However thinking about what is happening to their children is complex and connected with a woman's self-esteem and self-image. So, 'some people think, "oh well she must like it", erm some people think "why does she demean herself? why does she allow it to happen?", you know "how can she allow it to happen when she has got children?"' (Catherine).

And from Raisha:

I really believe that if a child can't respect their father, they can't respect anyone. He used to say to my son 'call your mum a bitch or a slag' and he would. And then he'd say 'see if *you* weren't like that *he* wouldn't say things like that' when he used to beat me he [son] used to sit on his knee. And he'd [husband] say 'look he's come to me' – I thought 'why doesn't he come to me – maybe I am bad, that's why he's not coming to me'. But of course it was because I was so upset that he went to *him*.

However Raisha was only able to gain that perspective when she looked back from a place of safety. At the time the abuse is going on, and a woman and children are living in that family culture, the conflicted views of what *is* reality impinge on everyday experience and impact on women's mothering.

Children of course are not passive onlookers or simply victims, in the way that women are also not passive in their relationships. The impact of living with their mother's abusive partner included the children taking control, as in Chrissie's case: 'my daughter just said to me one day "mum, snap out, got to snap out of this. He's hitting you all the time". And I did.'

Women's stories

In what follows I am going to explore in detail three women's stories (Sandra, Chrissie and Tilly) to illustrate the importance of a *psychological* material-discursive-intrapsychic perspective for understanding women's experiences of intergenerational transmission – that is, women's experiences of their parents and grandparents and their own children – and then identify how relevant this might be for accessing appropriate professional and effective support.

The neglected elements of psychology in feminist sociologists' accounts of domestic violence and abuse are, paradoxically, the same as those missing from traditional psychological approaches. That is, the intrapsychic perspective. This is probably because sociological feminism *and* mainstream psychology eschew this understanding of women's lives.

In the analysis of the stories presented below I suggest the ways in which a material-discursive-intrapsychic perspective makes a fundamental contribution to explaining the psychology of living with and leaving abusers.

The twenty-six women who took part in the DASH study were volunteers. Most were working-class and poor and almost all reported problematic backgrounds. The study does not claim to be representative or generalisable or to have tested robust hypotheses. The intention here is to look for insights into women's experiences.

What was evident in the women's stories was the impact of their family backgrounds upon survivors of abuse. Telling their stories and managing their memories helped them give their 'storied' experiences meaning (Reavey and Brown 2006). It also seemed to help the women make sense of their relationships with their children and their abusive partners and in some cases to make decisions to change their lives. Stories varied from cases where fathers and grandfathers physically and sexually abused the respondent, through stories of vulnerabilities of one or both parents where one of the parents had been abused by the grandparent or a partner, leading to narratives of neglect of the respondent.

Some stories were accounts of terrible abuse and neglect and many portions of text are unclear to the observer as they were constructed by the narrator to make their own sense.

A daughter in a mother's life

Sandra, mentioned earlier in this chapter, was only 22 at the time of the interview, at which point she had had two children and at least two abusive partners. She opted to talk about her own and her mother's life in order to

149

explain some things about her current situation. She was in care following her mother's breakdown, from the age of 9 to 12, and her sister was born about a year after she had been returned to her mother's care.

Sandra, talking further of her relationship with her mother, said:

> my sister were born when I was thirteen, so we went to [City] and ended up in bedsits and stuff and my mum were just like hallucinating that the man she were living with for nine years was talking to her in the street, do you know she'd thought she seen him? . . . she kept breaking down crying and stuff, and then I just, we had a meter with 50p's[7] in it and the fairground was just up the road do you know from our bedsit and I used to just nick some 50p's and that and she took me down saying 'she's right naughty' and 'she's nicking money off me' and 'I can't cope with her' and 'I don't want her' and all this and just handed me in.

Despite her mother's inability to look after her, Sandra had some sympathy for her mother (who was only 17 when she gave birth to Sandra) and was not prepared to tolerate her aunt and other relatives who said things like 'your mum's really bad for what she done . . . she put you in care. That's really bad.' Sandra continued her narrative about her mother, though with some disdain, saying that her mother tried to put her off men, saying 'sick stuff to me about men since I were a little kid . . . 'cos my dad used to beat her up and that'. Sandra, it is clear, had developed an implicit theory to explain her life through drawing on her early experiences.

Tilly, by contrast, did not express any empathy with her mother but even so drew on her own early life to explain her lived experience of sexual abuse and how it impacted on her later during adulthood:

Interviewer:	So when you say that in the past that you feel like you haven't been believed. . . . Who is it that hasn't believed you?
Tilly:	Well it were my own mum . . . things what were happening and basically she were abusing me 'cos she were just battering me, you know what I mean? It's the same sort of . . . like, that sort of thing doesn't happen, that doesn't happen, you know what I mean? So since then I've thought 'no one's ever going to believe me'.
Interviewer:	So you were actually getting abused from your mum?
Tilly:	And me dad. But different kinds of abuse. That's what she weren't believing [sexual abuse].

Tilly positions her mother as denying the sexual abuse she was experiencing, because 'that sort of thing doesn't happen', and thus Tilly considered that her mother had seriously let her down, so much so that Tilly considered that it had destroyed her own trust in other people.

> So it [the sexual abuse] were right from being ten year old so I thought from then that if they don't believe me and she's me own parent then nobody's going to believe me. . . . I mean, the only people I could tell who would believe me were my mum's mum and my mum's brother. They're both dead now. It's only recent that . . . three years and two years. They were the only two believed me, that I thought believed me. Like I go down to the [survivors] group and they say 'we believe you' and I go to the doctor's and she says 'I believe you' but I can't get it into my head that they do believe me. It's just one of them things, they keep saying 'we believe you' but I can't get . . . you know, that people do.

Tilly's distress was compounded by her own mother refusing to believe *her* mother (Tilly's grandmother) when she had confronted Tilly's mother with the fact that she was being sexually abused.

> I used to run away but then when she confronted my mum, which is her daughter, it were 'oh, don't take any notice of her, she's just bleeding stupid, she's just making it all up' so my nan didn't really have the right to do anything about it 'cos *she* weren't my mum, *she* weren't my parent, you know, but she always used to say 'if I could have done something I'd do it for you' but . . . so it's . . . you've got people who want to do things for you and can't and then the people that should be helping you and they didn't, they don't.

Tilly too was clear that her mother had had a role to play in her sense of disadvantaged adulthood. Her mother was very important to her, but Tilly believed her mother had let her down in a crucial way and thus destroyed her sense of worth and belief in herself.

What was happening to everyone at the time is unclear to the reader of the transcript and the extracts above. Tilly has storied her life and managed and condensed her memories in a way that helps *her* to make sense of what she believed (Reavey and Brown 2006). But the person in the middle of the story, Tilly's mother, is blamed by her daughter *and* by her own mother (Tilly's 'nan') for what went wrong in Tilly's life. Paradoxically the idealisation of Tilly's mother placed her on a pedestal to which no one could reasonably aspire (Sommerfeld 1989; Sayers 1990; Allan 2003). This will be discussed further in Chapter 8.

A father in a daughter's life

Sandra's father was in and out of prison. She told of how on one occasion when he was at his own home and she was escaping from her first abusive partner, with whom she had lived since she was 13, her father, to whom she had turned for some comfort, just said:

> 'you're a little prick' and I went 'you're a prick' and he just threw me straight across the living room up against the wall and I thought 'ooh here we go'. You know because me mum always said 'you can see him but watch out because he used to beat me'. And then when he threw me then I just got right scared. But this is because he was angry because I went to him in the first place because he had found out that [partner] had took cocaine and that he found out that [partner] had been in prison and then he was just dissing me for it instead of helping me.

Not only was Sandra's mother neglectful but she herself had been abused by Sandra's father (which Sandra may or may not have witnessed given her account of her early life). Turning to her father for support led to him simply beating her up, but Sandra 'justifies' her father's behaviour by saying that he disapproved of her choice of partner. The accounts above provide some indication of how loyalty to both mother and father, neglectful and abusive, is ubiquitous. There is attachment to close relationships that may appear to be irrational. This attachment is also present between many women who are abused and their abusers.

Children and men in a woman's life

Chrissie had five children, three by one and two by another violent man. Her story demonstrates that without good enough parenting your 'self' needs more and more love not only from children but from a man. Her story also shows how patriarchal discourses have positioned women as lovable only if they have a male partner, and that personal status and thus self-esteem are to be gained and sustained by being able to attract (and keep) a man.

Chrissie shows that she cares about her children but demonstrates her confusion brought about by the pressure to have *a man to give her 'love'*.

> *Chrissie*: It were February, Valentine's day I finally had enough. He
> [second abusive partner] actually kicked a bench into my
> leg and my little girl's leg and I left him in the house with
> t'kids while I went next door and phoned police. . . . People
> say to me I want to get out of this relationship but I'm
> scared because nobody will want me with five kids but that
> ain't t'case. Case is there's always somebody out there
> that's offering to give you some love and that.

Chrissie's dilemma, as with most women living with abuse, is that she cares what happens to her children but (believes) she needs a man for her 'self'. Paradoxically though, despite being positioned as necessary, men seem to be treated here as easily come by and interchangeable too. Clearly Valentine's Day was a significant one for her and it was therefore particularly acute that her partner did not demonstrate love on that day, and it underlined her sense of rejection and anger. However she also had a 'realistic' view that men are available 'out there' offering love. Her fantasy of men then is one in which they 'offer' love rather perhaps than have a need themselves or make demands. Also, as shown at the end of the extract below, for Chrissie it is necessary to have a man's approval for her attractiveness, and conversely a man's contempt rebounds immediately on her self-image and her behaviour, as she could be 'nasty' without a man as well as 'ugly'. Chrissie reported a conversation with her children:

> If you think about it and you think 'oh God' you look for a future and
> you say to your kids, like I talked to my kids first I said 'what would it
> be like without having a dad here and all that?' and they said 'brilliant
> Mum, you would be a good Mum, the one we've always wanted' and
> erm so I says 'well what would it be like, would you think I were nasty,
> would you think I were horrible?' and they said 'no, do what you want,
> it's your life, you do what you want' and his own child, he's black,
> thirteen on Saturday, and he hasn't seen his Dad two years today and
> erm he says to me 'right' he says 'Mum' he says 'you've got to build
> your confidence up'.

Sadly in this case Chrissie did not seem to have the emotional/psychological resources to do this and needed validation from a man. She said:

> and what it did mean is I were going in pubs and he [partner] were
> saying I were a mess so I started changing my appearance, wearing
> low cut tops, building my confidence up, getting a lot of confidence off

men and on New Year's Eve I actually kissed a bloke and it made me feel good because somebody else was showing interest in me. And he [abusive partner] always said to me 'you're ugly, you're not very good looking' and this lot.

Not only was this man physically violent to Chrissie but he also made her feel worthless as a woman, particularly within the context of heterosexual attractiveness, which was important for Chrissie and symbolic of patriarchal values generally. Furthermore her partner made a point of looking at other women as if they were attractive to him, which compounded Chrissie's reduced self-esteem.

So I thought 'well I'll go in a pub and I'll put a low cut top on', so this certain day I sees him looking at all these women, so I thought 'right if you can do it, I'll go and chat this bloke up' to build me confidence up so I did and people thought 'oh god she's turning into be a name for herself', and that but I weren't I just wanted . . . a bit of confidence off somebody. I went up to someone I says 'can you', I says to William 'can you give me a New Year's kiss?' so he went 'why?', he went 'you've got him'. Then [partner] come running in and give me a New Year's kiss, so he did he bombed it in, give me New Year's kiss and off. And he says to me 'I told you you were ugly', so I says 'well *he* don't think so', so he says 'but you'd never be able to live without me and without money, without anything'. So I thought about it and I says 'well, er who do you think you are God's gift to women?' and that just got me my confidence, he kept pulling me down and saying I were ugly and I just went and got one of my friends to say that he liked me and he did like me in the end, he became a bit more of a friend, so I built my confidence up, now and again I will go down in the dumps, it don't always happen.

Chrissie's validation of herself is obtained through the admiration of a man (or men) and in particular admiration and desire for her sexually (J. Kitzinger 1995; Van Roosmalen 2000). Patriarchal society and culture make it difficult for women to see themselves independently of how they are valued by men and patriarchal institutions. However there is little doubt that women who have had a reasonably secure and loving early life experience are more likely to negotiate their lives more effectively, independently and safely than women whose self-esteem has been damaged from the start by poor care in infancy (Goldner *et al.* 1990).

What is also interesting in Chrissie's account here is the way her partner interacts in this heterosexual 'game' with her – looking for other male competition for Chrissie's sexualised affection and then making sure he wins. They then insult each other although it seems at the end of this extract that the other man in the scenario she has described builds up her 'confidence' through becoming 'a bit more of a friend' – presumably by becoming a new sexual partner who will flatter her at first and make her feel better. This feeling of confidence though is unlikely to fill the gap left in her self-esteem for long.

Conclusions

Failure to experience good enough parenting to provide a secure emotional base and a sense of self-worth does not invariably lead to the risk that a woman will find an abusive partner. There are many potential outcomes from being brought up with abuse and violence (D.G. Dutton 2000; Israel and Stover 2009; Zinzow *et al.* 2009). However abusive and neglectful early life experiences, which leave a person with low self-esteem and limited emotional resources to deal with uncertainty, anxiety and fear of abandonment, lead to *vulnerabilities* (Anda *et al.* 2007). A mother who is being abused herself may not have the strength to support her children and, although the 'cycle' of abuse is not immutable, there is evidence (and a common-sense view too) that caring parenting is protective and a woman who is living with abuse is less likely to provide the care she might wish to give to her children. As argued in Chapter 4, the campaigns emphasising that domestic violence and abuse can happen to anyone regardless of background have provided an invaluable contribution to public, policy makers' and researchers' awareness of risk factors. However a general view that it can happen to anyone displaces the opportunities for support for those most at risk, and it is clear that women whose childhood involved abuse, neglect, poor attachment, inadequate parenting and the trauma of witnessing their father (or mother's partner) physically and emotionally abusing their mother will find this difficult to cope with if no extra support is given to them.

In the next and final chapter this will be considered again in the context of therapeutic interventions with women and with heterosexual couples where the man has been violent and abusive.

8

'DOING' DOMESTIC VIOLENCE: DILEMMAS OF CARE AND BLAME

Introduction

In this final chapter I (re)turn to psychology and a material-discursive-intrapsychic perspective on women's lives in the context of domestic violence and abuse. I specifically re-examine narrative and constructions of the self in a gendered context (Chodorow 1978) but more explicitly in constructions of the gendered *relationship*.

To do this I draw upon the work of symbolic interactionists (Simmel 1908/1950; Mead 1934; Goffman 1959/1990) and phenomenologists (Berger and Luckmann 1966; Butler 1988) to expose 'relationship' as 'performativity' of a gendered narrative. This work is also linked to psychoanalytic attachment theories (Bowlby 1980, 1990; Henderson *et al.* 2005; Ludlam and Nyberg 2007) and those of Klein and object relations (M. Klein 1959), to link the material, discursive and intra-psychic elements in relationship performance. This is then linked to open systems theory and systemic clinical approaches to work with couples in violent relationships.

To exemplify the approach, in addition to the women's stories, I draw upon data from the last phase of the DASH study which was the in-depth interviews with the health and social care professionals whose job it was to both 'care' and 'blame' in families where women and children lived with male violence.

The woman, the man and the relationship

Johnson and Ferraro (2000; see Chapter 2 in this volume) demonstrate how the four typologies they employ classify the *relationship* over and above an incident or series of incidents of violence. To recap: they emphasise how in some common couple violence one or the other will 'lash out' in the course of an argument. That is their way of being, Johnson and Ferraro propose, and this behaviour will not necessarily escalate. Some relationships though are characterised by 'intimate terrorism' which may or may not be violent but it is the abuse of power and control by one over the other and is part of a pattern within which fear builds up and characterises how those involved relate to each other over time. The third pattern they identify (violent resistance) has been described subsequently as the 'slow burn' in which the victim of intimate terrorism fights back, which sometimes results in murder. Their fourth pattern is 'mutual violent control' in which both parties battle for control over the other using violence, intimidation and other forms of abuse to gain advantage.

The identification of these descriptive categories was based on reviewing empirical evidence from (mostly) large-scale quantitative psychological studies of violence. Their analysis is important because it focuses upon *relationships* rather than engaging in either 'vilification' or 'victimisation'. Further, and unsurprisingly given their chosen paradigm, Johnson and Ferraro take an objective observer position in their descriptions of categories.

What is missing from their work is recognition of the discursive ways in which the roles of 'perpetrator' and 'victim' are constructed and regulated within relationships, which impact upon the storied and performative aspects of the actors' lived experience.

In Caroline Dryden's study of marriage, from the perspective of each partner, she argues (following Henriques, Hollway, Urwin, Venn and Walkerdine 1984/1998) that 'in any one given moment of life human action is "always already social"' (1999: 25). By this she suggests that we never think, act or make sense of our lives in any way that does not have a social meaning to it and a social context within which it can be performed. Her study of biographical accounts of marriages shows that women focus on the relationship, so that the marriage becomes a verbal balancing act as *through their talk they manage the 'status quo'*. That is they discursively keep the marriage going, presenting it to themselves and others as something that works, is good overall and has a future. Dryden positions this as women engaging in the 'sustained practice of self-blame', particularly when managing the presentations of problems in the relationship (Dryden 1999: 58). In contrast, this study shows up some of the men as presenting their *wives* (rather than the relationship) in a negative light, and although Dryden interpreted a high proportion of their discourse as misogynist, some men told her with relish that they saw themselves as 'typical heterosexual blokes' (in one case the man was fed up that he couldn't go out for a drink more frequently with his male friends, and one talked about his 'terrible temper' for which the couple were seeing a doctor (1999: 145)). Thus it was as if the men were performing (or in Dryden's words 'doing') masculinity, which had to be done *and could only work* in the context of the couple relationship. That social act of masculinity was managed through putting women down, but with the woman in the role of 'the wife' who could only perform her part in the presence of the 'third player', i.e. the relationship.

Following Simmel (1908/1950), the ways in which individuals act towards and communicate with each other are fraught with ambiguity, interpretations and developmental change. In other words not only do individuals in a relationship *experience* each other in the 'practical consciousness' sense (see Giddens 2003; and Chapter 6 in this volume) but they also reflect on each other and interpret the behaviours of the other (cf. 'discursive level' of consciousness) in the context of the relationship, which leads to the next set of actions and interpretations in the chain.

Subsequent symbolic interactionist and phenomenological sociologists (Berger and Luckmann 1995) have developed these ideas to elucidate three 'units' of analysis to be considered in any heterosexual couple relationship: the *woman*, the *man* and the *relationship* itself.

It is clear from the interview extracts employed throughout this book that women's narratives take account of all three components (me, him and 'it') positioned in dynamic relation to make sense of their own agency, and performativity, with the relationship as the 'object of belief' (Butler 1988). Just as 'identity as a survivor' of domestic violence and abuse is an important element in reflection and memories of storied selves, the abusive relationship becomes entwined in the storied memories in which the couple have 'performed' a violent relationship, and each has a perspective on the relationship that brought about that behaviour.[1]

Performing the abusive relationship

In addition to descriptions and discussions of the abusive men in their lives, the extracts from the interviews with women have that third element of the relationship as a crucial part of lived experience which also entered their decision-making. This is not necessarily about loving or hating a man but about what goes on in the 'space' between themselves and the abuser. One woman (who had had several violent relationships) suggested that men are violent:

> because really they [the men she had lived with] couldn't handle the relationships you know at end of day. You know the way they deal, dealt with anger. And drinking was just not the way, you know what I mean? and they tried to blame me for it, which it wasn't me it was them at end of day, you know what I mean. Like, well it's not my fault that they can't handle relationships is it at the end of the day?

Not only does Mel focus on the men's (inadequate) handling of the relationships but she makes it clear that she saw the context of *being in a relationship* as one in which men tried to blame her for the *relationship* rather than for any particular behaviour.

She continued:

I'd say 'well if you stopped drinking you would realise you were in a relationship' you know what I mean? or like as if to say 'well don't bother having anyone after me or someut, because you can't handle them'. That's what I said to him because he couldn't handle it, you know? none of them can, every man I've been with couldn't handle a relationship.

Mel's positioning of the relationship as separate from both the man *and* her self supports the concept of the relationship as the 'third player' in the context of living with violence.

Observing the performance of abuse

Professionals working with couples who live with violence and abuse frequently observe what is going on from a similar position to the one Mel demonstrates here (albeit as far as we know from being on the outside). That is the relationship is given an equal weighting in their understanding of how abuse happens and how the situation might be changed. Explanations of why women continue to live with violence and abuse also take a relational perspective in that early relationships are cited in implicit theories of causation. Talking of her experience of violent and abusive relationships from the perspective of being a health visitor, one woman says:

Well it's such a *power-based relationship* isn't it? They [women] feel weak, they feel powerless, they feel vulnerable, they feel *they can't exist without them [men]*, you know? No matter how bad it is this is still for them the only . . . you know the well, I think some of them might say anyway that their partner still cares for them and *loves* them and what ever that means. But they perhaps never had a positive loving figure in their life, perhaps *they have grown up in a not outright abusive situation* but certainly not very positive and behavioural role models, you know a lot of them. I think they don't know anything else, and haven't experienced it, or their self-esteem is very low for numerable reasons. That 'something' is better than nothing and nothing *is much too frightening you know to be without a partner is just unimaginable.*

(Health visitor, Interview 2)

That the relationship is central in the drama of domestic violence and abuse seemed to be implicitly understood. The health visitor's account above begins with a strong description of a power-based relationship which takes in some of what Dryden (1999) had observed, which is that it is women who maintain the relationship, and although this respondent is reporting on a combination of women's accounts she seems to hold a model in her mind of the kinds of stories that women tell of loving their abuser and believing he still cares for them. This respondent begins with a pro-feminist take on gender-power relations, then moves to a transmission of vulnerability model to explain women's powerlessness rather than one based on the rule of patriarchy *per se* (Dobash and Dobash 1979; Bettman 2009).

Thus in this respondent's account gender and power are enacted within relationships from childhood to adulthood, and patterns of relating stay with girls/women. At issue here though is whether listening to (many) women's voices (over time) takes the observer to a pro-feminist view (Hague and Mullender 2006) or to one which is regulated by a more clinical model, perceived by some feminist writers as woman blaming (Humphreys and Thiara 2003). A final point from this account is that the fear of living without a relationship is described as a greater one than the fear of the abuse and violence, which is a point also made by others. For example one social worker further suggested:

> My own personal opinion, I think women find it difficult 'cos they get *used to that relationship* and when they leave *that* relationship there's something missing and they don't know how to replace *that* and they feel like they can't cope without that person 'cos that person has had control and power over them for however long and to suddenly find yourself as an independent being must be very frightening and a lot of women can't cope with that and would rather return to the *safety of what they know* than what they don't know. 'Cos they don't have the confidence to cope with new *situations* or the support to do that. Yeah, I do personally find it very strange when they do go back to abusive partners but I understand why.
>
> (Social worker, Interview 1)

While implicitly acknowledging the long-term impact of abuse on self-esteem (Humphreys and Joseph 2004), and (even) an equivalent of Walker's 'learned helplessness' (Walker 2000), the respondent here focuses on the 'object', the relationship 'space', as being (ironically) one of 'safety' in that the woman *knows what to expect* in the familiar 'situation'. This suggests that the attachment may not be so much to the abusive man, but to the familiarity of how to live in that type of relationship context (which also lends weight to reinforce the view that women brought up in abusive and socially excluded families may be drawn to similar relationships in adulthood; see Chapter 7). This discourse is distinct from rhetoric about the abuser himself, as both of these commentators have focused on the woman as the manager of the relationship, albeit with less overt power than her male partner.

Another social worker similarly talked of the woman's 'status' in the relationship and again referred to an objectified 'situation' although in this version the respondent keeps the man's violence and intimidation in mind as a major factor in the woman's experience of the relationship. Note the respondent is talking about her *informal* knowledge of working with violence and abuse, as is the health visitor commentator above.

> I think I mean I've known, incidentally I was talking to a colleague about one recently, where the woman almost has a kind of *slave-like status* . . . within her relationship, where to ask her to make decisions for herself or to expect her to actually see herself as existing separately from her partner was, was almost impossible. I mean in that case it took many, many months of this particular refuge working with this woman to actually get her to even *consider herself as a separate individual who could make any sort of choices separate to the ones that her partner was making* for her. . . . I think it's quite complex, I think it's partly the kind of you know economics with many women, but I think it's also all those kind of emotional factors about . . . you know identity, but also huge fear and intimidation . . . and you know women being very, very frightened to leave *situations* where they don't know if, if they're going to be found and what will happen to them if they are.
>
> (Social worker, Interview 17)

Health and social care workers hold implicit theories that acknowledge the lack of clarity and complexity in abusive and violent relationships, which are different from the messages from social work academics in particular (Mullender 1997). The description of the woman unable to see herself as separate from her partner suggests not so much 'learned helplessness' and/ or PTSD (J.C. Campbell 1990) but that the woman's agency shrinks into a joined sense of identity with her abuser; that implicitly some health professionals have noticed a distortion of attachment (Bifulco 2002; Henderson *et al.* 2005).

Taking the intra-psychic on board

The focus on the performance of a relationship, rather than an individual, sheds light on the power of unconscious patterns of thinking and being from the early weeks and months of life for both women and men, whose relationship with an object/mother and others (M. Klein 1959) ensured (or not) a 'good enough' (Winnicott 1953) sense of self/integrity (see discussion of Erikson's work in Chapter 7) through which the individual had also been able (or not) to develop a secure and healthy attachment (Bowlby 1990; Blizard and Bluhm 1994; Bifulco *et al.* 2000).

This is not to say that a focus on the psychodynamics of the relationship means that the violent and abusive man no longer bears responsibility for his actions – of course he does. Neither is thinking about the relationship equivalent to saying that women are never at fault through their own violence and abuse (D.G. Dutton and Nicholls 2005).

The implications here are first that relationship performance provides a means of making sense of many women's attachment to the violent man through understanding the way the relationship is positioned (G.A. Harris 2006); and second directing possibilities for clinical and therapeutic practice with the couple relationship which makes clear where responsibilities lie while seeing what needs to change (Vetere and Cooper 2004). This conceptualisation challenges the reactive process of vilification of the abuser and the interventions that stem from this position (Corvo and Johnson 2003), moving towards a recognition of the need for ensuring safety before treatment (Vetere and Cooper 2001), treating the long-term effects of abuse through exploration of attachment with a focus on building resilience (Simeon *et al.* 2007) and allowing for reparation (van Wormer 2009). How might this be achieved in practice?

Ambiguity, ambivalence and the psychosocial context

There is much evidence from the work of feminist psychologists that heterosexism and patriarchal values are embedded in the culture to the extent that they both regulate and become integrated in behaviour and thinking for both women and men (see Ussher 1989; C. Kitzinger and Wilkinson 1993; Nicolson 1996; Malson 1997). In the case of domestic abuse, 'women learn early on to feel at fault for interpersonal conflict and to feel responsible for making it better – their social training for connectedness, accommodation and cooperation prioritizes relationship above all else, including the self' (Almeida and Durkin 1999: 314). 'Women are made to feel that there is nothing more essential than having a man and children' (1999: 314), as stated explicitly by Chrissie in particular in Chapter 7 whose story revealed that only by being desired by a man could she feel alive.

Why should this be the case?

Nancy Chodorow (1978), anthropologist and feminist psychoanalyst, has argued that women's mothering underlies the gender-power systems based upon the organisation of the division of labour in heterosexual partnerships. 'Heterosexual marriage, which usually gives men rights in women's sexual and reproductive capacities and formal rights in children, organises sex. Both together organise and reproduce gender as an unequal social relation' (Chodorow 1978: 10). Her thesis is that women's mothering makes them 'pivotal actors' (1978: 11) in the sphere of social reproduction, that is of gender-power relations and inequalities within and without those relationships.

While there are many theories to explain women's mothering role and the in-built inequalities, Chodorow argues that these mostly fall down by failing to recognise the immutable psychological qualities of the role. Chodorow goes on to propose that mothering is more than a set of behaviours and, in order to be a 'good enough' mother, specific relational capacities are required which involve a 'sense of self-in-relationship' (1978: 33). Thus mothering cannot be taught, nor can structural gendered inequalities force women to provide adequate mothering, nor can health and social care authorities force a woman to be 'good enough' unless 'she, *to some degree* and *on some unconscious or conscious level,*[2] has the capacity and sense of self as maternal to do so' (1978: 32).

The importance of this thesis for understanding women's experience of living with domestic violence and abuse rests upon women's relational capacities in so far as women who themselves had 'good enough' mothering relate to men (and their children) in a maternal way that involves a sense that her 'self' is in 'relation' and as such experienced and understood to be engaged in surveillance/self-surveillance (see Chapter 4 of this volume; Vaz and Bruno 2003) through the prism of the relationship (object of belief) (Butler 1988).

Following Bowlby (1990) (and others arguing from a similar perspective) Chodorow links the psychological capacities which comprise mothering to the primary attachment experience and she also distinguishes boys' and girls' experiences of this in terms of their attachment to their father and mother as part of the oedipal drama (Freud 1925; Chodorow 1978: 206; Gay 2007). As discussed in Chapters 6 and 7 above, women who have had a secure attachment (Bowlby 1990) and developed the opportunity to have a trust in others and a sense of autonomy in their selfhood (Erikson 1968/ 1977) will be less likely to reproduce in their adult relationships the 'slave-like' status described so graphically by the social worker quoted above and apparent in many of the women's self-narratives.

Containing anxiety: the psychological place of safety

The mothering capacity and women's self-in-relation must also be traced back to the description in Chapter 7 (above) of the work of Melanie Klein, particularly the ways in which the infant relates to the 'object' mother, both taking in and expelling parts of her 'self' from and onto the object. Klein (and other object-relations and psychoanalytic theorists) propose the intra-psychic and social essence of human psychology. That is we experience our world in relation to others, although those relations are not objective truths but emotional relations influenced by the early object relations and the unconscious phantasies that are part of psychological growth and survival.

One fundamental feature of Klein's work that has informed the role of the psychoanalytic therapist has been the concept of 'containment' of anxiety. According to Klein, a mother aware of her infant's extreme anxiety will 'hold' it for the baby and transform it into a more manageable form and then return these feelings which she will have made safe. Thus the infant experiences trust in another (cf. Erikson) and in herself too.

During infancy and childhood the responsible adults/parents can modify the feelings of persecutory anxiety by holding the boundaries between phantasy and reality, while acknowledging the feelings persecutory phantasies of anxiety may represent. This includes not only containment of the child's fears but also of their aggression, cruelty and sadism, all of which are part of normal primitive behaviours seen in infancy (J. Segal 1992). In other words the carer of the infant will tolerate the infant's frustrations, rages, upsets and fears, try to understand them and give back to the infant a sense of security from those fears. Some carers, who have not had their own anxieties and frustrations so contained, still experience primitive fears and will exacerbate the infant's feelings rather than containing and comforting. What happens to women whose mothers and fathers not only fail to contain their anxieties but exacerbate them?

This is not making a case to 'blame' the mother/parent/carer but a case for how support might be offered to them to soothe their own primitive fears and enable them to do the same for their own children.

This process of 'containment' is invaluable for working with women living with and surviving domestic abuse and violence on several levels. First, it relates to the early experiences of some of the more vulnerable women who have been brought up unable to 'hold' a strong, trusting and autonomous self, insecurely attached and highly anxious, as with almost all the women who tell their stories in this book. In crucial ways their extreme and uncontained anxieties, exacerbated through living with violence, act to prevent their leaving the relationship. Second, Klein's theory concerning containment relates to the ways in which mothering takes place. Women who have had some experience of good enough mothering may, for a variety of reasons, enter and remain in one or more relationships with 'vulnerable' men where they act in a mothering role to contain the anxieties not just for those men but for the relationship (including the wider relationship of the family).

Third, the counsellor or psychotherapist performs a very similar role *vis-à-vis* the client or patient seeking help – that is, to 'hold' (or contain) the unacceptable and distressing feelings that a person might experience brought about by trauma or pain that resonates with early anxieties from infancy (Klein 1959). Morgan (2001) describes a dynamic process whereby two people who have developed a 'couple state of mind' are *integrated* emotionally while holding an awareness of being *separate* and *different* from each other. Therapy may enable them to view themselves from a 'third position' provided the therapist receives, contains and metabolises their anxieties and subsequently offers them back to the couple in a 'safer' form.

Containing anxiety for themselves and others

Catherine had eventually left her husband for good with no regrets but it had taken 'four or five years' before she could tell anyone what was happening to her. She seemed to be emotionally compelled to hold her fear and emotional pain. Her marriage had lasted seven years and 'the domestic abuse started after the first year of marriage, when I moved to [city]'. She had been loath to tell her family what was happening to her because:

> it's embarrassing and you know there's always that hope things might change and I'll have made all this fuss. And then I have heard of other people that have told their families and the families have turned against them because they have gone back to the abuser.

Catherine was well aware what was happening to her but she was ashamed, didn't trust her family to support her and hinted that she might well return to her husband even though she had said she had felt so much better through getting free from him. The strength of her ability not only to contain her own and the relationship anxieties but also to 'protect' the relationship from outside criticism and further embarrassment is significant.

Mary, who had remained married to an abusive and violent man for over thirty years, demonstrated her containment of the relationship. 'I'm the one who carries the embarrassment. My husband has not really faced up to the fact that he's got a very serious problem and he's never acknowledged it as a problem.' Clearly her description shows how she is in fact looking after the emotional needs of the man who is experiencing (in her view) intolerable pain and anxieties, in order to care for the relationship which she values.

Marilyn, who had had two abusive partners, had lived twice in a state of anxiety and it had almost become routine in her life. Even so she managed to contain her anxiety as part of a process of containing the relationship. She described her current relationship which she had left five weeks previously:

> you daren't stay at the shops or go shopping with your friends for too long because is he going to phone? What is he going to do? I've been shopping with my friends and he's told me if I don't come home he's going to cut my throat. I've had to run and leave my friends. I'm

scared to have my friends in the house because my friends are dying to say something to him and the whole time you're living on your nerves and it's mental abuse and how they treat you. Being told to cook something to eat at two in the morning by the scruff of my neck. Controlled totally until I've had no option but to leave my house because if not I would have had a total mental breakdown.

In experiencing his blatant control over her life and containing *his* feelings, his terrorism continued. In the end, because she had enough awareness to realise she had reached the end of her tether could hold no further anxiety, she managed to leave him. However her first reaction seems to have been to *contain* her own, her friends' and *the anxiety in the relationship* rather than confront it or walk away from the abuser.

From care to blame

Domestic violence remains a criminal offence in which the perpetrator is unequivocally to blame. Pro-feminist arguments support a criminalisation rather than a therapeutic discourse (Ferraro 1996; Mirrlees-Black 1999) and have appropriately taken issue with the view that women (victims) should shoulder all or some of the blame for being attacked at home or in the public domain (I. Anderson *et al.* 2001; Anastasio and Costa 2004; Capezza and Arriaga 2008).

Psychological aspects of abusive relationships are at best neglected by the criminalisation discourse presently influential in strategies of governments, but mostly psychology is ignored. The Home Office consultation paper referred to in Chapter 1 (Home Office 2009) (as with almost every other similar document) touches only upon the psychological repercussions from *surviving* domestic abuse.

So for example they talk of women's need for help to overcome what has happened to them. They do, pertinently, talk of the importance of influencing social attitudes to women and girls (see discussion of this in Chapter 5) as well as educating young women and men in 'mutual respect' (Home Office 2009: 29). However the dearth of psychological research available in the UK, as well as the limitations of the large-scale North American studies using survey methods, continues to constrain the discourses available to those governmental agencies considering policy and practice.

Providing support and (physical) sanctuary works for women who have the confidence to know they want (and need) to leave their abusers. But what about those women whose accounts, above and throughout this book (see Chapters 6 and 7), are ambivalent for many reasons? Women who say that what they actually needed was 'a break'? Women who are so oppressed that they seek out men who will abuse them because they do not recognise they have a choice? What about women whose lives are intertwined with their abusive partner in such a way that they cannot make sense of what they want to do? What about women whose religious convictions, extended family or belief in 'love' make leaving impossible? These women are oppressed by patriarchy but their 'take' on what they want will remain unheard so long as the pro-feminist versus mainstream psychology stand-off persists (particularly in that the pro-feminist lobby is currently ahead of the game in its influence).

One front-line social worker voiced some of the frustrations expressed by many of those whose training (as with policy) tends to be informed by the pro-feminist activists and campaigners (see Chapters 2 and 3).

> I think it's a hard, hard cycle to break out of . . . and maybe some of the abused women, I don't know it sounds a bit funny maybe to say, 'do they deserve it?' I don't think they deserve it, maybe they invite it. Sometimes, it's not an excuse that . . . but maybe it's a reason why it happens.
>
> (Social worker, Interview 5)

When faced with the dominant discourse that gender-power relations are the only cause of domestic violence and abuse to be considered (and therefore leaving the man is the solution) it becomes difficult for the professional to link this theory with lived experience and consequences for practice. Commentators, particularly from the front line, find themselves forced back into politically (and psychologically) problematic explanations of women's behaviour when that behaviour doesn't appear to be in women's own interests.

The dominant regulatory political and activist discourses *separate* the abuser from the abused and the woman from the man. There is no middle ground. Women are positioned as living with abuse *solely* because material constraints bind them into that particular life. While this is probably mostly true in, say, Taliban-ruled Afghanistan, and for Shi'a women under Karzai, for countless other women in developing countries (see Chapter 1) as well as a great many in the developed world, material constraints are not the only factors that bind women to abusive relationships (Palmer 1998; Sen 1998; Kim *et al.* 2007; Schuler *et al.* 2008).

Most women in western democracies have the freedom, legally and morally, to live independently of men. But many abused women do not leave. There are more complex reasons why women live with abusers and stay despite the possibility of leaving, as demonstrated in Chapters 6 and 7 and above in this chapter in particular. Any discussion of this area, of why women stay, draws accusations of being anti-feminist, 'anti-women', or simply naïve, so that such a discussion has become 'taboo'. But this does a disservice to some of the most vulnerable women who continue to live with abusers and need support to change their lives – either to stop the abuse in that relationship or leave it.

The 'relationship', as the third unit of analysis, pulls in consideration of material, discursive and intra-psychic elements of domestic abuse and violence as well as showing possibilities for change. Focusing on the relationship provides a forum for academic debate capable of transcending the pro-feminist versus psychologist positions of 'men use fear to control' versus 'men have problems' and/or 'violence is symmetrical'.

Examining the role of the relationship in domestic violence and abuse displays the activist pro-feminist position as potentially reinforcing discourses of *surveillance* and self-surveillance with echoes of regulation (Foucault 1976; Armstrong 1995). As with formula stories (Loseke 2001; see Chapter 4) the regulation of women within this discursive framework requires that they, or those closest to them, take action if they find they are living with abuse.

These discourses of criminalisation and surveillance obscure the emotional and intra-psychic levels of experience. So for example the Home Office consultation paper (referred to above) urges 'people' to feel confident to intervene in cases of violence to women, to 'pick up the early signs' of violence, so that those suffering would 'receive help and support they need quickly in order to overcome the physical and mental impact of being a victim of violence' (Home Office 2009: 3).

Many women *do* of course need material resources to support them to leave an abuser. They need to know they will be able to leave safely, that the abuser will be prevented from perpetrating their actions towards them any more, that their children will be safe and emotionally and financially secure. Women need to feel that they are not alone in any sense of that word – in their experience or in the aftermath. They need to have all sense of shame lifted from them so they may continue with their lives as survivors not perpetual victims.

Conclusions

Women, for historical, cultural and psychological reasons, try to make things work and frequently carry the responsibility for the state of their relationships and take the blame if they fail. They also take the blame if they stay with an abuser despite everything that is known about leaving violent relationships.

Living with abuse as an adult and witnessing the experience of abusers as a child are intrinsically linked. This is not to say that the one inevitably results in the other, but we are psychologically, emotionally and socially influenced by the material constraints of our individual worlds. Not all men are abusive or violent and not all women experience abuse or tolerate it for long if they do. There are individual differences and it is these individual differences that enable the hope that prevention and healing are possible.

NOTES

Introduction

1 www.Uk.news.yahoo.com 1 September 2009.
2 Some writers have recognised that 'cycle of violence' has been used to refer to both the interpersonal exacerbation of a violent situation and the intergenerational transmission of violence.
3 All names and identifying details and events have been changed.
4 Between 1999 and 2002 I was the principal investigator on a study of women's help-seeking behaviours on behalf of themselves and their children following domestic violence ('DASH' which stands for **D**omestic **A**buse women **S**eeking **H**elp). This book is independent from and extends beyond that project although some examples will be used to illustrate and underline some key issues.

1 Domestic violence

1 The trial was underway at the time of writing.
2 http://www.afghan-web.com/woman/afghanlaw.html
3 http://www.stopvaw.org/Prevalence_of_Domestic_Violence.html
4 http://www.feminist.com/violence/spot/dv.html
5 Conversely of 426 male homicide victims, only eight were killed by their partners.
6 The survey took place across five countries (Bangladesh, Brazil, Peru, Thailand and Tanzania) in either the capital or a large city and one provincial location; a rural setting in Ethiopia and a single large city in each of Japan, Namibia, Serbia and Montenegro and the whole of Samoa.
7 From a Christian organisation providing information about violence to women across developing nations.
8 http://www.cafod.org.uk/gender/domestic-violence
9 http://www.cafod.org.uk/conflict-and-peace/free-of-violence
10 http://www.cafod.org.uk/kenya/there-is-no-light
11 http://www.wethewomen.org/entry/domestic-violence-in-korea/
12 Now re-named 'Refuge'.
13 http://www.surrey.police.uk/news_item.asp?area=&itemID=8216&division=3
14 These are local partnerships of voluntary and statutory agencies who come together to develop multi-agency strategies in their regions.
15 http://england.shelter.org.uk/get_advice/advice_topics/families_and_relationships/domestic_violence/what_is_domestic_violence
16 http://www.yorkshirepost.co.uk/news/Frail-father-banished-to-attic.531151.jp

17 Yahoo! UK & Ireland News, 28th August 2009.
18 http://www.the-news.net/cgi-bin/article.pl?id=850-6
19 This was publicised as 'torture' rather than domestic violence.
20 http://archive.thisisbradford.co.uk/2007/9/18/202428.html
21 http://www.womensaid.org.uk/domestic-violence-survivors-handbook.asp?
section=00010001000800010031003#Woman%20and%20men,%20victims
%20and%20survivors

2 What is domestic abuse?

1 All names and identifying details of women in the DASH study described or
quoted in this book have been changed.
2 http://www.telegraphindia.com/1050612/asp/look/story_4851495.asp
3 http://uk.news.yahoo.com/21/20090331/tuk-woman-bit-off-boyfriend-s-tongue-
6323e80.html
4 hubpages.com/hub/Where-Are-They-Now-John-Wayne-Bobbit
5 www.crimeandjustice.org.uk/opus191
6 Personal correspondence and conversations with Erin Pizzey and others working
in the area of domestic violence.
7 www.renewamerica.us/columns/roberts/080324

3 Psychology, feminism and ideology

1 www.homeoffice.gov.uk/about-us/news/domestic-violence-report
2 http://www.womensaid.org.uk/domestic-violence-articles.asp?section=
00010001002200390001&itemid=1279
3 Although the word and concept of 'therapy' is not permitted within the
framework.
4 http://www.des.emory.edu/mfp/301/301JamesOnSelf.pdf

4 The social construction of domestic abuse

1 http://dictionary.reference.com/browse/myth
2 http://www.niwaf.org/Domesticviolence/myths.htm
3 http://www.hupd.harvard.edu/domestic_violence.php
4 http://www.menweb.org/battered/batfact.htm
5 http://www.harrysnews.com/tgDemonizingMen.htm
6 http://menshealth.uws.edu.au/documents/DV%20demonising%20men.htm
7 Now renamed 'Refuge'.
8 http://www.independent.co.uk/news/uk/this-britain/george-carman-was-a-wife
beating-drunk-says-son-663284.html
9 http://www.reuters.com/article/newsOne/idUSL0919437820080709?rpc=64

5 Public perceptions and moral tales

1 We decided to use the term 'domestic violence' because we considered that this
would be more commonly understood by the general population.
2 A total of 1,340 questionnaires were returned, representing a response rate of
40.8 per cent.

3 I am translating 'nagging' as women disagreeing with a man's behaviour or decision.
4 A tabloid weekly newspaper in the UK.
5 http://news.bbc.co.uk/1/hi/uk/271848.stm
6 These stories are reported across various news and 'showbiz' websites. Two examples are: www.sfgate.com/cgi-bin/blogs/sfgate/detail?blogid=7&entry_id=10003; telegraph.co.uk/news/uknews/1531799/
7 Royal Courts of Justice, 17 March 2008, Case: FD06DO3721, Mr Justice Bennett.
8 telegraph.co.uk/news/uknews/1584085
9 www.officialpiersmorgan.com/2009/04/page/2
10 Royal Courts of Justice, 17 March 2008, Case: FD06DO3721, Mr Justice Bennett.
11 www.guardian.co.uk/uk/2008/mar/18/law.divorce1
12 http://www.bbc.co.uk/politics97/diana/panorama.html
13 www.guardian.co.uk/uk/mccartneydivorce
14 en.wikipedia.org/wiki/O._J._Simpson
15 www.heyugly.org/DomesticViolence.php
16 www.heyugly.org/DomesticViolence.php
17 www.mtv.com/news/articles/1604577/20090209/brown__chris__18_.jhtml
18 howhype.com/story/rhianna_s_alleged_return_to_chris_brown_infuriates

6 Lived experience and the 'material-discursive-intrapsychic' self

1 See Nicolson (1998) for a further discussion in the context of a longitudinal qualitative study of depression across the transition to motherhood.
2 Giddens (2003: 7) notes however that the practical level of consciousness lacks a theoretical place in Freudian psychoanalysis.

7 Domestic abuse across generations

1 Intergenerational cycles here do not refer to Walker's 'cycle of violence' model as described in Chapter 3.
2 I use this reference as it is a 'reader' with original essays by Freud himself.
3 A British television programme.
4 My emphasis.
5 I am making a general comment here. Winnicott and Fairbairn, whose 'school' was named 'object relations', took a somewhat distinct perspective on object relations from that of Klein, whose work was referred to as 'Kleinian'. However the emphasis for the purposes of the case I am making is similar – it is a focus on the importance of the very first relationships for human psychology.
6 When a person is under extreme pressure they will return psychically to that infantile state.
7 That is, fifty pence, which is a coin used in electric or gas meters.

8 'Doing' domestic violence

1 NB I only have original data from the woman's and not the man's point of view.
2 Chodorow's emphasis.

REFERENCES

Abrams, K.M. and G.E. Robinson (1998) Stalking. Part I: an overview of the problem. *Canadian Journal of Psychiatry* 43(5): 473–476.

Adams, D. (1986) Treatment models of men who batter: a profeminist analysis. In K. Yllö and M. Bograd (eds) *Feminist Perspectives on Wife Abuse*. Newbury Park, CA: Sage, 176–199.

Ainsworth, M.D.S. (1996) Attachments and other affectional bonds across the life cycle. In C. Murray Parkes, J. Stevenson-Hinde and P. Marris (eds) *Attachment Across the Life Cycle*. London: Routledge, 33–51.

Allan, J. (2003) Mother blaming: a covert practice in therapeutic intervention. *Australian Social Work* 57(1): 57–70.

Allison, C.J., K. Bartholomew, O. Mayseless and D.G. Dutton (2008) Love as a battlefield: attachment and relationship dynamics in couples identified for male partner violence. *Journal of Family Issues* 29(1): 125–150.

Almeida, R.V. and T. Durkin (1999) The cultural context model: therapy for couples with domestic violence. *Journal of Marital and Family Therapy* 25(3): 313–324.

American Psychological Association (1996) *Violence and the Family*. Washington, DC: American Psychological Association.

Anastasio, P.A. and D.M. Costa (2004) Twice hurt: how newspaper coverage may reduce empathy and engender blame for female victims of crime. *Sex Roles* 51(9): 535–542.

Anda, R.F., V.J. Felitti, J.D. Bremner, J.D. Walker, C. Whitfield, B.D. Perry *et al.* (2006) The enduring effects of abuse and related adverse experiences in childhood. A convergence of evidence from neurobiology and epidemiology. *European Archives of Psychiatry and Clinical Neuroscience* 256(3): 174–186.

Anda, R.F., D.W. Brown, V.J. Felitti, J.D. Bremner, S.R. Dube and W.H. Giles (2007) Adverse childhood experiences and prescribed psychotropic medications in adults. *American Journal of Preventive Medicine* 32(5): 389–394.

Anderson, I., G. Beattie and C. Spencer (2001) Can blaming victims of rape be logical? Attribution theory and discourse analytic perspectives. *Human Relations* 54(4): 445–467.

Anderson, K.L. (1997) Gender, status, and domestic violence: an integration of feminist and family violence approaches. *Journal of Marriage and Family* 59(3): 655–669.

Anderson, K.L. (2005) Theorizing gender in intimate partner violence research. *Sex Roles* 52(11): 853–865.

Anderson, K.L. and D. Umberson (2001) Gendering violence: masculinity and power in men's accounts of domestic violence. *Gender and Society* 15(3): 358–380.

Andrews, B. and G.W. Brown (1988) Marital violence in the community. A biographical approach. *The British Journal of Psychiatry* 153(3): 305–312.

Anslow, J. (2008) Myth, Jung and the McC women. *British Journalism Review* 19(2): 58–65.

Archer, J. and S.M. Coyne (2005) An integrated review of indirect, relational, and social aggression. *Personality and Social Psychology Review* 9(3): 212–230.

Arendt, H. (2008) From Eichmann in Jerusalem: a report on the banality of evil. In N. Scheper-Hughes and P. Bourgois (eds) *Violence in War and Peace*. Oxford: Blackwell, 236–243.

Arias, I., J. Dankwort, U. Douglas, M.A. Dutton and K. Stein (2002) Violence against women: the state of batterer prevention programs. *Journal of Law, Medicine and Ethics* 30(3 Suppl): 157–165.

Armistead, N.E. (1974) *Reconstructing Social Psychology*. Harmondsworth: Penguin.

Armstrong, D. (1995) The rise of surveillance medicine. *Sociology of Health and Illness* 17(3): 393–404.

Audit Commission (2009) *When it Comes to the Crunch: How Councils are Responding to the Recession*. London: Audit Commission.

Auster, C. and S. Ohm (2000) Masculinity and femininity in contemporary American society: a reevaluation using the Bem sex-role inventory. *Sex Roles* 43(7): 499–528.

Babcock, J.C., N.S. Jacobson, J.M. Gottman and T.P. Yerington (2000) Attachment, emotional regulation, and the function of marital violence: differences between secure, preoccupied, and dismissing violent and nonviolent husbands. *Journal of Family Violence* 15(4): 391–409.

Babcock, J.C., C.E. Green and C. Robie (2004) Does batterers' treatment work? A meta-analytic review of domestic violence treatment. *Clinical Psychology Review* 23(8): 1023–1053.

Bacchus, L., G. Mezey and S. Bewley (2002) Women's perceptions and experiences of routine enquiry for domestic violence in a maternity service. *BJOG* 109(1): 9–16.

Bacchus, L., G. Mezey and S. Bewley (2006) A qualitative exploration of the nature of domestic violence in pregnancy. *Violence Against Women* 12(6): 588–604.

Bagshaw, D. and D. Chung (2000) *Women, Men and Domestic Violence*. Commonwealth of Australia.

Baldry, A.C. (2003) Bullying in schools and exposure to domestic violence. *Child Abuse and Neglect* 27(7): 713–732.

Bandura, A. (1977) Self-efficacy: toward a unifying theory of behavioral change. *Psycholical Review* 84(2): 191–215.

Banks-Wallace, J. (1998) Emancipatory potential of storytelling in a group. *Journal of Nursing Scholarship* 30(1): 17–22.

Banyard, V.L., E.G. Plante and M.M. Moynihan (2004) Bystander education: bringing a broader community perspective to sexual violence prevention. *Journal of Community Psychology* 32(1): 61–79.

Barnett, O., C.L. Miller-Perrin and R.D. Perrin (2005) *Family Violence across the Lifespan: An Introduction*. London: Sage.

Barzelatto, J. (1998) Understanding sexual and reproductive violence: an overview. *International Journal of Gynecology and Obstetrics* 63(Suppl 1): S13–S18.

Bates, L. and W. Brown (1998) Domestic violence: examining nurses' and doctors' management, attitudes and knowledge in an accident and emergency setting. *Australian Journal of Advanced Nursing* 15(3): 15–22.

Bayer, J.K., H. Hiscock, O.C. Ukoumunne, A. Price and M. Wake (2008) Early childhood aetiology of mental health problems: a longitudinal population-based study. *Journal of Child Psychology and Psychiatry* 49(11): 1166–1174.

Bem, S. (1993) *The Lenses of Gender*. New Haven: Yale University Press.

Bentzel, S.B. and R.O. York (1988) Influence of feminism and professional status upon service options for the battered woman. *Community Mental Health Journal* 24(1): 52–64.

Berger, P.L. and T. Luckmann (1966) *The Social Construction of Reality: A Treatise on the Sociology of Knowledge*. Garden City, NY: Anchor Books.

Berger, P.L. and T. Luckmann (1995) *The Social Construction of Reality*. Harmondsworth: Penguin.

Berns, N. (1999) 'My problem and how I solved it': domestic violence in women's magazines. *Sociological Quarterly* 40(1): 85–108.

Bettman, C. (2009) Patriarchy: the predominant discourse and fount of domestic violence. *Australian and New Zealand Journal of Family Therapy* 30(1): 15–28.

Bhatt, R.V. (1998) Domestic violence and substance abuse. *International Journal of Gynecology and Obstetrics* 63(Suppl 1): S25–S31.

Bifulco, A. (2002) Attachment style measurement: a clinical and epidemiological perspective. *Attachment and Human Development* 4(2): 180–188.

Bifulco, A. and P. Moran (1998) *Wednesday's Child: Research into Women's Experience of Neglect and Abuse in Childhood and Adult Depression*. London: Routledge.

Bifulco, A., O. Bernazzani, P.M. Moran and C. Ball (2000) Lifetime stressors and recurrent depression: preliminary findings of the Adult Life Phase Interview (ALPHI). *Social Psychiatry and Psychiatric Epidemiology* 35(6): 264–275.

Bifulco, A., P. Moran, R. Baines, A.S. Bunn and K. Stanford (2002) Exploring psychological abuse in childhood: II. Association with other abuse and adult clinical depression. *Bulletin of the Menninger Clinic* 66(3): 241–258.

Binney, G., G. Harkell and J. Nixon (1981) *Leaving Violent Men: A Study of Refuges and Housing for Abused Women*. Bristol: Women's Aid Federation England.

Blizard, R.A. and A.M. Bluhm (1994) Attachment to the abuser: integrating object-relations and trauma theories in treatment of abuse survivors. *Psychotherapy: Theory, Research, Practice, Training* 31(3): 383–390.

Borg, C. (2003) *Domestic Violence Against Women: Perceptions of the Maltese General Public*. Valetta: Ministry for Social Policy.

Bostock, J., M. Plumpton and R. Pratt (2009) Domestic violence against women: understanding social processes and women's experiences. *Journal of Community and Applied Social Psychology* 19(2): 95–110.

Bowlby, J. (1979) *The Making and Breaking of Affectional Bonds*. London: Tavistock.

175

Bowlby, J. (1980) *Attachment and Loss*. New York: Basic Books.

Bowlby, J. (1990) *A Secure Base: Parent–Child Attachment and Healthy Human Development*. New York: Basic Books.

Breckenridge, J. and J. Mulroney (2007) Leaving violent relationships and avoiding homelessness – providing a choice for women and their children. *New South Wales Public Health Bulletin* 18(5–6): 90–93.

Briere, J. and C.E. Jordan (2004) Violence against women: outcome complexity and implications for assessment and treatment. *Journal of Interpersonal Violence* 19(11): 1252–1276.

Broverman, I.K., D.M. Broverman, F.E. Clarkson, P.S. Rosenkrantz and S.R. Vogel (1970) Sex-role stereotypes and clinical judgments of mental health. *Journal of Consulting and Clinical Psychology* 34(1): 1–7.

Brown, A. and M. Testa (2008) Social influences on judgments of rape victims: the role of the negative and positive social reactions of others. *Sex Roles* 58(7): 490–500.

Brown, S.D. (2001) Psychology and the art of living. *Theory Psychology* 11(2): 171–192.

Brownmiller, S. (1975/1993) *Against Our Will: Men, Women and Rape*. New York: Ballantine Books.

Brush, L.D. (1990) Violent acts and injurious outcomes in married couples: methodological issues in the National Survey of Families and Households. *Gender and Society* 4(1): 56–67.

Buchbinder, E. and Z. Eisikovits (2003) Battered women's entrapment in shame: a phenomenological study. *American Journal of Orthopsychiatry* 73(4): 355–366.

Bullock, C.F. and J. Cubert (2002) Coverage of domestic violence fatalities by newspapers in Washington state. *Jounal of Interpersonal Violence* 17(5): 475–499.

Bureau of Justice Statistics Special Report (1995) *Violence Against Women: Estimates from the Redesigned Survey*. Washington, DC: US Bureau of Justice.

Burkitt, I. (1999) Between the dark and the light: power and the material contexts of social relations. In D.J. Nightingale and J. Cromby (eds) *Social Constructionist Psychology: A Critical Analysis of Theory and Practice*. Milton Keynes: Open University Press, 67–82.

Butler, J. (1988) Performative acts and gender constitution: an essay in phenomenology and feminist theory. *Theatre Journal* 40(4): 519–531.

Byrne, R.W. (2003) Imitation as behaviour parsing. *Philosophical Transactions of the Royal Society* 358: 529–536.

Caffo, E. and C. Belaise (2003) Psychological aspects of traumatic injury in children and adolescents. *Child and Adolescent Psychiatric Clinics of North America* 12(3): 493–535.

Camacho, C.M. and L.F. Alarid (2008) The significance of the victim advocate for domestic violence victims in municipal court. *Violence and Victims* 23(3): 288–300.

Campbell, A. (2002) *A Mind of Her Own: The Evolutionary Psychology of Women*. Oxford: Oxford University Press.

Campbell, J.C. (1990) Battered woman syndrome: a critical review. *Violence Update* 1(4): 10–11.

Capezza, N. and X. Arriaga (2008) Why do people blame victims of abuse? The role of stereotypes of women on perceptions of blame. *Sex Roles* 59(11): 839–850.

Caprioli, M. and M.A. Boyer (2001) Gender, violence, and international crisis. *Journal of Conflict Resolution* 45(4): 503–518.

Carll, E.K. (2003) News portrayal of violence and women: implications for public policy. *American Behavioral Scientist* 46(12): 1601–1610.

Carlson, B.E. (2005) The most important things learned about violence and trauma in the past 20 years. *Journal of Interpersonal Violence* 20(1): 119–126.

Carrillo, R. (2002) Overview of international human rights standards and other agreements and responses of the judicial system to violence against women. *International Journal of Gynecology and Obstetrics* 78(Suppl 1): S15–S20.

Chapple, C.L. (2003) Examining intergenerational violence: violent role modeling or weak parental controls? *Violence and Victims* 18: 143–162.

Chew-Graham, C., C. Bashir, K. Chantler, E. Burman and J. Batsleer (2002) South Asian women, psychological distress and self-harm: lessons for primary care trusts. *Health and Social Care in the Community* 10(5): 339–347.

Chodorow, N. (1978) *The Reproduction of Mothering.* Berkeley: University of California Press.

Chodorow, N. (1994) *Femininities, Masculinities, Sexualities: Freud and Beyond.* London: Free Association Books.

Choi, P.Y.L. (1995) What is this news on the menstrual cycle and premenstrual syndrome? Introduction. *Social Science and Medicine* 41(6): 759–760.

Choi, S. and J.P. Ryan (2006) Completing substance abuse treatment in child welfare: the role of co-occurring problems and primary drug of choice. *Child Maltreatment* 11(4): 313–325.

Chrisler, J.C. and S. Ferguson (2006) Violence against women as a public health issue. *Annals of the New York Academy of Sciences* 1087: 235–249.

Cody, A. (1996) Helping the vulnerable or condoning control within the family: where is nursing? *Journal of Advanced Nursing* 23(5): 882–886.

Cohn, F. (2008) The veil of silence around family violence: is protecting patients' privacy bad for health? *Journal of Clinical Ethics* 19(4): 321–329.

Coker, A.L., P.H. Smith, R.E. McKeown and M.J. King (2000) Frequency and correlates of intimate partner violence by type: physical, sexual, and psychological battering. *American Journal of Public Health* 90(4): 553–559.

Cook, J. and S. Bewley (2008) Acknowledging a persistent truth: domestic violence in pregnancy. *Journal of Royal Society of Medicine* 101(7): 358–363.

Corvo, K. and P.J. Johnson (2003) Vilification of the 'batterer': how blame shapes domestic violence policy and interventions. *Aggression and Violent Behavior* 8(3): 259–281.

Craig, M.E., J. Robyak, E.J. Torosian and J. Hummer (2006) A study of male veterans' beliefs toward domestic violence in a batterers intervention program. *Journal of Interpersonal Violence* 21(9): 1111–1128.

Criminal Statistics for England and Wales (1997) London: HMSO.

Crossley, M.L. (2003) Formulating narrative psychology: the limitations of contemporary social constructionism. *Narrative Inquiry* 13(2): 287–300.

Daly, M. (1984) *Gyn/Ecology.* London: Women's Press.

Danielsson, I., N. Olofsson and K.G. Gådin (2005) [Consequences of violence – a public health issue. Strong connection between violence/threat and illness in both women and men]. *Lakartidningen* 102(12–13): 938–940, 942.

Dankoski, M., M. Keiley, V. Thomas, P. Choice, S. Lloyd and B. Seery (2006)

Affect regulation and the cycle of violence against women: new directions for understanding the process. *Journal of Family Violence* 21(5): 327–339.

Danziger, K. (1997) *Naming the Mind: How Psychology Found its Language.* London: Sage.

Dasgupta, S.D. (2000) Charting the course: an overview of domestic violence in the South Asian community in the United States. *Journal of Social Distress and the Homeless* 9(3): 173–185.

Dasgupta, S.D. (2002) A framework for understanding women's use of nonlethal violence in intimate heterosexual relationships. *Violence Against Women* 8(11): 1364–1389.

Davhana-Maselesele, M. (2007) We are still trapped in the cycle of violence against women and children. *Curationis* 30(4): 3.

Davis, K. and B. Taylor (2002) Voices from the margins. Part 1: narrative accounts of indigenous family violence. *Contemporary Nurse* 14(1): 66–75.

Davis, R.E. (2002) 'The strongest women': exploration of the inner resources of abused women. *Qualitative Health Research* 12(9): 1248–1263.

DeJonghe, E.S., G.A. Bogat, A.A. Levendosky and A. von Eye (2008) Women survivors of intimate partner violence and post-traumatic stress disorder: prediction and prevention. *Journal of Postgraduate Medicine* 54(4): 294–300.

Dekeseredy, W.S. and M. Dragiewicz (2007) Understanding the complexities of feminist perspectives on woman abuse: a commentary on Donald G. Dutton's Rethinking Domestic Violence. *Violence Against Women* 13(8): 874–884.

Department of Health (2001) *Domestic Violence: A Resource Manual for Health Care Professionals.* London: NHS Executive.

Diamond, M.A. and S. Allcorn (2004) Moral violence in organisations: hierarchic dominance and the absence of potential space. *Organisational and Social Dynamics* 4(1): 22–45.

Dobash, R.E. and R.P. Dobash (1977/1978) Wife – the 'appropriate' victims of marital violence. *Victimology* 2(3–4): 426–442.

Dobash, R. and R. Dobash (1979) *Violence Against Wives: A Case Against the Patriarchy.* New York: Free Press.

Dobash, R.E. and R.P. Dobash (1984) The nature and antecedents of violent events. *British Journal of Criminology* 24(3): 269–288.

Dobash, R.E., R.P. Dobash, K. Cavanagh and R. Lewis (2004) Not an ordinary killer; just an ordinary guy: when men murder an intimate woman partner. *Violence Against Women* 10(6): 577–605.

Dobash, R.P., R.E. Dobash, M. Wilson and M. Daly (1992) The myth of sexual symmetry in marital violence. *Social Problems* 39(1): 71–91.

Dodge, K.A., J.E. Bates and G.A. Pettit (1990) Mechanisms in the cycle of violence. *Science* 250: 1678–1683.

Douki, S., F. Nacef, A. Belhadj, A. Bouasker and R. Ghachem (2003) Violence against women in Arab and Islamic countries. *Archives of Women's Mental Health* 6(3): 165–171.

Doumas, D.M., C.L. Pearson, J.E. Elgin and L. McKinley (2008) Adult attachment as a risk factor for intimate partner violence: the 'Mispairing' of partners' attachment styles. *Journal of Interpersonal Violence* 23(5): 616–634.

Downs, D.A. and J. Fisher (2005) Battered women syndrome: tool of justice or false hope in self-defence cases? In D.R. Loseke, R.J. Gelles and M.M. Cavanaugh (eds) *Current Controversies on Family Violence*. London: Sage, 241–256.

Dryden, C. (1999) *Being Married, Doing Gender: A Critical Analysis of Gender Relationships in Marriage*. London: Routledge.

Dryden, C., K. Doherty and P. Nicolson (2010) Accounting for the hero: a critical psycho-discursive approach to children's experience of domestic violence and the construction of masculinities. *British Journal of Social Psychology* 49(1): 189–205.

Dutton, D.G. (2000) Witnessing parental violence as a traumatic experience shaping the abusive personality. *Journal of Aggression, Maltreatment and Trauma* 3(1): 59–67.

Dutton, D. (2003) MCMI results for batterers: a response to Gondolf. *Journal of Family Violence* 18(4): 253–255.

Dutton, D.G. and K. Corvo (2006) Transforming a flawed policy: a call to revive psychology and science in domestic violence research and practice. *Aggression and Violent Behavior* 11(5): 457–483.

Dutton, D.G. and P.R. Kropp (2000) A review of domestic violence risk instruments. *Trauma Violence Abuse* 1(2): 171–181.

Dutton, D.G. and T.L. Nicholls (2005) The gender paradigm in domestic violence research and theory: Part 1 – The conflict of theory and data. *Aggression and Violent Behavior* 10: 680–714.

Dutton, M.A., K.J. Burghardt, S.G. Perrin, K.R. Chrestman and P.M. Halle (1994) Battered women's cognitive schemata. *Journal of Traumatic Stress* 7(2): 237–255.

Edleson, J.L. (1999) The overlap between child maltreatment and woman battering. *Violence Against Women* 5(2): 134–154.

Edley, N. (2001) Analysing masculinity: interpretative repertoires, ideological dilemmas and subject positions. In M.W.S. Yates and S. Taylor (eds) *Discourse as Data: A Guide for Analysis*. London: Sage, 189–228.

Ehrenreich, B. and D. English (1989) *For Her Own Good: One Hundred and Fifty Years of the Experts' Advice to Women*. New York: Doubleday/Anchor Books.

Ehrensaft, M.C., J. Brown, E. Smailes, H. Chen and J.G. Johnson (2003) Intergenerational transmission of partner violence: a 20-year prospective study. *Journal of Consulting and Clinical Psychology* 71(4): 741–753.

Ellsberg, M.C. (2006a) Violence against women and the Millennium Development Goals: facilitating women's access to support. *International Journal of Gynecology and Obstetrics* 94(3): 325–332.

Ellsberg, M.C. (2006b) Violence against women: a global public health crisis. *Scandinavian Journal of Public Health* 34(1): 1–4.

Ellsberg, M., L. Heise, R. Pena, S. Agurto and A. Winkvist (2001) Researching domestic violence against women: methodological and ethical considerations. *Studies in Family Planning* 32(1): 1–16.

Enosh, G. and E. Buchbinder (2005) The interactive construction of narrative styles in sensitive interviews: the case of domestic violence research. *Qualitative Inquiry* 11(4): 588–617.

Erez, E. (2002) Domestic violence and the criminal justice system: an overview. *Online Journal of Issues in Nursing* 7(1).

Ericksen, J.R. and A.D. Henderson (1992) Witnessing family violence: the children's experience. *Journal of Advanced Nursing* 17: 1200–1209.

Erikson, E. (1968/1977) *Childhood and Society*. London: Paladin.

Erlick Robinson, G. (2003) Violence against women in North America. *Archives of Women's Mental Health* 6(3): 185–191.

Esqueda, C. and L. Harrison (2005) The influence of gender role stereotypes, the woman's race, and level of provocation and resistance on domestic violence culpability attributions. *Sex Roles* 53(11): 821–834.

Essex, E.L., D. Petras and C.R. Massat (2007) Predictors of loneliness among court-involved and substance abusing mothers. *Women and Criminal Justice* 17(2): 63–74.

Ezer, T. (2008) Lessons from Africa: combating the twin epidemics of domestic violence and HIV/AIDS. *HIV AIDS Policy Law Review* 13(2–3): 57–62.

Fairbairn, W.R.D. (1944/1952) Endopsychic structures considered in terms of object relationship. In *Psychoanalytic Studies of the Personality*. London: Routledge & Kegan Paul, 82–136

Faludi, S. (1991) *Backlash*. New York: Crown.

Fanslow, J. and R. Norton (1994) Violence against women: priorities for public health research in New Zealand. *New Zealand Medical Journal* 107(972): 63–64.

Faramarzi, M., S. Esmailzadeh and S. Mosavi (2005) A comparison of abused and non-abused women's definitions of domestic violence and attitudes to acceptance of male dominance. *European Journal of Obstetrics and Gynecology and Reproductive Biology* 122(2): 225–231.

Featherstone, B. and L. Trinder (1997) Familiar subjects? Domestic violence and child welfare. *Child and Family Social Work* 2(3): 147–159.

Felson, R.B. (2002) *Violence and Gender Re-examined*. Washington, DC: American Psychological Association.

Fennema-Notestine, C., M.B. Stein, C.M. Kennedy, S.L. Archibald and T.L Jernigan (2002) Brain morphometry in female victims of intimate partner violence with and without posttraumatic stress disorder. *Biological Psychiatry* 52(11): 1089–1101.

Fergusson, D.M. and L.J. Horwood (1998) Exposure to interparental violence in childhood and psychosocial adjustment in young adulthood. *Child Abuse and Neglect* 22(5): 339–357.

Fernandez, M. (2006) Cultural beliefs and domestic violence. *Annals of the New York Academy of Sciences* 1087: 250–260.

Ferraro, K.J. (1996) The dance of dependency: a genealogy of domestic violence discourse. *Hypatia* 11(4): 77–91.

Ferraro, K.J. (1997) Battered women: strategies for survival. In P. Carderelli (ed.) *Violence Between Intimate Partners: Patterns, Causes and Effects*. Boston: Allyn and Bacon, 124–240.

Ferraro, K.J. and J.M. Johnson (1983) How women experience battering: the process of victimization. *Social Problems* 30(3): 325–339.

Ferro, A. and R. Basile (eds) (2009) *The Analytic Field: A Clinical Concept*. London: Karnac.

Fincham, F.D. and S.R.H. Beach (1999) Conflict in marriage: implications for working with couples. *Annual Review of Psychology* 50(1): 47–77.

Fisher, C.B. and M. Oransky (2008) Informed consent to psychotherapy: protecting the dignity and respecting the autonomy of patients. *Journal of Clinical Psychology* 64(5): 576–588.

Flitcraft, A.H. (1995) Clinical violence intervention: lessons from battered women.

Journal of Health Care for the Poor and Underserved 6(2): 187–195; discussion 195–197.

Fontes, L.A. (2004) Ethics in violence against women research: the sensitive, the dangerous, and the overlooked. *Ethics and Behavior* 14(2): 141–174.

Forrester, M. and C. Ramsden (2000) Discursive ethnomethodology: analysing power and resistance in talk. *Psychology, Crime and Law* 6: 281–304.

Foucault, M. (1976/1990) *The History of Sexuality, Volume 1: An Introduction.* New York: Vintage.

Fraser, N. (1989) *Unruly Practices: Power, Discourse, and Gender in Contemporary Social Theory.* Minneapolis: University of Minnesota Press.

Frattaroli, S. and S.P. Teret (2006) Understanding and informing policy implementation: a case study of the domestic violence provisions of the Maryland Gun Violence Act. *Evaluation Review* 30(3): 347–360.

French, M. (1979) *The Women's Room.* London: Sphere Books.

Freud, S. (1925) Some psychical consequences of the anatomical distinction between the sexes. In *Standard Edition of the Complete Works of Sigmund Freud*, ed. James Strachey. London: Hogarth, 19: 248–258.

Freud, S. (1926/1921) The question of lay analysis. In J. Strachey (ed.) *The Standard Edition of the Complete Psychological Works of Sigmund Freud* (Vol. XX). London: Hogarth Press.

Friedan, B. (1963) *The Feminine Mystique.* New York: Laurel.

Frost, M. (1999) Health visitors' perceptions of domestic violence: the private nature of the problem. *Journal of Advanced Nursing* 30(3): 589–596.

Gallagher, H.L. and C.D. Frith (2003) Functional imaging of 'theory of mind'. *Trends in Cognitive Sciences* 7(2): 77–83.

Galvani, S. (2006) Alcohol and domestic violence: women's views. *Violence Against Women* 12(7): 641–662.

Gannon, L. (1999) *Women and Aging: Transcending the Myths.* London: Routledge.

Garcia-Moreno, C., L. Heise, H.A. Jansen, M. Ellsberg and C. Watts (2005) Public health. Violence against women. *Science* 310(5752): 1282–1283.

Garriga, R.M. (2007) [Patriarchate as a cause of violence; the difficulty to identify abusive relationships in one's own home]. *Revista de Enfermeria* 30(7–8): 42–44.

Gay, P. (2007) *The Freud Reader.* London: Vintage.

Gelles, R.J. (1980) Violence in the family: a review of research in the seventies. *Journal of Marriage and the Family* 42(4): 873–885.

Gelles, R.J. (1997) *Intimate Violence in Families.* London: Sage.

Gelles, R.J. (2000) Public policy for violence against women: 30 years of successes and remaining challenges. *American Journal of Preventive Medicine* 19(4): 298–301.

Gelles, R.J. and M. Straus (1988) *Intimate Violence.* New York: Simon and Schuster.

Gerber, G. (1991) Gender stereotypes and power: perceptions of the roles in violent marriages. *Sex Roles* 24(7–8): 439–458.

Giddens, A. (2003) *The Constitution of Society.* Cambridge: Polity Press.

Gilligan, C. (1993) *In a Different Voice: Psychological Theory and Women's Development.* Cambridge, MA: Harvard University Press.

Gilligan, J. (2000) *Violence: Reflections on Our Deadliest Epidemic.* London: Jessica Kingsley.

Gillis, A.R. and H. John (1983) Bystander apathy and the territorial imperative. *Sociological Inquiry* 53(4): 449–460.

Gillis, J.R., S.L. Diamond, P. Jebely, V. Orekhovsky, E.M. Ostovich, K. MacIsaac, *et al.* (2006) Systemic obstacles to battered women's participation in the judicial system: when will the status quo change? *Violence Against Women* 12(12): 1150–1168.

Gilson, S.F. (1998) The YWCA Women's Advocacy Program: a case study of domestic violence and sexual assault services. *Journal of Community Practice* 4(4): 1–26.

Goffman, I. (1959/1990) *The Presentation of Self in Everyday Life*. Harmondsworth: Penguin.

Goldner, V. (1999) Morality and multiplicity: perspectives on the treatment of violence in intimate life. *Journal of Marital and Family Therapy* 25(3): 325–336.

Goldner, V., P. Penn, M. Sheinberg and G. Walker (1990) Love and violence: gender paradoxes in volatile attachments. *Family Process* 29(4): 343–364.

Gondolf, E.W. (1987) Changing men who batter: a developmental model for integrated interventions. *Journal of Family Violence* 2(4): 335–349.

Gondolf, E.W. (2007) Theoretical and research support for the Duluth model: a reply to Dutton and Corvo. *Aggression and Violent Behavior* 12(6): 644–657.

Good, J.M.M. (2007) The affordances for social psychology of the ecological approach to social knowing. *Theory Psychology* 17(2): 265–295.

Gordon, L. (1988) *Heroes of Their Own Lives: The Politics and History of Family Violence*. New York: Viking.

Grace, S. (1995) *Policing Domestic Violence in the 1990s*. London: HMSO.

Gracia, E. (2004) Unreported cases of domestic violence against women: towards an epidemiology of social silence, tolerance, and inhibition. *Journal of Epidemiology and Community Health* 58(7): 536–537.

Green, L. (2008) Living in a state of fear. In N. Scheper-Hughes and P. Bourgois (eds) *Violence in War and Peace*. Oxford: Blackwell, 186–195.

Griffiths, H. and J. Halna (2003) Feminist qualitative methodology: evaluating policing of domestic violence. In T. Skinner, M. Hester and E. Malos (eds) *Researching Gender Violence: Feminist Methodology in Action*. Devon: Willan Publishing, 22–43.

Gubrium, J.F. and J.A. Holstein (1998) Narrative practice and the coherence of personal stories. *Sociological Quarterly* 39(1): 163–187.

Haaken, J. (2010) *Hard Knocks: Domestic Violence and the Psychology of Storytelling*. Hove, UK: Routledge.

Haaken, J. and N. Yragui (2003) Going underground: conflicting perspectives on domestic violence shelter practices. *Feminism Psychology* 13(1): 49–71.

Hacking, I. (1999) *The Social Construction of What?* Cambridge, MA: Harvard University Press.

Hagerman-White, C. (2006) *Combating Violence Against Women: Stocktaking Study on the Measures and Actions Taken in Council of Europe Member States*. Strasbourg: Directorate of Human Rights.

Hague, G. and A. Mullender (2006) Who listens? The voices of domestic violence survivors in service provision in the United Kingdom. *Violence Against Women* 12(6): 568–587.

Hague, G., E. Malos and W. Dear (1996) *Multi-Agency Work and Domestic Violence*. Bristol: Policy Press.

Haight, W.L., W.S. Shim, L.M. Linn and L. Swinford (2007) Mothers' strategies for protecting children from batterers: the perspectives of battered women involved in child protective services. *Child Welfare* 86(4): 41–62.

Hamberger, L.K. (1997) Female offenders in domestic violence – a look at actions in their context. *Journal of Aggression, Maltreatment and Trauma* 1(1): 117–129.

Hammond, N. (1989) Lesbian victims of relationship violence. *Women and Therapy* 8(1): 89–105.

Hanmer, J., S. Griffiths and D. Jerwood (1998) *Arresting Evidence: Domestic Violence and Repeat Victimisation* (No. 104). London: Home Office, Policing and Reducing Crime Unit.

Hanna, C. (1996) No right to choose: mandated victim participation in domestic violence prosecutions. *Harvard Law Review* 109: 1850–1909.

Hare, S.C. (2006) What do battered women want? Victims' opinions on prosecution. *Violence and Victims* 21(5): 611–628.

Harre, R. and P.F. Secord (1972) *The Explanation of Social Behaviour*. Oxford: Blackwell.

Harris, G.A. (2006) Conjoint therapy and domestic violence: treating the individuals and the relationship. *Counselling Psychology Quarterly* 19(4): 373–379.

Harris, M., R.D. Fallot and R.W. Berley (2005) Qualitative interviews on substance abuse relapse and prevention among female trauma survivors. *Psychiatric Services* 56(10): 1292–1296.

Harris, R.J. and C.A. Cook (1994) Attributions about spouse abuse: it matters who the batterers and victims are. *Sex Roles* 30(7): 553–565.

Harrison, L.A. and C.W. Esqueda (1999) Myths and stereotypes of actors involved in domestic violence: implications for domestic violence culpability attributions. *Aggression and Violent Behavior* 4(2): 129–138.

Hattendorf, J. and T.R. Tollerud (1997) Domestic violence: counseling strategies that minimize the impact of secondary victimization. *Perspectives in Psychiatric Care* 33(1): 14–23.

Hearn, J. (1998) *The Violences of Men*. London: Sage.

Heimann, P. (1950) On countertransference. *International Journal of Psychoanalysis* 31: 81–84. Reprinted in S.T. Levy and A.C. Furman (eds) *Influential Papers from the 1950s*. London: Karnac, 27–34, 2003.

Heise, L.L., J. Pitanguy and A. Germain (1994) *Violence Against Women. The Hidden Health Burden*. Washington, DC: World Bank Discussion Papers 255.

Heise, L., M. Ellsberg and M. Gottemoeller (1999) *Ending Violence Against Women*. Population Reports, Series L. No. 11.

Henderson, A., K. Bartholomew and D.G. Dutton (1997) He loves me; he loves me not: attachment and separation resolution of abused women. *Journal of Family Violence* 12(2): 169–191.

Henderson, A., K. Bartholomew, S.J. Trinke and M.J. Kwong (2005) When loving means hurting: an exploration of attachment and intimate abuse in a community sample. *Journal of Family Violence* 20(4): 219–230.

Hendy, H.M., K. Weiner, J. Bakerofskie, D. Eggen, C. Gustitus and K.C. McLeod (2003) Comparison of six models for violent romantic relationships in college men and women. *Journal of Interpersonal Violence* 18(6): 645–665.

Henning, K. and L. Feder (2004) A comparison of men and women arrested for domestic violence: who presents the greater threat? *Journal of Family Violence* 19(2): 69–80.

Henriques, J., W. Hollway, C. Urwin, C. Venn and V. Walkerdine (1984/1998) *Changing the Subject: Psychology, Social Regulation and Subjectivity*. London: Routledge.

Hepburn, A. and S. Wiggins (eds) (2007) *Discursive Research in Practice: New Approaches to Psychology and Interaction*. Cambridge: Cambridge University Press.

Herman, J.L. (1992a) *Trauma and Recovery: From Domestic Abuse to Political Terror*. London: Pandora.

Herman, J.L. (1992b) Complex PTSD: a syndrome in survivors of prolonged and repeated trauma. *Journal of Traumatic Stress* 5(3): 377–391.

Herman, J.L. (2004) From trauma and recovery: the aftermath of violence – from domestic abuse to political terror. In N. Scheper-Hughes and P. Bourgois (eds) *Violence in War and Peace: An Anthology*. Oxford: Blackwell, 368–371.

Heyzer, N. (1998) Working towards a world free from violence against women: UNIFEM's contribution. *Gender and Development* 6(3): 17–26.

Hill, P.S. and H.T. Ly (2004) Women are silver, women are diamonds: conflicting images of women in the Cambodian print media. *Reproductive Health Matters* 12(24): 104–115.

Hollway, W. and T. Jefferson (2000/2001) *Doing Qualitative Research Differently: Free Association, Narrative and the Interview Method*. London: Sage.

Holt, S., H. Buckley and S. Whelan (2008) The impact of exposure to domestic violence on children and young people: a review of the literature. *Child Abuse and Neglect* 32(8): 797–810.

Home Office (2003) *SAFETY AND JUSTICE: The Government's Proposals on Domestic Violence*. London: HMSO.

Home Office (2006) *Lessons Learned from the Domestic Violence Enforcement Campaigns*. London: HM Government.

Home Office (2009) *Together We Can End Violence Against Women and Girls: A Consultation Paper*. London: HM Government.

Hossein, K. (2007) *A Thousand Splendid Suns*. London: Bloomsbury.

Humphreys, C. (1999) Avoidance and confrontation: social work practice in relation to domestic violence and child abuse. *Child and Family Social Work* 4(1): 77–87.

Humphreys, C. (2007) A health inequalities perspective on violence against women. *Health and Social Care in the Community* 15(2): 120–127.

Humphreys, C. and S. Joseph (2004) Domestic violence and the politics of trauma. *Women's Studies International Forum* 27(5–6): 559–570.

Humphreys, C. and R. Thiara (2003) Mental health and domestic violence: 'I call it symptoms of abuse'. *British Journal of Social Work* 33(2): 209–226.

Humphreys, C., A. Mullender, P. Lowe, G. Hague, H. Abrahams and M. Hester (2001) Domestic violence and child abuse: developing sensitive policies and guidance. *Child Abuse Review* 10(3): 183–197.

Humphreys, C., A. Mullender, R. Thiara and A. Skamballis (2006) 'Talking to my mum': developing communication between mothers and children in the aftermath of domestic violence. *Journal of Social Work* 6(1): 53–63.

Hunter, M.S. (1990) Psychological and somatic experience of the menopause: a prospective study. *Psychosomatic Medicine* 52(3): 357–367.

Hyman, A. and R.A. Chez (1995) Mandatory reporting of domestic violence by health care providers: a misguided approach. *Women's Health Issues* 5(4): 208–213.

Iliffe, G. and L.G. Steed (2000) Exploring the counselor's experience of working with perpetrators and survivors of domestic violence. *Journal of Interpersonal Violence* 15(4): 393–412.

Israel, E. and C. Stover (2009) Intimate partner violence: the role of the relationship between perpetrators and children who witness violence. *Journal of Interpersonal Violence*. Only available electronically – 0886260509334044.

Jacobson, N.S. (1994) Rewards and dangers in researching domestic violence. *Family Process* 33(1): 81–85.

Jecker, N.S. (1993) Privacy beliefs and the violent family. Extending the ethical argument for physician intervention. *Jama* 269(6): 776–780.

Jenkin, A. and J. Millward (2006) A moral dilemma in the emergency room: confidentiality and domestic violence. *Accident and Emergency Nursing* 14(1): 38–42.

Jennings, J.L. (1987) History and issues in the treatment of battering men: a case for unstructured group therapy. *Journal of Family Violence* 2(3): 193–213.

Johnson, M.P. (2006) Conflict and control: gender symmetry and asymmetry in domestic violence. *Violence Against Women* 12(11): 1003–1018.

Johnson, M.P. and K.J. Ferraro (2000) Research on domestic violence in the 1990s: making distinctions. *Journal of Marriage and the Family* 62: 948–963.

Jones, L., M. Hughes and U. Unterstaller (2001) Post-traumatic stress disorder (PTSD) in victims of domestic violence: a review of the research. *Trauma, Violence, & Abuse* 2(2): 99–119.

Kasturirangan, A., S. Krishnan and S. Riger (2004) The impact of culture and minority status on women's experience of domestic violence. *Trauma, Violence, & Abuse* 5(4): 318–332.

Kearney, M.H. (2001) Enduring love: a grounded formal theory of women's experience of domestic violence. *Research in Nursing and Health* 24: 270–282.

Kelly, L. (1988) *Surviving Sexual Violence*. Minneapolis: University of Minnesota Press.

Kelly, L. (1996) When does the speaking profit us? Reflections of the challenges of developing feminist perspectives on abuse and violence by women. In M. Hester, L. Kelly and J. Radford (eds) *Women, Violence and Male Power*. Buckingham: Open University Press, 34–49.

Kelly, L. (2001) The interconnectedness of domestic violence and child abuse: challenges for research, policy and practice. In A. Mullender and R. Morley (eds) *Children Living with Domestic Violence: Putting Men's Abuse of Women on the Child Care Agenda*. London: Whiting and Birch, 43–56.

Kelly, L. and J. Radford (1990) 'Nothing really happened': the invalidation of women's experiences of sexual violence. *Critical Social Policy* 10(30): 39–53.

Kilpatrick, K.L. and L.M. Williams (1998) Potential mediators of post-traumatic stress disorder in child witnesses to domestic violence. *Child Abuse and Neglect* 22(4): 319–330.

Kim, J.C., C.H. Watts, J.R. Hargreaves, L.X. Ndhlovu, G. Phetla, L.A. Morison, *et al.* (2007) Understanding the impact of a microfinance-based intervention on women's empowerment and the reduction of intimate partner violence in South Africa. *American Journal of Public Health* 97(10): 1794–1802.

Kimmel, M.S. (2002) 'Gender symmetry' in domestic violence: a substantive and methodological research review. *Violence Against Women* 8(11): 1332–1363.

Kimura, M. (2008) Narrative as a site of subject construction: the 'comfort women' debate. *Feminist Theory* 9(1): 5–24.

Kirkwood, C. (1993) *Leaving Abusive Partners: From the Scars of Survival to the Wisdom for Change.* London: Sage.

Kitzinger, C. and S. Wilkinson (1993) The precariousness of heterosexual feminist identities. In M. Kennedy, C. Lubelska and V. Walsh (eds) *Making Connections: Women's Studies, Women's Movements, Women's Lives.* Oxford: Blackwell, 24–38.

Kitzinger, J. (1995) 'I'm sexually attractive but I'm powerful': young women negotiating sexual reputation. *Women's Studies International Forum* 18(2): 187–196.

Klein, E., J. Campbell, E. Soler and M. Ghez (1997) *Ending Domestic Violence.* London: Sage.

Klein, M. (1959) Our adult world and its roots in infancy. In M. Klein, *Envy and Gratitude and Other Works 1946–1963.* London: Virago, 1993, 247–263.

Klein, R.C. (1998) *Family Violence: Multi-Disciplinary Perspectives.* London: Routledge.

Kohlberg, L. (1973) The claim to moral adequacy of a highest stage of moral judgment. *Journal of Philosophy* 70(18): 630–646.

Kopper, B.A. (1996) Gender, gender identity, rape myth acceptance, and time of initial resistance on the perception of acquaintance rape blame and avoidability. *Sex Roles* 34(1): 81–93.

Krantz, G. and C. Garcia-Moreno (2005) Violence against women. *Journal of Epidemiology and Community Health* 59(10): 818–821.

Kropp, P.R. (2004) Some questions regarding spousal assault risk assessment. *Violence Against Women* 10(6): 676–697.

Kropp, P.R. and S. Hart (2000) The Spousal Assault Risk Assessment (SARA) guide: reliability and validity in adult male offenders. *Law and Human Behavior* 24(1): 101–118.

Kurri, K. and J. Wahlstrom (2001) Dialogical management of morality in domestic violence counselling. *Feminism Psychology* 11(2): 187–208.

Kurz, D. (1989) Social science perspectives on wife abuse: current debates and future directions. *Gender and Society* 3(4): 489–505.

Kwiatkowska, A. (1998) Gender stereotypes and beliefs about family violence in Poland. In R.C. Klein (ed.) *Family Violence: Multi-Disciplinary Perspectives.* London: Routledge, 129–154.

Larsen, T., P. Brodersen, A. Larsen and F. Bendtsen (1985) [Violence against women in their partnerships. IV. Pattern of contact with public institutions]. *Ugeskr Laeger* 147(22): 1801–1804.

Latané, B. and J. Darley (1969) Bystander 'apathy'. *American Scientist* 57(2): 244–268.

Lee, R.M. and E.A. Stanko (2003) *Researching Violence.* London: Routledge.

Letellier, P. (1994) Gay and bisexual male domestic violence victimization:

challenges to feminist theory and responses to violence. *Violence and Victims* 9(2): 95–106.

Liebling, A. and B. Stanko (2001) Allegiance and ambivalence. Some dilemmas in researching disorder and violence. *British Journal of Criminology* 41(3): 421–430.

Loseke, D.R. (2001) Lived realities and formula stories of 'battered women'. In J.H.J. Gubrium (ed.) *Institutional Selves: Personal Troubles in Organizational Context*. Tampa: Oxford University Press, 107–126.

Loseke, D.R. (2005) Through a sociological lens: the complexities of family violence. In D.R. Loseke, R.J. Gelles and M.M. Cavanaugh (eds) *Current Controversies on Family Violence*. London: Sage, 35–48.

Loseke, D.R. and S.E. Cahill (1984) The social construction of deviance: experts on battered women. *Social Problems* 31(3): 296–310.

Loseke, D.R. and D. Kurt (2005) Men's violence toward women is the serious social problem. In D.R. Loseke, R.J. Gelles and M.M. Cavanaugh (eds) *Current Controversies on Family Violence*. London: Sage, 79–96.

Loseke, D.R., R.J. Gelles and M.M. Cavanaugh (eds) (2005) *Current Controversies on Family Violence*. London: Sage.

Ludermir, A.B., L.B. Schraiber, A.F. D'Oliveira, I. Franca-Junior and H.A. Jansen (2008) Violence against women by their intimate partner and common mental disorders. *Social Science and Medicine* 66(4): 1008–1018.

Ludlam, M. and V. Nyberg (eds) (2007) *Couple Attachments: Theoeretical and Clinical Studies*. London: Karnac.

Luyt, R. (2003) Rhetorical representations of masculinities in South Africa: moving towards a material-discursive understanding of men. *Journal of Community and Applied Social Psychology* 13(1): 46–69.

Malik, N.M., J. Silverman, K. Wang and C. Janczewski (2008) Domestic violence and dependency courts: the Greenbook demonstration experience. *Journal of Interpersonal Violence* 23(7): 956–980.

Malson, H.M. (1997) Anorexic bodies and the discursive production of feminine excess. In J.M. Ussher (ed.) *Body Talk: The Material and Discursive Regulation of Sexuality, Madness, and Reproduction*. London: Routledge, 243–245.

Mann, R.M. (2000) *Who Owns Domestic Abuse? The Local Politics of a Social Problem*. Buffalo: University of Toronto Press.

Margolin, B., G. Burman and R.S. John (1993) America's angriest home videos: behavioral contingencies observed in home reenactments of marital conflict. *Journal of Consulting and Clinical Psychology* 61(1): 28–39.

Markowitz, F.E. (2001) Attitudes and family violence: linking intergenerational and cultural theories. *Journal of Family Violence* 16(2): 205–218.

Marris, P. (1996) The social construction of uncertainty. In C. Murray Parkes, J. Stevenson-Hinde and P. Marris (eds) *Attachment Across the Life Cycle*. London: Routledge, 77–92.

Martin, S.G. (2002) Children exposed to domestic violence: psychological considerations for health care practitioners. *Holistic Nursing Practice* 16(3): 7–15.

Martin, S. (2009) Psychological perspectives on domestic violence: feminism in a tight spot. *Psychology of Women Section of the British Psychological Society Annual Conference*. Cumberland Lodge.

Martin, S.H. and R. Bachman (1997) The relationship of alcohol to injury in assault cases. In M. Galanter (ed.) *Recent Developments in Alcoholism, Volume 13: Alcohol and Violence*. New York: Plenum Press, 41–56.

Martin, S.L., K.E. Moracco, J. Garro, A.O. Tsui, L.L. Kupper, J.L. Chase, *et al.* (2002) Domestic violence across generations: findings from Northern India. *International Journal of Epidemiology* 31(3): 560–572.

Mateas, M. and P. Sengers (2002) Narrative intelligence. *Advances in Consciousness Research* 46: 1–26.

McAdams, D.P., J. Reynolds, M. Lewis, A.H. Patten and P.J. Bowman (2001) When bad things turn good and good things turn bad: sequences of redemption and contamination in life narrative and their relation to psychosocial adaptation in midlife adults and in students. *Personality and Social Psychology Bulletin* 27(4): 474–485.

McCarroll, J.E., S. Castro, E.M. Nelson, Z. Fan, P.K. Evans and A. Rivera (2008) Characteristics of domestic violence incidents reported at the scene by volunteer victim advocates. *Military Medicine* 173(9): 865–870.

McCarry, M. (2005) Conducting social research with young people: Ethical consideration. In T. Skinner, M. Hester and E. Malos (eds) *Researching Gender Violence: Feminist Methodology in Action*. Collumpton, Devon: Willan Publishing, 87–104.

McConaghy, J.S. and R.R. Cottone (1998) The systemic view of violence: an ethical perspective. *Family Process* 37(1): 51–63.

McCosker, H., A. Barnard, and R. Gerber (2004) Phenomenographic study of women's experiences of domestic violence during the childbearing years. *Online Journal of Issues in Nursing* 9(1): 12.

McFarlane, J.M., J.Y. Groff, J.A. O'Brien and K. Watson (2005) Prevalence of partner violence against 7,443 African American, White, and Hispanic women receiving care at urban public primary care clinics. *Public Health Nursing* 22(2): 98–107.

McLeod, J. and S. Balamoutsou (1996) Representing narrative process in therapy: qualitative analysis of a single case. *Counselling Psychology Quarterly* 9(1): 61–76.

Mead, G.H. (1934) *Mind, Self and Society*. Chicago: University of Chicago Press.

Mechanic, M.B. (2004) Beyond PTSD: mental health consequences of violence against women: a response to Briere and Jordan. *Journal of Interpersonal Violence* 19(11): 1283–1289.

Meyers, M. (1994) News of battering. *Journal of Communication* 44(2): 47–63.

Meyers, M. (1997) *News Coverage of Violence Against Women*. London: Sage.

Miller, P.J., R. Potts, H. Fung, L. Hoogstra and J. Mintz (1990) Narrative practices and the social construction of self in childhood. *American Ethnologist* 17(2): 292–311.

Miller, S.L. (1994) Expanding the boundaries: toward a more inclusive and integrated study of intimate violence. *Violence and Victims* 9(2): 183–194.

Mirrlees-Black, C. (1999) Domestic violence: findings from a new British Crime Survey self-completion questionnaire. Home Office Research Study 191. http://www.homeoffice.gov.uk/rds/pdfs/hors191.pdf

Mirrlees-Black, C. and C. Byron (1999) Results of a questionnaire attached to the British Crime Survey. http://homeoffice.gov.uk/crimpol/crimreduc/domestic violence/

Moe, A.M. (2007) Silenced voices and structured survival: battered women's help seeking. *Violence Against Women* 13(7): 676–699.

Moran, L.J. and B. Skeggs (2003) *Sexuality and the Politics of Violence and Safety*. London: Routledge.

Morgan, M. (2001) First contacts: the therapist's 'couple state of mind' as a factor in the containment of couples seen for consultations. In F. Grier (ed.) *Brief Encounters with Couples: Some Analytical Perspectives*. London: Karnac, 17–32.

Morley, R. and A. Mullender (1992) Hype or hope? The importation of pro-arrest policies and batterers' programmes from North America to Britain as key measures for preventing violence against women in the home. *International Journal of Law, Policy and the Family* 6(2): 265–288.

Morley, R. and A. Mullender (2001) Domestic violence and children. In A. Mullender and R. Morley (eds) *Children Living with Domestic Violence: Putting Men's Abuse of Women on the Child Care Agenda*. London: Whiting and Birch, 24–42.

Motz, A. (2008) *The Psychology of Female Violence: Crimes Against the Body*. London: Routledge.

Muehlenhard, C.L. and L.A. Kimes (1999) The social construction of violence: the case of sexual and domestic violence. *Personality and Social Psychology Review* 3(3): 234–245.

Muhlbauer, V. (2006) Domestic violence in Israel. *Annals of the New York Academy of Sciences 1087* (Violence and Exploitation Against Women and Girls): 301–310.

Mullender, A. (1996) *Rethinking Domestic Violence: The Social Work and Probation Response*. London: Routledge.

Mullender, A. (1997) Domestic violence and social work: the challenge to change. *Critical Social Policy* 17(50): 53–78.

Mullender, A. and G. Hague (2005) Giving a voice to women survivors of domestic violence through recognition as a service user group. *British Journal of Social Work* 35(8): 1321–1341.

Mullender, A. and R. Morley (eds) (2001) *Children Living with Domestic Violence: Putting Men's Abuse of Women on the Child Care Agenda*. London: Whiting and Birch.

Murray, S. and A. Powell (2009) 'What's the problem?': Australian public policy constructions of domestic and family violence. *Violence Against Women* 15(5): 532–552.

Nasrullah, M., S. Haqqi and K.J. Cummings (2009) The epidemiological patterns of honour killing of women in Pakistan. *European Journal of Public Health* 19(2): 193–197.

National Family Violence Survey (1985) http://www.childtrends.org/Files/NFVS1985.pdf

Neft, N. and A.D. Levine (1997) *Where Women Stand: An International Report on the Status of Women in 140 Countries*. New York: Random House.

Niarchos, C. (1995) Women, war, and rape: challenges facing the International Tribunal for the Former Yugoslavia. *Human Rights Quarterly* 17(4): 649–690.

NiCarthy, G. (1987) *The Ones Who Got Away*. Seattle: Seal.

Nicolson, P. (1996) *Gender, Power and Organisation: A Psychological Perspective*. London: Routledge.

Nicolson, P. (1998) *Postnatal Depression: Psychology, Science and the Transition to Motherhood*. London: Routledge.

Nicolson, P. (2009) The social construction of domestic abuse: a double-edged sword? *The Psychology of Women Section of the British Psychological Society Annual Conference*. Cumberland Lodge.

Nicolson, P. and R. Wilson (2004) Is domestic violence a gender issue? Views from a British city. *Journal of Community and Applied Social Psychology* 14(4): 266–283.

Nienhuis, N.E. (2005) Theological reflections on violence and abuse. *Journal of Pastoral Care and Counseling* 59(1–2): 109–123.

Nightingale, D. and J. Cromby (1999) *Social Constructionist Psychology: A Critical Analysis of Theory and Practice*. Milton Keynes: Open University Press.

O'Brien, E.M., M.C. Black, L.R. Carley–Baxter and T.R. Simon (2006) Sensitive topics, survey nonresponse, and considerations for interviewer training. *American Journal of Preventive Medicine* 31(5): 419–426.

O'Donovan, K. (1991) Defences for battered women who kill. *Journal of Law and Society* 18(2): 219–240.

O'Farrell, T.J., V. Van Hutton and C.M. Murphy (1999) Domestic violence before and after alcoholism treatment: a two-year longitudinal study. *Journal of Studies on Alcohol* 60: 317–321.

Ogawa, J.R., L.A. Sroufe, N.S. Weinfield, E.A. Carlson and B. Egeland (1997) Development and the fragmented self: longitudinal study of dissociative symptomatology in a nonclinical sample. *Development and Psychopathology* 9(4): 855–879.

Ouellette, S.C. (2008) Notes for a critical personality psychology: making room under the critical psychology umbrella. *Social and Personality Psychology Compass* 2(1): 1–20.

Pahl, J. (1985) *Private Violence and Public Policy*. Boston: Routledge & Kegan Paul.

Palmer, C. (1998) The Taliban's war on women. *Lancet* 352(9129): 734.

Papadopoulos, D. (2008) In the ruins of representation: identity, individuality, subjectification. *British Journal of Social Psychology* 47: 139–165.

Parker, I. (1996) Against Wittgenstein: materialist reflections on language in psychology. *Theory Psychology* 6(3): 363–384.

Parker, I. (2002) *Critical Discursive Psychology*. London: Palgrave.

Parker, I. (2003) Psychoanalytic narratives: writing the self into contemporary cultural phenomena. *Narrative Inquiry* 13(2): 301–315.

Parker, R.N. (1993) The effects of context on alcohol and violence. *Alcohol Health and Research World (Special issue: Alcohol, aggression, and injury)* 17: 117–122.

Pearshouse, R. (2008) Sexual assault, domestic violence and HIV: promoting women's rights through legislation. *HIV AIDS Policy Law Review* 13(2–3): 63–64.

Peckover, S. (2002) Supporting and policing mothers: an analysis of the disciplinary practices of health visiting. *Journal of Advanced Nursing* 38(4): 369–377.

Peckover, S. (2003) 'I could have just done with a little more help': an analysis of women's help-seeking from health visitors in the context of domestic violence. *Health and Social Care in the Community* 11(3): 275–282.

Peled, E. and J.L. Edleson (1994) *Ending the Cycle of Violence: Community Responses to Children of Battered Women*. Newbury Park, CA: Sage.

Peled, E., Z. Eisikovits, G. Enosh and Z. Winstok (2000) Choice and empowerment for battered women who stay: toward a constructivist model. *Social Work* 45(1): 9–25.

Pence, E., M. Paymar and T. Ritmeester (eds) (1993) *Education Groups for Men Who Batter: The Duluth Model.* New York: Springer.

Perilla, J.L. (1999) Domestic violence as a human rights issue: the case of immigrant Latinos. *Hispanic Journal of Behavioral Sciences* 21(2): 107–133.

Piaget, J. (1932) *The Moral Judgment of the Child.* London: Kegan Paul.

Pillemer, K. (2005) Elder abuse is caused by the deviance and dependence of abusive caregivers. In D.R. Loseke, R. Gelles and M. Cavanaugh (eds) *Current Controversies on Family Violence.* Thousand Oaks, CA: Sage, 207–219.

Pizzey, E. (1974/1977) *Scream Quietly or the Neighbors Will Hear.* Short Hills, NJ: R. Enslow Publishers.

Pizzey, E. and J. Shapiro (1982) *Prone to Violence.* Feltham, Middlesex: Hamlyn.

Quigley, B.M. and K.E. Leonard (2000) Alcohol and the continuation of early marital aggression: neurobiological, psychosocial, and developmental correlates of drinking. *Alcoholism: Clinical and Experimental Research* 24(7): 1003–1010.

Ragin, D.F., M. Pilotti, L. Madry, R.E. Sage, L.E. Bingham and B.J. Primm (2002) Intergenerational substance abuse and domestic violence as familial risk factors for lifetime attempted suicide among battered women. *Journal of Interpersonal Violence* 17(10): 1027–1045.

Raymond, J. (2002) The new UN trafficking protocol. *Women's Studies International Forum* 25(2): 491–502.

Reavey, P. and S.D. Brown (2006) Transforming past agency and action in the present. *Theory and Psychology* 16(2): 179–202.

Renker, P.R. and P. Tonkin (2006) Women's views of prenatal violence screening: acceptability and confidentiality issues. *Obstetrics and Gynecology* 107(2, Part 1): 348–354.

Renzetti, C.M. (1997) Confessions of a reformed postivist: feminist participatory research as good social science. In M.D. Schwartz (ed.) *Researching Sexual Violence Against Women.* London: Sage, 131–143.

Renzetti, C. (1998) Violence and abuse in lesbian relationships: theoretical and empirical issues. In R.K. Berger (ed.) *Issues in Intimate Violence.* Thousand Oaks, CA: Sage, 117–127.

Richardson, J. and G. Feder (1996) Domestic violence: a hidden problem for general practice. *British Journal of General Practice*, April: 239–242.

Richardson, J., J. Coid, A. Petruckevitch, W.S. Chung, S. Moorey and G. Feder (2002) Identifying domestic violence: cross sectional study in primary care. *British Medical Journal* 324(7332): 274.

Riger, S. (2001) Transforming community psychology. *American Journal of Community Psychology* 29(1): 69–81.

Riley, D. (1983) *War in the Nursery: Theories of the Child and Mother.* London: Virago.

Ristock, J.L. (2003) Exploring dynamics of abusive lesbian relationships: preliminary analysis of a multisite, qualitative study. *American Journal of Community Psychology* 31(3): 329–341.

Rivett, M. (2001) Comment – working systemically with family violence: controversy, context and accountability. *Journal of Family Therapy* 23: 397–404.

Rodriguez, M.A., E. McLoughlin, G. Nah and J.C. Campbell (2001) Mandatory reporting of domestic violence injuries to the police: what do emergency department patients think? *Jama* 286(5): 580–583.

Rodriguez, M.A., W.R. Sheldon and N. Rao (2002) Abused patient's attitudes about mandatory reporting of intimate partner abuse injuries to police. *Women Health* 35(2–3): 135–147.

Romito, P. (2008) *A Deafening Silence: Hidden Violence Against Women and Children*. Bristol: Policy Press.

Romkens, R. (2006) Protecting prosecution: exploring the powers of law in an intervention program for domestic violence. *Violence Against Women* 12(2): 160–186.

Rosenbaum, A. and P.A. Leisring (2001) Group intervention programs for batterers. *Journal of Aggression, Maltreatment and Trauma* 5(2): 57–71.

Russell, D.H. (1991) Rape and child sexual abuse in Soweto: an interview with community leader Mary (Masechaba) Mabaso. *South African Sociological Review* 3(2).

Russell, D.H., N.R. Van de Ven and R. Gena (1988) *Crimes Against Women*. Oakland, CA: Black Iris Press.

Ryan, C., M. Anastario and A. DaCunha (2006) Changing coverage of domestic violence murders: a longitudinal experiment in participatory communication. *Journal of Interpersonal Violence* 21(2): 209–228.

Saltzman, L.E., Y.T. Green, J.S. Marks and S.B. Thacker (2000) Violence against women as a public health issue: comments from the CDC. *American Journal of Preventive Medicine* 19(4): 325–329.

Sandis, E.E. (2006) United Nations measures to stop violence against women. *Annals of the New York Academy of Sciences* 1087: 370–383.

Saunders, D.G. (2002) Are physical assaults by wives and girlfriends a major social problem? A review of the literature. *Violence Against Women* 8(12): 1424–1448.

Sayers, J. (1990) Psychoanalytic feminism: deconstructing power in theory and therapy. In I. Parker and J. Shotter (eds) *Deconstructing Social Psychology*. London: Routledge, 196–207.

Schechter, S. (1982) *Women and Male Violence: The Visions and Struggles of the Battered Women's Movement*. Cambridge, MA: Southend Press.

Schore, A.N. (2005) Back to basics: attachment, affect regulation, and the developing right brain: linking developmental neuroscience to pediatrics. *Pediatrics in Review* 26(6): 204–217.

Schuler, S.R., S.M. Hashemi, A.P. Riley and S. Akhter (1996) Credit programs, patriarchy and men's violence against women in rural Bangladesh. *Social Science and Medicine* 43(12): 1729–1742.

Schuler, S.R., L.M. Bates and F. Islam (2008) Women's rights, domestic violence, and recourse seeking in rural Bangladesh. *Violence Against Women* 14(3): 326–345.

Schwartz, M. (ed.) (1997) *Researching Sexual Violence Against Women: Methodological and Personal Perspectives*. London: Sage.

Seave, P.L. (2006) Disarming batterers through restraining orders: the promise and the reality in California. *Evaluation Review* 30(3): 245–265.

Segal, H. (1964) *Introduction to the Work of Melanie Klein*. London: Hogarth Press.

Segal, J. (1992) *Melanie Klein*. London: Sage.

Seligman, M.E.P. (1972) Learned helplessness. *Annual Review of Medicine* 23(1): 407–412.

Seligman, M.E. (1975) *Helplessness: On Depression, Development, and Death.* Oxford: W.H. Freeman.

Sen, P. (1998) Development practice and violence against women. *Gender and Development* 6(3): 7–16.

Shurman, L.A. and C.M. Rodriguez (2006) Cognitive-affective predictors of women's readiness to end domestic violence relationships. *Journal of Interpersonal Violence* 21(11): 1417–1439.

Simeon, D., R. Yehuda, R. Cunill, M. Knutelska, F.W. Putnam and L.M. Smith (2007) Factors associated with resilience in healthy adults. *Psychoneuroendocrinology* 32(8–10): 1149–1152.

Simmel, G. (1908/1950) *The Sociology of Georg Simmel.* Glencoe, IL: Free Press.

Skinner, T., M. Hester and E. Malos (eds) (2005) *Researching Gender Violence: Feminist Methodology in Action.* Collumpton, Devon: Willan Publishing.

Smith, A. (2001) Domestic violence laws: the voices of battered women. *Violence and Victims* 16(1): 91–111.

Smith, J.P. and J.G. Williams (1992) From abusive household to dating violence. *Journal of Family Violence* 7(2): 153–165.

Smith, J.S., S.L. Rainey, K.R. Smith, C. Alamares and D. Grogg (2008) Barriers to the mandatory reporting of domestic violence encountered by nursing professionals. *Journal of Trauma Nursing* 15(1): 9–11.

Smith, M.E. (2003) Recovery from intimate partner violence: a difficult journey. *Issues in Mental Health Nursing* 24(5): 543–573.

Sokoloff, N.J. and I. Dupont (2005) Domestic violence at the intersections of race, class, and gender: challenges and contributions to understanding violence against marginalized women in diverse communities. *Violence Against Women* 11(1): 38–64.

Sommerfeld, D. (1989) The origins of mother blaming: historical perspectives on childhood and motherhood. *Infant Mental Health Journal* 10(1): 14–24.

Sonkin, D.J. (1986) Clairvoyance vs. common sense: therapist's duty to warn and protect. *Violence and Victims* 1(1): 7–22.

Sorensen, B. (1998) Explanations for wife beating in Greenland. In R.C. Klein (ed.) *Family Violence: Multi-Disciplinary Perspectives.* London: Routledge, 153–175.

Spillius, E. (2007) *Encounters with Melanie Klein: Selected Papers of Elizabeth Spillius.* London: Free Association Books.

Squire, C. (1990) Feminism as antipsychology: learning and teaching in feminist psychology. In E. Burman (ed.) *Feminists and Psychological Practice.* London: Sage, 76–88.

Stanko, B.A. (2007) From academia to policy making: changing police responses to violence against women. *Theoretical Criminology* 11(2): 209–219.

Stanko, E.A. (1985) *Intimate Intrusions: Women's Experiences of Male Violence.* London: Routledge & Kegan Paul.

Steinmetz, S.K. (1978) Violence between family members. *Marriage and Family Review* 1(3): 1–16.

Steinmetz, S. (2005) Elder abuse is caused by the perception of stress associated with providing care. In D.R. Loseke, R.J. Gelles and M.M. Cavanaugh (eds) *Current Controversies on Family Violence.* London: Sage, 191–206.

Steinmetz, D. and H. Tabenkin (2008) [Screening for domestic violence in primary care setting]. *Harefuah* 147(12): 978–981, 1029, 1030.

Stenius, V.M. and B.M. Veysey (2005) 'It's the little things': women, trauma, and strategies for healing. *Journal of Interpersonal Violence* 20(10): 1155–1174.

Stith, S.M., K.H. Rosen, K.A. Middleton, A.L. Busch, K. Lundeberg and R.P. Carlton (2000) The intergenerational transmission of spouse abuse: a meta-analysis. *Journal of Marriage and the Family* 62(3): 640–654.

Stith, S., K.H. Rosen and E.E. McCollum (2003) Effectiveness of couples treatment for spouse abuse. *Journal of Marital and Family Therapy* 29(3): 407–426

Stoppard, J. (2000) *Understanding Depression: Feminist Social Constructionist Approaches*. London: Routledge.

Storrs, E. (2004) 'Our scapegoat': an exploration of media representations of Myra Hindley and Rosemary West. *Theology and Sexuality* 11(1): 9–28.

Stover, C.S. (2005) Domestic violence research: what have we learned and where do we go from here? *Journal of Interpersonal Violence* 20(4): 448–454.

Straka, S.M. and L. Montminy (2006) Responding to the needs of older women experiencing domestic violence. *Violence Against Women* 12(3): 251–267.

Straus, M.A. (1979) Measuring intra-family conflict and violence: the Conflict Tactics (CT) scales. *Journal of Marriage and the Family* 41(1): 75–88.

Straus, M.A. (1980) Victims and aggressors in marital violence. *American Behavioral Scientist* 23: 681–704.

Straus, M.A. (2005) Women's violence toward men is a serious problem. In D.R. Loseke, R.J. Gelles and M.M. Cavanaugh (eds) *Current Controversies on Family Violence*. London: Sage, 55–78.

Straus, M.A. (2008) Dominance and symmetry in partner violence by male and female university students in 32 nations. *Children and Youth Services Review* 30(3): 252–275.

Straus, M.A., R.J. Gelles and S. Steinmetz (1981) *Behind Closed Doors: Violence in the American Family*. New York: Anchor Press.

Street, A.E., L.E. Gibson and D.R. Holohan (2005) Impact of childhood traumatic events, trauma-related guilt, and avoidant coping strategies on PTSD symptoms in female survivors of domestic violence. *Journal of Traumatic Stress* 18(3): 245–252.

Stuart, L.M. (1997) Domestic violence: old problems, new approaches. *Links*, 4.

Suffla, S., A. Van Niekerk and N. Arendse (2008) Female homicidal strangulation in urban South Africa. *BMC Public Health* 8: 363.

Sullivan, M., R. Bhuyan, K. Senturia, S. Shiu-Thornton and S. Ciske (2005a) Participatory action research in practice: a case study in addressing domestic violence in nine cultural communities. *Journal of Interpersonal Violence* 20(8): 977–995.

Sullivan, M., K. Senturia, T. Negash, S. Shiu-Thornton and B. Giday (2005b) 'For us it is like living in the dark': Ethiopian women's experiences with domestic violence. *Journal of Interpersonal Violence* 20(8): 922–940.

Sully, P. (2002) Commitment to partnership: interdisciplinary initiatives in developing expert practice in the care of survivors of violence. *Nurse Education in Practice* 2(2): 92–98.

Sully, P. (2008) Domestic violence and children: the case for joined-up working. *Journal of Family Health Care* 18(1): 9–13.

REFERENCES

Sutherland, C., D. Bybee and C. Sullivan (1998) The long-term effects of battering on women's health. *Women's Health* 4(1): 41–70.

Swan, S.C. and D.L. Snow (2006) The development of a theory of women's use of violence in intimate relationships. *Violence Against Women* 12(11): 1026–1045.

Swan, S.C. and T.P. Sullivan (2009) The resource utilization of women who use violence in intimate relationships. *Journal of Interpersonal Violence* 24(6): 940–958.

Sykes, G.M. and D. Matza (1957) Techniques of neutralization: a theory of delinquency. *American Sociological Review* 22(6): 664–670.

Taft, C. and C. Murphy (2007) The working alliance in intervention for partner violence perpetrators: recent research and theory. *Journal of Family Violence* 22(1): 11–18.

Taft, C.T., P.A. Resick, J. Panuzio, D.S. Vogt and M.B. Mechanic (2007) Examining the correlates of engagement and disengagement coping among help-seeking battered women. *Violence and Victims* 22(1): 3–17.

Tjaden, P. and N. Thoennes (2000) Prevalence and consequences of male-to-female and female-to-male intimate partner violence as measured by the National Violence Against Women Survey. *Violence Against Women* 6(2): 142–161.

Tuckett, D. (1989) A brief view of Herbert Rosenfeld's contribution to the theory of psychoanalytic technique. *International Journal of Psycho-Analysis* 70: 619–625.

Ussher, J.M. (1989) *The Psychology of the Female Body*. London: Routledge.

Ussher, J.M. (ed.) (1997) *Body Talk*. London: Routledge.

Ussher, J.M. (2006) *Managing the Monstrous Feminine: Regulating the Reproductive Body*. London: Routledge.

Usta, J., J.A. Farver and L. Zein (2008) Women, war, and violence: surviving the experience. *Journal of Women's Health (Larchmt)* 17(5): 793–804.

Van Roosmalen, E. (2000) Forces of patriarchy: adolescent experiences of sexuality and conceptions of relationships. *Youth Society* 32(2): 202–227.

van Wormer, K. (2009) Restorative justice as social justice for victims of gendered violence: a standpoint feminist perspective. *Social Work* 54(2): 107–116.

Vaz, P. and F. Bruno (2003) Types of self-surveillance: from abnormality to individuals 'at risk'. *Surveillance and Society* 1(3): 272–291.

Verhulst, F.C. (2000) Editorial. *Journal of Child Psychology and Psychiatry* 41(3): 275–276.

Vetere, A. and J. Cooper (2001) Working systemically with family violence: risk, responsibility and collaboration. *Journal of Family Therapy* 23(4): 378–396.

Vetere, A. and J. Cooper (2003) Setting up a domestic violence service. *Child and Adolescent Mental Health* 8(2): 61–67.

Vetere, A. and J. Cooper (2004) Wishful thinking or Occam's razor? A response to 'Dancing on a razor's edge: systemic group work with batterers'. *Journal of Family Therapy* 26(2): 163–166.

Vives-Cases, C., D. Gil-Gonzalez and M. Carrasco-Portino (2009) Verbal marital conflict and male domination in the family as risk factors of intimate partner violence. *Trauma, Violence, & Abuse* 10(2): 171–180.

Walby, S. (2004) *The Cost of Domestic Violence*. London: Department of Trade and Industry and Women and Equality Unit.

Walker, L.E. (1977) Who are the battered women? *Frontiers: A Journal of Women Studies* 2(1): 52–57.

Walker, L.E. (1979) *The Battered Woman*. New York: Harper and Row.

Walker, L.E. (1984) Battered women, psychology, and public policy. *American Psychologist* 39(10): 1178–1182.

Walker, L.E. (1989) Psychology and violence against women. *American Psychologist* 44(4): 695–702.

Walker, L.E. (1999) Psychology and domestic violence around the world. *American Psychologist* 54(1): 21–29.

Walker, L.E. (2000) *The Battered Woman Syndrome*. New York: Springer.

Walsh, S. and P. Nicolson (1997) Exploring the interface: applications of feminist theory, practice and research. *Feminism Psychology* 7(2): 211–213.

Watson, J. (2000) *Male Bodies: Health, Culture and Identity*. Buckingham: Open University Press.

Weidel, J.J., E. Provencio-Vasquez, S.D. Watson and R. Gonzalez-Guarda (2008) Cultural considerations for intimate partner violence and HIV risk in Hispanics. *Journal of the Association of Nurses in AIDS Care* 19(4): 247–251.

Westland, G. (1978) *Current Crises of Psychology*. London: Heinemann.

White, H. and P. Chen (2002) Problem drinking and intimate partner violence. *Journal of Studies on Alcohol* 63(2): 205–214.

Wilcox, P. (2000) Lone motherhood: the impact on living standards on leaving a violent relationship. *Social Policy and Administration* 34(2): 176–190.

Wilson, A. (2006) *Dreams, Questions, Struggles: South Asian Women in Britain*. London: Pluto Press.

Winnicott, D. (1953) Transitional objects and transitional phenomena. *International Journal of Psychoanalysis* 34: 89–97.

Winnicott, D. (1969) The use of an object. *International Journal of Psycho-Analysis* 50: 711–716.

Wolf, N. (1991) *The Beauty Myth*. New York: Doubleday.

Wolfe, D.A. (1994) Factors associated with the development of post-traumatic stress disorder among child victims of sexual abuse. *Child Abuse and Neglect* 18: 37.

Wood, J.T. (2001) The normalization of violence in heterosexual romantic relationships: women's narratives of love and violence. *Journal of Social and Personal Relationships* 18(2): 239–261.

Worden, A.P. and B.E. Carlson (2005) Attitudes and beliefs about domestic violence: results of a public opinion survey: II. Beliefs about causes. *Journal of Interpersonal Violence* 20(10): 1219–1243.

WHO (2006) *WHO Multi-Country Study on Women's Health and Domestic Violence against Women*. Geneva: World Health Organization.

Yardley, L. (1996) Reconciling discursive and materialist perspectives on health and illness: a reconstruction of the biopsychosocial approach. *Theory and Psychology* 6(3): 485–508.

Yardley, L. (1997) *Material Discourses of Health and Illness*. London: Routledge.

Yeager, K. and A. Seid (2002) Primary care and victims of domestic violence. *Primary Care* 29(1): 125–150, vii–viii.

Yllö, K.A. (1998) Through a feminist lens: gender, power, and violence. In K.V. Hansen and A.I. Garey (eds) *Families in the US: Kinship and Domestic Politics*. Philadelphia: Temple University Press, 608–618.

Yllö, K.A. (2005) Through a feminist lens: gender diversity, and violence: extending the feminist framework. In D.R. Loseke, R.J. Gelles and M.M. Cavanaugh (eds) *Current Controversies on Family Violence*. London: Sage, 19–34.

Yoshihama, M. (2005) A web in the patriarchal clan system: tactics of intimate partners in the Japanese sociocultural context. *Violence Against Women* 11(10): 1236–1262.

Zink, T., C.J. Jacobson, Jr., S. Regan and S. Pabst (2004) Hidden victims: the healthcare needs and experiences of older women in abusive relationships. *Journal of Women's Health (Larchmt)* 13(8): 898–908.

Zinzow, H.M., K.J. Ruggiero, H. Resnick, R. Hanson, D. Smith, B. Saunders *et al.* (2009) Prevalence and mental health correlates of witnessed parental and community violence in a national sample of adolescents. *Journal of Child Psychology and Psychiatry* 50(4): 441–450.

INDEX